Dowsing
— for answers

By
Wilma Davidson

GREEN
MAGIC

Green Magic
Long Barn
Sutton Mallet
Somerset TA7 9AR
England
www.greenmagicpublishing.com

Typeset by Academic and Technical, Bristol
www.acadtech.co.uk

ISBN 978-0-9552908-4-8

GREEN MAGIC

Contents

Acknowledgements

I would like to say a 'Big Thankyou' to my children Janice, Gail and Mike for their constant support, and a special thankyou to my son Mike and his wife Debs, who designed the cover for *Dowsing for Answers*. To Peter Gotto and his team at Green Magic Publishing, I would like to say thankyou very much for doing a great job in making this book possible.

I would also like to thank John, Helen and the staff at the British Society of Dowsers who have been ever-ready to offer advice and assistance. My thanks also go to those who have given me permission to quote from their work in this field.

Wilma Davidson

Introduction

When you learn to dowse, a whole new world of possibilities is opened up, as dowsing is not simply a tool used to find underground water supplies, or to dowse the sex of an unborn baby – this amazing tool can be used in every-day life to give answers to all sorts of basic questions.

This well respected tool has been used by many governments during wars to find unexploded bombs and mines, and several large oil companies use the services of a dowser to find oil, so dowsing is not simply a new age craze; it is an invaluable tool there to answer your questions.

In this book I have tried to highlight the many uses of dowsing to help make life easier, so when your need confirmation, your pendulum will give you the answer. This little tool will answer your questions on health, diagnose car or computer problems etc., but will not answer any questions for self gain! So it will not confirm which horse will win a race, or which are the lucky lottery numbers! Next time you can't remember if you have already added salt to the potatoes, or the length of time required to cook a certain dish, then your pendulum will confirm the answer.

Every year there is an increase in the number of different alternative therapies available and it's often difficult trying to establish the best therapy to treat a specific health problem, so by dowsing you will find the most beneficial treatment. The same applies to mineral and vitamin supplements, as often we see an advertisement promising wonderful health benefits, so before spending money on the wrong supplement, you can dowse to find which minerals are short in your body. How many of us have bottles of pills in our cupboard which were bought in expectation of an energy boost which never happened?

If you are greatly concerned about the effects of hidden chemicals in your food, fluoride in your drinking water, or eating food which has been genetically engineered, this is where the pendulum excels itself. Now you can also confirm if food or drink contains the artificial sweetener aspartame, harmful preservatives or colourants. Another bonus is that it will tell you if the food is fresh, if it contains harmful bacteria or if it has been irradiated.

Are you alarmed about the health effects of electromagnetic fields in your area? Your pendulum will give positive confirmation if your cell phone is emitting harmful rays, if the cell phone mast nearby is damaging health, if the overhead power lines or electricity pylons are a health hazard, or of the presence of nuclear energy. If you are concerned about the effect on your health from eating food cooked in a microwave oven, then ask your pendulum the question, and it will confirm your suspicions.

Dowsing is easy to learn and most people can dowse, but perhaps the most difficult part of dowsing is remembering to use the pendulum! Learning the basics of dowsing only takes a few minutes, and the more you use the skill, the more you become in tune with your pendulum. Children enjoy dowsing and will spend happy hours in the garden dowsing for hidden sweets.

You can use your pendulum to check garden soil or which compost to use for certain plants. It is also a great help in diagnosing pet problems, so if your dog develops a limp, or your cat's coat becomes dull, you can use the pendulum to find the cause and the cure.

To say it is to everyone's advantage to learn to dowse is an understatement as it is a 'must' in an emergency, since it can diagnose the wounds of casualties in an accident, or locate fresh drinking water which has not been contaminated by chemicals or terrorists. So get dowsing, and you'll be so glad you've mastered this skill.

1

Dowsing – an invaluable tool

Dowsing is an amazing gift from our Creator, it's 'Free', and is available to all of us to answer questions about our food, health, and everyday problems in our life.

This ancient art has been used since the days of early man, as a tool to locate cures for illnesses, edible plants, and to find a healthy site to build a home. We are all born with the ability to dowse and around 85% of adults and children can dowse successfully. Those who seem unable to dowse are often sleeping over a negative energy line which creates an energy blockage. Considering that dowsing is such a useful and flexible help line which is on call 24 hours a day, and gives reliable results to questions when properly phrased, it is surprising how few people are aware of its many benefits.

Today dowsing is beginning to be recognized as a reliable and well respected tool used in industry, and in some areas of Germany there is a certification programme. I understand in the United States, the American Society of Dowsers members are discussing an accepted standard of dowsing, and the issue of diplomas to certify dowsers who are experienced and capable of giving reliable results.

Dowsing can be used anywhere, either indoors or outdoors, and can be done with or without a pendulum or rod, and the big bonus is that, like Healing, it is Free! No special talent is necessary to become a dowser, and it is now being taught in many countries.

Ask any group of people if they can dowse, and invariably the answer will be 'Oh that's when you hold a needle over the expectant mother's tummy, to diagnose the sex of the unborn baby' or 'It's used by farmers to find water'. Yes to both uses.

But it can be used for dozens and dozens of everyday situations, as long as it is not for self gain.

It can be used to find harmful invisible energies, such as electromagnetic energy rays, radon gas, and geopathic stress lines from underground water, and will give an accurate answer very much faster than any scientific equipment available today.

Dowsing is almost 100% accurate at diagnosing illnesses, their cause and treatment, and it will also confirm the root of allergies, painful aches, or emotional problems. It is thought by many dowsers to be a form of esoteric energy science and, either with a pendulum or with rods, is a way of accessing information which we are not able to access on a normal conscious level. This tool, by some unexplained ability, can help each one of us to tap into our Higher Self, and enable us to access information which would normally be far out of our reach.

One explanation of this gift is that the dowser is connected to the object they are about to dowse by an invisible field of subtle energy. This explanation makes a lot of sense, as we all have an invisible link with every person we meet. When we send absent healing, we send out an invisible subtle energy link, so it makes sense that when we dowse we do exactly the same thing.

To date, there has not yet been an instrument invented, other than the pendulum or rods, which can contact a higher energy than the physical plane, as scientific instruments are designed to measure energy on the earth plane.

Until a scientific genius, with the aid of the spirit world, invents a piece of scientific equipment which can link to other vibrations, science will not be able to get answers to resolve the mystery of dowsing.

Some time ago two scientists tried to measure the healing vibration I channel, and although they spent a lot of time and effort, and gave a lot of thought to the exercise, they failed. My spirit guides told me that man is unable to measure these higher vibrations of energy, as they could not comprehend the scale of this higher vibration of energy because it is unknown to them.

It is known that dowsers use the pineal gland when dowsing. This little known gland is the central point of our consciousness, and is also responsible for production of melatonin, created while we are asleep.

Before telling you details of the many uses of dowsing, how to diagnose all health problems and find suitable remedies, I want to tell you a few facts about the history of dowsing, so you will appreciate that it is not some new-age gadget, but is a tool respected by our forefathers.

It is sad that some people are suspicious of dowsing and don't realize it has been used to save lives for centuries, and that many governments have been using this tool for years to help win wars. The British government used dowsers during the 1940s war against Germany, to find unexploded mines with delayed action fuses, which had sunk deep into the ground. One well known dowser was stationed at Portsmouth to detect magnetic mines. He saved many lives as, without his dowsing skills, many people would not have been alive when the war ended.

The United States Government trained groups of marines to dowse, before going to Vietnam, to enable them to find booby traps, unexploded mines, Vietcong tunnels, and groups of Vietcong rebels, and their ammunition stores.[2]

Proof that this versatile tool has been used by our ancestors for thousands of years is confirmed by ancient drawings of men using dowsing rods, found in prehistoric caves. Murals of dowsers were found in the Caves of Tasseli in the foothills of the Atlas Mountains, where they'd been drawn 8,000 years previously, and the age has been checked by the carbon 14 Process.[3]

Other proof shows the Chinese Emperor Tu, in 200 BC, was a skilled dowser, and perhaps the most famous of all dowsers was Queen Cleopatra, who used her personal dowser to find gold.

To prove to you the accuracy of dowsing, here is one of the most outstanding demonstrations of map dowsing which took place in America in 1959, when a Californian dowser Verne

Cameron demonstrated to the US Navy that he could accurately locate the position and depth of submarines in the Pacific Ocean. Hard though it may be to believe, he could also distinguish between the US and Russian submarines, so if this man could find the location of the US nuclear submarines using dowsing, then the Russians, who are keen dowsers, could also locate the US submarines – somewhat disconcerting dowsing you'll agree!

Today Ministries of Agriculture in several countries have dowsers on their staff, as have most large oil companies. It is widely used in Russia where geologists have been known to dowse from aircraft to find lead strips located several hundred feet underground – quite a feat![3]

Dowsing is a very popular subject in Russia, and programmes are regularly shown on television in Moscow at peak viewing times. Postgraduates can learn scientific dowsing to be used in industry, but it will probably be many years before this happens in the West.

Russia has always been a forward thinking country in the world of science, as remember they were the first country to accept the dangers of the microwave oven nearly sixty years ago. The sale and use of these ovens was banned for several decades until recently, while we in the West do not acknowledge the hazard.

In centuries gone by man was much more in tune with the Earth, and used his dowsing skill to find harmful earth energies, poisonous plants, and food, but this skill went underground when the church intervened, and discouraged it as evil in the sixteenth century. At that time dowsers were persecuted, as it was considered the same category as witchcraft, but fortunately today most churches accept it is a tool which can save lives and, provided it is only used for good, it is favoured.

The Roman Catholic Church in 1942 decreed that dowsing could be used in God's work to find water, to diagnose food illness, and to check energies in the home. It also stated that dowsing must not be used for evil work or self gain and should only be used in love.

4

Would you like to learn to dowse? I will explain the basics later and, if you enjoy this new-found skill, you can learn more about dowsing at local adult centre classes, or a local dowsing group. There are dowsing societies and local dowsing groups in many towns in the UK, USA and other countries.

How does dowsing work? The honest answer is that nobody really knows how it works. Ask any dowser to explain to you how dowsing works and, if they are honest, they'll say they don't really know the answer. There are two very different theories, so accept the one that feels most comfortable to you.

These are only guesswork, as nobody has a correct explanation how dowsing succeeds in giving such exact answers to questions, often on subjects we know nothing about. All we know for certain is that the brain is involved in the exercise.

The human brain has two separate sides, and when we dowse we use one side of the brain to ask the question, and then it switches off to allow the other side to answer, so a lot of brain activity is used during dowsing. The brain has four separate activities, Alpha, Beta, Theta, and Delta. We use our normal wide awake state which is Beta to ask the question, then switch to Delta to search our subconscious to find the answer.

Some dowsers firmly believe the skill is linked with changes in muscle response and brain rhythms, but what instigates these muscle responses? Many dowsers are convinced the other side of the brain, which is the dominant side of the brain, links into our memory bank which holds all knowledge.

Do you believe in Life After Life? The other explanation is that there is someone in the spirit world who is giving us the answers. Whoever or Whatever the source of the answers, it does a great job of helping us to reach the intangible. Dowsing is very much like many other forms of exercise, in that the more you use your dowsing technique, the more confident and tuned in you become. We are all a part of the universal energy, and have this wonderful invisible link, which allows us to use our subtle energy field to get answers from the universal energy or helpful spirits. The really amazing fact about dowsing is that the dowsing questions travel through time and space to their destination, and the reply travels back to us – a truly exceptional service!

When you dowse, you are, without realizing it, teaching your mind to open the door between your conscious and your intuitive side. Modern man is very logical, as constantly moving technology has given us emails, texting, computers, the internet, etc., so we have more or less lost touch with Nature, and our basic gifts. Are we being blinded by modern equipment so that we only accept a tool to be reliable if we can feel it, hear it, or see it? To give you some examples of how the pendulum can be used for health problems, here are a few suggestions. I will talk about its uses in the home later.

A few uses for dowsing

1. Diagnosing back problems
2. Causes of allergies
3. Finding the cause of an illness
4. Checking the body's level of minerals
5. Balancing the chakras
6. Choosing the correct flower remedy
7. Checking food colourants
8. Locating aspartame in food
9. Finding cause of infertility
10. Checking energy level of your body

You too can dowse – the pendulum

So how do you use this amazing dowsing tool?

Dowsing can be done with either a pendulum or rods. The pendulum can be anything which is heavy enough to swing on a chain or string. You can use a fishing weight or a front door key on a piece of string, or a pendant with a gold chain, or perhaps you'd prefer to use a favourite crystal or other stone. In other words it does not make any difference what item you choose to use, as literally anything which will swing will do the job. I have on occasions used my dog leash, when I have wanted to dowse during a walk along the beach, and it works just as well as a smart looking pendulum.

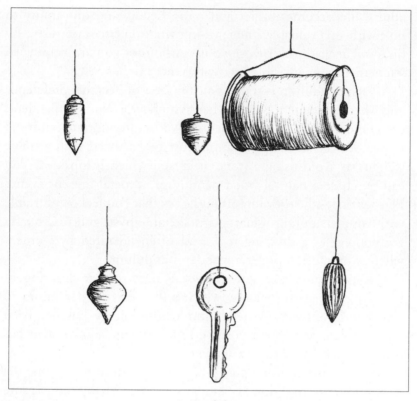

▲ *Pendulums*

Experienced dowsers often work without a pendulum, and dowse simply by placing their first finger and thumb together, while mentally asking the question, and when they receive the answer, their finger starts moving in another direction. Other dowsers use a different technique whereby they hold their hands an inch apart in front of their body, in a position which looks as though they are about to pray and, with hands slightly apart, move one hand upwards and the other one downwards. They continue to move the hands up and down while mentally asking the question and when the answer comes to them, their hands start to go in a reverse movement.

Please do not feel nervous or uneasy about dowsing, as we are all born with intuition and a Higher Self; but as we become adults, life becomes busier and more hectic, and our ability to link with this valuable source of information becomes rusty. By building a relationship with your pendulum, you are helping to strengthen your invisible link with your Higher Self.

Which pendulum you use is all a matter of personal preference and what feels right to you. Perhaps you have a favourite pendent, or grandfather's gold watch fob. The important point to remember is that the pendulum must be balanced with a stable weight, so avoid using a stone or crystal which is lopsided. You can purchase a natural wood pendulum, a metal one, or even a Perspex one – the only important fact is that you feel comfortable with your pendulum. Quartz crystals, amethyst, and rose quartz are popular as a dowsing tool, and often favoured by women, whereas men often prefer a wooden pendulum.

It is important to remember crystals need regular cleansing, as they collect negative energy, which will cause the pendulum to give wrong answers. A pendulum whose energy has not been cleansed cannot create a positive link with the source, as it has been blocked by negative energy.

You sometimes hear a person say 'My pendulum gives me the wrong answers' or 'I don't trust it any more'. Usually this is a sure sign the pendulum is in need of an energy bath, the questions have been phrased wrongly, or the person is sleeping over geopathic stress and their energies need to be cleansed and rebalanced.

Most people find they can master the art of dowsing within a few minutes, and this includes even the most skeptical people! The secret of dowsing is to establish your 'Yes', 'No', and 'Don't Know' Signs, and once you have confirmed them, you are able to start using the pendulum.

How do you hold the pendulum?

1. Start by holding the chain or cord of the pendulum between your first fingertip and thumb.
2. If preferable, you can hold the chain over your middle finger between the joints and steady it with your thumb.

3. Another option is to hold it over your first finger and steady with your thumb.

Experiment with holding the pendulum in different positions, and once you have found a comfortable way to hold the pendulum, you are ready to start dowsing. Do not worry if you are left handed, as you can hold the pendulum with either hand. The main thing always to remember is to hold it in a relaxed grip, as holding in a vicelike grip means tension enters into the exercise. Try to relax and allow it to happen, and if you don't get any response from your pendulum, try again.

When I first started dowsing I was desperately keen to do it properly, so I dowsed and asked my pendulum which way it would like to be held! I got a positive answer that it preferred to be held over my middle finger, so I have used that method ever since. I was so over enthusiastic about my new found skill, that I dowsed and asked my Jasper pendulum where it would like to be stored. Would it prefer to be in a velvet purse, a little cardboard box, a jewellery box, or a leather purse?. I was so keen to please my new friend, that I even dowsed and asked what colour of leather it preferred.

I got a positive Yes to the colour Red, so bought it a little red purse. Afterwards when I thought about it, I realized that although I was a bit daft getting so enthusiastic about the pendulum's preferences, it all made sense. Leather is a natural material, so will have more affinity with the stone and have better energy than a man-made material, and red is the colour of energy.

What is the best length of the chain?

Once you have decided the most comfortable way to hold your pendulum it is time to find the best length of chain to use, so what is the best length? Most dowsers find a short length is more controllable than a long length, and work with 21 to 27 centimeters, but in the end, it is all about what is right for you. I have seen dowsers work happily with a 10 to 15 cm length, but as pendulum dowsing is very much an art, rather than a science, the dowser influences the results.

The only rule concerning the chain or string is that it must be lighter in weight than the crystal or whatever you have chosen for your pendulum.

As an enthusiastic beginner, I found out this fact when I was playing golf with my neighbour and, on returning to the car, she realized she had lost her car keys on the course. I was quick to offer to dowse to find which part of the course to look, but as I did not have a pendulum with me, I took the lace out of my golf shoe and tied it to my friend's wedding ring. Alas complete failure, as the shoe lace was heavier than the pendulum, so would not swing. An added problem was that it was a windy day, so the pendulum blew about in the wind and the exercise was a complete failure. I did learn a valuable lesson that the pendulum should always be heavier than the chain, so don't make the same mistake as I did!

When you start dowsing you should mentally say 'It will only be used for Good' and ask permission to dowse. That's the technicalities over! So now you have to ask the question 'Please show me my "Yes" sign'. Your 'Yes' sign may be a clockwise circle, an anticlockwise circle or alternatively it may swing back and forward, so please don't worry if your friend has a different sign, as there are variations.

Until you have built up a relationship with your pendulum, which comes with use, each time you use it you should ask to confirm your 'Yes', 'No' and 'Don't Know' signs, particularly if you use a different pendulum.

Once you have established your 'Yes' sign, it is time to repeat the exercise to learn your No sign. Again it can be either clockwise or anticlockwise or back and forward. The other sign you should learn is the 'Don't Know' sign, as this one will appear when you have asked a question to which you should not know the answer, e.g. 'Is my neighbour having an affair with the milkman?' It will not answer personal questions when you do not have a right to know the answer – it may answer but will probably be wrong! The 'Don't Know' sign is also used when you have phrased a

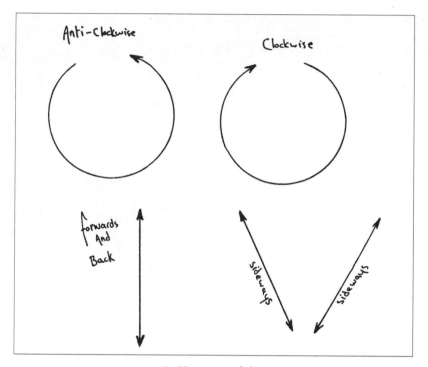

▲ *Using a pendulum*

question in such a way that the answer could be 'Yes' or 'No' and will also use this sign when you ask a question which relates to freewill. If you ask a question 'Should I take more calcium?' you have freewill to decide so the spirit world will never influence. If you ask the question 'Does my body need extra calcium?' or 'Is my body short of calcium?' or 'Will my body benefit from extra calcium?' it will then give you the answer. Never start a question with 'Should I' or 'Can I', as you must choose.

Congratulations. You can now dowse! To use the pendulum simply mentally ask questions, e.g. 'Is my body short of zinc?' or 'Am I sleeping over a geopathic stress line?'.

You will soon become tuned in to your pendulum, so that it almost becomes like an extension of yourself, and you may feel that you instinctively know the answer before the pendulum moves. Many dowsers experience a feeling of tingling in

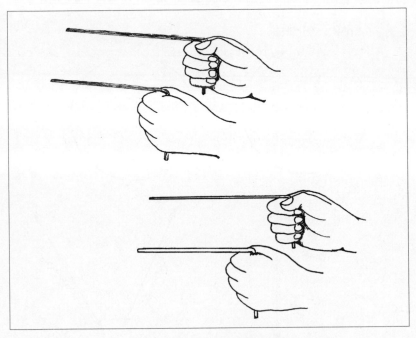

▲ *How to hold the rods*

their hand or wrist, if the answer is going to be positive. I get a feeling like needles and pins which starts at the end of my smallest finger and travels up the side of my hand, so please don't worry if you get a twitch in a finger or wrist, as it is probably a sign.

A good rule is to always remember to disconnect yourself from the pendulum after dowsing, to close the energy door. This can be done by visualizing a White light coming from the universe, down through your head, and through your body, and going deep into the ground, to give you a strong root.

Don't influence the pendulum!

When you are particularly keen for the pendulum to give you either a negative or positive answer to a specific question, try to keep your mind blank, as it is very easy to influence the answer. So be aware of this pitfall, and avoid being too keen to receive the answer you want to get.

Always remember to detach yourself when you ask the question, and wait patiently for the answer. Here are some examples of what *not* to do!

Never ask a question such as 'Will I pass my driving test next month?' or 'Will my son John pass his final university exam?' while you are willing the pendulum to give you the answer you want to hear. You must always avoid mentally saying 'Please please say Yes!' as it is so easy to mentally influence the answer. Perhaps you want to ask if a relative has prostate cancer, so while asking the question you may mentally be thinking 'Please say No', and when you are mentally sending out these thoughts, you will almost certainly get the wrong answer. It is sometimes not easy but try to avoid wishful thinking, and try not to have a preconceived idea of the answer. Always try to keep your mind blank when you ask the question, even if you are 100% certain you know the answer.

Cleansing the pendulum

Regularly cleansing your pendulum is important, as stones and crystals collect negative energy from anyone who has handled them, or from the environment. Some people place the crystal in a tumbler of water with a pinch of sea salt and leave it overnight, but I have heard some dowsers say this is wrong, so dowse and ask if the pendulum will be harmed by being soaked in salt seawater overnight.

If you are able to channel healing or reiki energy, then you can cleanse the pendulum by holding it in your hand, while mentally running the healing energy through the stone. This is a quick method which can be done anywhere.

Another option is to leave the pendulum on the windowsill overnight for the energy of the moon to cleanse it. This is okay if you are certain it will not be stolen by a passing person. In the end it is really all about intent, so whatever method you use will work, as the power of positive thought is very powerful.

Perhaps you'll have a preference for dowsing rods rather than the pendulum, so make yourself a pair of rods, or borrow a pair to experiment with before purchasing your own. Once you are confident they will work well for you, they can be purchased from many new-age shops and from dowsing societies or local group.

Many dowsers make their own rods by cutting the neck from metal coat hangers, and then they are left with an L shaped piece of metal. These DIY dowsers remove the ink refill from a cheap pen, and slide it over the end of the metal, to make a handle, as the metal being very thin is difficult to grip. When you have made your L shaped rods and you are ready to start dowsing, you should hold them by the shorter length, which should be facing downwards, and the longer length should be pointing straight ahead. Keep your elbows close to your sides and hold one rod in each hand, although when you become experienced, you may prefer to work with only one rod.

It is also possible to use metal hangers intact, as by holding them with the handle facing forward and the length close to your body, you will find they swing to answer your questions.

Enthusiastic dowsers often make their own personalized rods from a tree branch, and have a strong preference for the Y shaped rod, made from either hazel, birch, willow or apple tree.

When using rods, you must ask to be shown your 'Yes', 'No', and 'Don't Know' sign. You mentally ask the question exactly the same as you would when using a pendulum. Rods are preferred by many dowsers for outdoor work, as the wind will not influence their behaviour, whereas a pendulum can be blown about by wind.

To use the rods to find underground water, a broken pipe, or negative energy line, simply ask the rods to swing to show you the sign when you cross over the line, or when you are close to a missing object or a missing person. You can also use the rods to ask questions about health problems or medication, so they are as reliable and effective as the pendulum, but for indoor work the pendulum is more convenient.

14

Asking for protection

Protection is all about containing your energy in a safely sealed area, to protect you from both the environment and external influences. It is so easy to unwittingly stand close to someone in the supermarket, who has had a violent row with their husband or boss, and so has an abundance of negative energy, or someone who suffers from depression or is on drugs, so their energy is heavy. These situations can affect your energy, which is why you sometimes feel flat or tired after being in a busy place. You should also put on your protection before treating a patient. as it is important to keep your energies cleansed when dowsing.

To avoid a drain on your energy, before you start dowsing it is advisable to mentally say a few words of prayer for protection, or mentally place a White light around yourself to close the door to negative energy.

An alternative is to visualize a bubble of White light, and see yourself jump into the bubble, so you are surrounded by this protective light, then zip it up so you are secure.

Unprotected dowsing is a 'No-No,' so always think protection before you dowse, and cleanse your energies after you have finished dowsing.

Cleansing your energies and your aura

To cleanse your body's energies of any negativity, you should visualize a White light coming from the Creator or Universal Energy, down through the crown of your head, flushing through your entire body, so all negative energy is washed away, as the light carries on down through your feet and deep into the ground. Then visualize another beam of White light, again coming in through your head and filling your body with pure White light, so that your energies are now cleansed.

Keeping your aura healthy by protecting it from energy vultures and noxious rays is essential for dowsers, so next you should cleanse your aura, as this is the energy field of your body, and is where negative energy collects. Regular cleansing is a must and you will find that after you cleanse your aura you feel energized.

We each have a physical body which is composed of matter, and we also each have an energy body known as the aura, sometimes called the subtle body, which is close to the body, and coexists with our solid body. The body and the aura interact, and illnesses usually start on the outer layer of the aura and work their way through to the body, so an imbalance in the energy of the aura reflects on the body, as they are constantly exchanging energy. This explains why the colours of the aura are constantly changing, depending on our state of health at that particular time, so keeping the energy of the aura cleansed and balanced is essential to good health.

Start by visualizing yourself under a waterfall, with the fresh water cascading down from above, so it is showering your aura, and washing away any negative energy which may have gathered there. An alternative method is to visualize a White light coming from above, and see it completely surround your body, and going down under your feet. When you do this exercise regularly, you will find it only takes a moment and you won't have to think too hard to get it right!

It is so easy to become drained of energy, if you are spending a long time using the pendulum to heal someone or to clear negative energy from a building, so cleansing and protecting your energies is an important part of spiritual work.

Permission to dowse

It is important to mentally ask permission before you use the pendulum to heal anyone, and it is polite to ask a person's permission before you dowse information about them. It is very easy to invade someone's privacy, without intending to intrude.

Most dowsers ask permission from their source before dowsing, by asking three questions recommended by the late Terry Ross.[4]

Can I?, Should I?, May I? So what does all this dowsing jargon mean?

1. Can I? This question is asking if you are able to dowse. Perhaps your immune system or energies are low.
2. Should I? This question asks if the time or conditions are right – perhaps the energy of the site is very negative and dowsing at the wrong time could get the wrong answer.
3. May I? This is asking for permission to dowse.

Dowsing for health

Dowsing is a quick and accurate tool to establish exactly what is causing an illness, uncomfortable symptoms, or allergies. If you or your child develop a strong pain in the tummy, you can dowse to establish if it is caused by cramp, or a grumbling appendix, food poisoning, or simply excess stress. It is also possible to establish if the pain will go away without medical treatment, or if it will respond to herbal remedies.

Using the pendulum to heal

Before giving a person healing, it is beneficial to cleanse and balance their energies, cleanse their aura, balance the negative and positive ions in their body, balance their chakras and polarity, and check for the presence of geopathic stress. These should always be checked before you treat a patient or relative, as these energy blockages will stop the body responding to healing, medication, alternative therapies, or treatments. This can all be done by the pendulum, and all that's needed is positive thought, so that you expect it to happen, since if you doubt that the pendulum can be used for this work, then negative energy slips into the exercise. Once the body's energies have been cleansed, balanced, and energy blockages cleared, the patient's body is then able to start the process of healing itself.

Please don't ever start to dowse while thinking 'I know this won't work but I may as well try it' because, if you think along those lines, you are doomed to failure, as although the power of positive thought is extremely powerful, sadly the power of negative thought is also powerful.

Using the pendulum to treat illness and energy problems

I want to remind you that before using the pendulum to treat illnesses or any energy problems, it is essential to cleanse its energy, so that you get the correct results, because when the pendulum has negative energy it will give the wrong answers. Sorry to nag, but can I also remind you to please place protection around yourself before you start the exercise.

How do you get the pendulum to send medication or do other tasks?

1. The first step is to ensure your pendulum is clear of negative energy, so run some healing or reiki energy through it, and ask the pendulum to please carry out the task.
2. Hold the pendulum, and give it a gentle nudge to get it moving slowly back and forward, and then mentally ask it to please show you your 'Yes' sign when the task is completed.
3. Thank the pendulum, and then dowse to ask if the aura is cleansed, or whatever the task requested is completed.
4. Remember that you should have protection around you before doing this task, and when finished you must run a beam of light through your body to earth you, and cut the connection.

Once you have done this form of healing a few times, you will find that you automatically protect and cleanse your energy, but at first it is sometimes difficult to remember all the things you are supposed to do!

The pendulum is capable of giving healing to a person in the room or is equally effective when used for distant healing. It can be used to cleanse the aura, balance the chakras, balance polarity, or give a new energy link with the earth, as this can be broken if the person has been exposed to powerful geopathic stress.

Strange though it may sound, the pendulum can be used to send medication to a person whose body is short of minerals or vitamins. If you have dowsed, and found that your patient's body is short of iodine, you can ask the pendulum to channel iodine to top up the iodine level in your patient's body or to remove excess, which can be the case in certain schizophrenic patients. Yes, it all sounds very far fetched but it does work. I can assure you that your pendulum can do this work. I have been successfully sending medication to friends and family for many years with great results. I am fortunate that, as a medium, I get a little voice telling me what minerals are lacking, and what to send.

When you are concerned that a person is ill, simply lacking in energy, or has a low immune system, an alternative option to channeling individual minerals or amino acids to them is to ask the pendulum the question 'Are you able to channel the right amount of all the nutrients needed at this moment in my patient's body?' The answer should be 'Yes,' so you can then ask the pendulum 'Please send my patient all the missing nutrients to bring them to the correct level', or words to that effect, and don't forget to ask to be shown the 'Yes' sign when the task is finished. Then check again to establish the work has been done, by asking if the patient's body is short of any nutrients. This exercise must be done regularly as channeled medication must be topped up every few days.

Your pendulum is an excellent tool to clear drinking water and food of toxins, chemicals, and harmful bacteria, clear negative energy from a person or building, balance black ley lines, or clear buildings of geopathic stress.

Yin and Yang

It is so easy for the body's energies to be out of balance, so the Yin and Yang must be kept well balanced for good health and vitality.

Ask the pendulum if the energies are out of balance, and if you receive a 'Yes' then hold the pendulum, and ask it to please balance the person's body energies.

Summary

Don't be too surprised if, when you discover that you can dowse, you become very enthusiastic and want to dowse all sorts of questions. The wonderful thing about dowsing is that it is a free tool which has been given to all of us to use in everyday situations. It has a long history as records show it was used by man 8,000 years ago, and the pendulum and rods must surely be the only tools in existence which have remained effective all those years.

Dowsing has been used by armies in many countries to help fight wars and, as I mentioned earlier, platoons of US marines were taught to dowse to find Vietcong tunnels during the Vietnam war, and the British government used dowsers during World War 2 to find mines. These facts confirm that dowsing is not simply a play thing, as it has over the years saved many lives.

It only takes a few minutes to learn the basic principles of dowsing, and it is a great feeling of excitement when you discover you can dowse. Once you start to use your pendulum regularly, you will build up a rapport with it, so that you know the answer before it starts to move.

Like any skill, the basics are important, so to ensure you and your pendulum work well as a team, you must cleanse its energy each time you use it. It is also important to choose the wording of your questions.

Always remind yourself that we humans are born with free will, and the pendulum will not give you an answer when you can choose the outcome, so remember never to start a question with the words 'Should I?' as you have the choice.

Another basic rule is 'Protection' as it is important to place a white light of protection around yourself before you dowse, to protect from any negative energies. Many dowsers don't bother to protect themselves, but it is better to be safe than sorry, and as long as you remember the basics, you and your pendulum will make a great team!

Endnotes

1. Bird. Christopher, *Divining Hand 'Observer for the US Forces*, March 13 1967. New Age Press Incorporated. 1989. ISBN 08761 30902.
2. Gordon, Rolf, *Are You Sleeping in a Safe Place?*, 6th edition. Available from Dulwich Health, 130 Gipsy Hill, London SE19 1PL, UK.
3. Davies, Rodney, *Discover Your Psychic Powers*. Aquarian Press/Thorson. 1991. ISBN 1-85538-073-0.
4. Ross, Edward T., and Wright Richard D., *The Diving Mind*. Destiny Books. Rochester, Vermont. ISBN 0-89281-263-X.

2

Dowsing which therapy or treatment is right for you. Using the pendulum to balance the body's polarity and ions

The human body has negative and positive ions, and often when a person is ill these ions are out of balance. You may assume that when they are balanced, negative and positive are in equal numbers, but that is not the case, as there should always be more negative than positive, so this is a job for the pendulum. What are ions? They are minute charges of static electricity in the air, and are an important part of the fabric of our atmosphere, and negative ions are generally accepted as being charged forms of oxygen and water.[1]

We ladies have all at some time cursed an ion imbalance, as too many positive ions are the culprits that cause your skirt to cling to your legs, when they create static electricity around you! Another example of ion imbalance is when you dust the screen of the television set, and the dust goes straight back on to the screen. There should always be more negative than positive of these minute molecules, but like other energies there can be an imbalance and that's when you get illness, as it can instigate a range of illnesses including skin rash, migraine, asthma, behaviour problems, and mood swings.

You've probably heard policemen joke about how they dread being on duty when there is a full moon as the police station becomes a hectic place, as the madmen are loose in town! This makes a lot of sense as ion levels are linked to the energy of the moon. Too many positive ions in the body create excess serotonin. This stress neurohormone charges the mind to become overactive, so are your child's ADHD symptoms worse when the moon is full?

When a lot of static electricity is present, it is caused by an excess of positive ions, and they can be measured on a scale of ions per cubic centimetre of space.

This imbalance is often found in buildings, cars, office equipment, synthetic carpets, and clothing made of man made fabrics. All of these are notorious for ion imbalance. Negative ions work to balance the ions, and can be aided by an ionizer, but the pendulum will do the job of balancing the ions temporarily if asked.

Most of us at one time have experienced a light electric shock when we touched someone's jacket or ran our fingers through the carpet pile – that's ions!

All can be resolved by asking the pendulum the questions

1. Is there too high a level of positive ions in this room?
2. Are there more positive than negative ions in this room?

If you receive confirmation that the level is wrong, you can then ask your pendulum 'Please balance the level of negative and positive ions and show me the "Yes" sign when complete'. Unfortunately this is only a temporary cure, for as soon as you switch on your computer or television the ion problem returns.

Do you spend a lot of time working on your computer? Do you find that your eyes feel dry, the skin on your hands feels dry, or you have an annoying rash on your face? Then perhaps you need an ionizer. I recently purchased a small pyramid-shaped model from Healthy House, which is ideal for my small office, and has resolved my dry hands and itchy eyes problem. If you would like more detailed information about ions, I recommend the website of Zenion Industries Inc. www.zenion.com as they have an excellent report on ions.

As well as the ionizer producing negative ions and working to balance the positive and negative ions in a room, it has been discovered that it can eliminate the infection Acinetobacter which is a constant health threat to many patients.

Results of research carried out at St. James's Hospital in Leeds, UK, showed hard to believe results, as the ionizer had succeeded in eliminating this powerful bacterium which plagues hospitals.

More confirmation comes from Sharp, whose research showed the ions from their air conditioning systems inactivates viruses including influenza.[2]

Isn't it amazing how often there is a simple answer to curing an illness, when scientists have worked for long periods researching to find a cure, and to no avail?

This brings an interesting thought into my mind: if the ionizer can remove harmful viruses, is it possible that these viruses would not be in hospitals if the levels of ions were kept at the correct level?

Travelling farther along this line of thought, I wonder if viruses can only survive where there is a shortage of negative ions in the atmosphere? When you stop and think about this idea, you realize that hospitals have an enormous amount of electrical equipment which creates positive ions, and most of us have many electrical gadgets, and some of these items like the phone, cooker, computer, printer, toaster, and kettle are constantly switched on, ready for use.

Now you can ask your pendulum a few questions about ions and ionizers.

1. Can the negative ions from an ionizer remove some harmful viruses?
2. Do viruses only survive where there is a shortage of negative ions?

The pendulum can cleanse the aura

To cleanse the person's aura, simply hold the pendulum, and give it a gentle swing to start it moving, then mentally ask it to please cleanse the person's aura, mentioning their Christian name. This should only take a couple of minutes to finish, so ask the pendulum to please show you the 'Yes' sign when the aura has been cleansed, then say thank you.[3]

Once the aura has been cleansed, you can ask the pendulum if there are any cracks in the aura, and if the aura needs to be healed. Cracks can appear in the aura if the person has been involved in an accident, or a traumatic experience. You can ask the pendulum to please heal the aura, and repair the cracks, and to show you the 'Yes' sign when the work has been done.

Balance the chakras with your pendulum

Start by asking the pendulum if the energies of any of the person's seven main chakras are out of balance.

If you receive a 'Yes,' then you can ask which chakra is out of balance.

You can also ask if two chakras are out of balance.

Once you have established if any of the chakras are out of balance, you can then ask if any of the chakras are in need of healing? If the answer is 'Yes', you can ask the pendulum to heal the chakra.

Hold the pendulum and ask that it please balances the chakras and shows you the 'Yes' sign when finished. Now that it is balanced, it is the time to heal any sick chakra.

The seven main chakras

1. The crown chakra	5. The solar plexus
2. The third eyebrow	6. The spleen chakra
3. The throat chakra	7. The base chakra
4. The heart chakra	

A chakra is an energy vortex or energy centre, linked to the working of a specific area of the body, so if a chakra is out of balance, then there could be health problems in that part of the body. Each chakra is a different colour which creates energy in that area of the body, a fascinating subject.

The pendulum and your health

I want now to talk about using your pendulum to diagnose the health problem, then establish the most suitable therapy or treatment.

Is backache a problem?

Are you plagued with backache? Then try using your pendulum or dowsing rods to locate the problem. By asking your pendulum the following questions or similar ones about your backache, you will be able to locate the problem, and also establish the most suitable treatment.

1. Is the problem muscular?
2. Is the pain caused by a soft tissue injury?
3. Will the problem respond to physiotherapy?
4. Is a disc out of place?
5. Is the pelvis out of alignment?

If you suffer from back or shoulder pain, as well as the questions above, perhaps you'd like to ask if the problem is caused by normal wear and tear, or whether you have damaged a tendon. You can add other questions to the list, depending on the history or source of the pain.

Make a list of the possible causes to dowse and ask each question separately, until you receive a positive answer. Once you have tracked down the cause of the pain, you can then diagnose the best method to treat it. You can ask if the injury would respond to massage, chiropractic treatment, osteopathy, acupuncture, or shiatsu.

Start by asking the question 'Would massage treatment improve my backache?' then change the wording and ask 'Would massage relieve my back pain?' then ask the same question of other therapies, and once you have received a few positive answers, you can make a list of the these different therapies, and dowse which is the most effective treatment.

You can then dowse to find out which minerals or vitamins you should take to help heal the injury, so ask the following questions:

1. 'Would Vervain help to relieve my back problem?' Vervain helps you to relax, and improves the quality of sleep, which can be disturbed by discomfort. This in turn creates stress and tension, so slowing the healing process.
2. Ask 'Is my body short of copper?'. A shortage of copper is often the cause of aches in joints. Many aches and pains are linked to a shortage of this mineral, and this is the reason many sufferers swear by their copper bracelet. Between 60% and 80% of copper, or other minerals or chemicals placed on the skin, go directly to the bloodstream.
3. Ask if your back problem would be helped by any of the following: glucosomine, chondroiten, boswellia, or zinc.

These are all available from most health shops. By using the pendulum, you should be able to get a clear picture of both the problem and best treatment, and so save money by only buying pills or ointments which will improve the problem. Also you will not waste money on therapies which will not improve the problem, as it is so easy to have several sessions of treatment before you begin to realize it is not making any noticeable improvement of the problem. Whatever your health problem, it is possible to diagnose it with the pendulum and find the right treatment and the right therapist for you.

Diagnosing a health problem

I want to remind you that I am a healer, and not a qualified medical doctor, so before following my advice, please consult a medical doctor.

When you feel ill, and you suffer lots of annoying symptoms which are vague, so the doctor finds it difficult to diagnose the cause of your illness, then often by dowsing you can locate the problem area. Start by dowsing to check the different sections of the body, and ask the following questions.

1. Is my lymphatic system properly balanced?
2. Are my endocrine glands working correctly?
3. Is there a problem in my respiratory system?
4. Is the cardiovascular system working efficiently?
5. Are my symptoms caused by disruption of one of these systems?
6. Is the pineal gland working effectively? (this is linked to the hormone melatonin)

When you have established which system is not properly balanced, you can look at a health atlas, and make a list of all the parts of the body within that system, so you can dowse each part to locate the problem

Which therapy or treatment is most beneficial to an illness

Interest in complementary therapies has grown rapidly over the past decade and the proof is the number of therapists practicing, and the amazing number of different therapies available – and new ones seem to keep arriving!

Sales of crystals, herbs and oils are now big business, as people become aware of the benefits of using these treatments, and literally billions of pounds and dollars are spent each year around the world on these items. It is important to know that you are purchasing the right product for your needs, so that is where dowsing is able to lend a helping hand.

Five years ago in the UK, Eileen Inge Herzberg, in her book *Know Your Complementary Therapies*, stated that back in 1998, there were five million patients each year using complementary practitioners. That number has increased dramatically since then, and there are roughly 60,000 therapists, and probably about a third of them are either spiritual healers or reiki healers.[4]

Therapists are making a healthy living, as in UK alone we spend nearly £2 billion on alternative and complementary therapy, and if you add these figures to those of the USA, Canada, Europe, and Australia, we are talking about a multi billion industry which is here to stay.

More confirmation comes from the results of a poll by the Institute of Complementary Medicine, on behalf of the BBC, as these figures suggest that one in every five adults in the UK used some form of this medicine.[5]

Dowse and ask if your pet would respond to healing treatment. Phrase the question several different ways and you will find that all give a positive 'Yes'. As popularity has increased and more and more people appreciate the benefits, many are bringing their children for treatment and animals, including dogs, cats and horses, enjoy it.

I have had the pleasure of giving healing to many different animals, and as well as dogs, cats, and loppy eared rabbits, I have given healing to rodents including brown and white rats and a ferret who was very receptive to the healing energy. I have also given healing to many dogs who were entered for the world famous Crufts Dog Show, as their owners believed the healing treatment gave their coat an extra shine and their eyes became brighter!

If any of your pets develop aches or pains, dowse and ask if there is an alternative therapy or medicine which will relieve their heath problem, as most animals prefer this treatment to visiting the vet. When they enter the door of the surgery, they sense the fear of other animals, and many start to shake, or dig their paws firmly on the pavement and try hard to refuse to enter the surgery.

Although complementary therapists are not usually medically trained doctors, they are very dedicated, and their training is expensive and often lengthy. It can involve attending many lectures, and some therapists have to go before an examination board to ensure their skills are sufficient to become qualified. Always try to choose a therapist who is a member of an organization linked to that particular therapy, as membership usually includes insurance cover and a strict Code of Conduct.

With so many therapies to choose from, how do you decide which will be most effective in treating your health problem? That's where the pendulum is a big help, as simply by asking which of the therapies listed below would be beneficial to your problem, you will be able to make a short list of them, and then choose the right one for your needs at this time.

Chart of alternative therapies

aromatherapy	iridology
acupuncture	Indian head massage
colour therapy	kinesiology
crystal healing	neurolinguistic programming (NLP)
chiropractor	thought field therapy
Dr Bach flower remedies	reflexology
emotional freedom technique (EFT)	reiki healing
homeopathy	shiatsu
herbalism	spiritual healing
hypnotherapy	sound therapy

These are only a few of the many therapies available, so add to the list any others which you feel may be helpful, then dowse to ask which therapies would be beneficial to treat the specific ailment. Dowse the following questions:

To find which therapies would be beneficial for the illness ask

1. Would this therapy be beneficial to my illness?
2. Would the therapy reduce my symptoms?

As you will find several of them would be beneficial, you can then narrow down the choice by asking the following questions:

3. Which of these therapies on the short list would be the most beneficial!
4. How many treatments will be required?

Once you have established the therapy you wish to use, you can look in the telephone directory to find a list of therapists, and then dowse to find the most suitable one. Alternatively you can contact the organization for that particular therapy, and request a list of qualified members for you to dowse. Yoga, meditation, tai chi, and Alexander technique are all self-help therapies and can be done either at home or in a group.

Yoga is an excellent exercise to relieve stress and give your body an opportunity to relax, so if you suffer from stress, or have a very busy life, dowse and ask if your body would benefit from yoga sessions?

Meditation is a wonderful way to give your mind a complete rest, as it shuts off from all everyday things and commitments, leaving you feeling completely relaxed and rejuvenated, so dowse and ask if your body and mind would benefit from meditation.

Tai chi is all about control and discipline, so is the ideal exercise for those who enjoy gentle exercise, but are in control of their body. Dowse and ask if it is the right exercise for you.

The Alexander technique is a method of using your body in the correct manner so that no energy is wasted in movements. This is not so much an exercise as a way of life, as once you have mastered the technique, you will never look back! This method of movement (which teaches you to walk, stand, and sit properly, and arise from a chair without putting strain on your neck) is taught in many stage schools. Dowse and ask if the Alexander technique would be beneficial to you. How often have you been to the theatre and seen the actress gets up from a chair, and seem to glide across the stage, or sit down so elegantly, and get up from a chair as though everything in her body is in balance – and it is! You too could do that!

Dowsing aromatherapy oils

Aromatherapy is all about being nice to yourself, and this treatment comes high on the 'feel good' chart, even when you don't need a treatment for illness or aches and pains. To lie back and enjoy a soothing massage or facial is great, and soaking in a bath of warm water with fragrance of aromatherapy oils.

Never underestimate the Power of Touch, as it can be a wonderful healing tool, and if exposure to pollution or electro-magnetic fields is making you feel flat, it's time to give yourself an aromatherapy treat. This treatment is helpful to those who suffer from depression, insomnia, ADHD, anxiety, stress, head-aches, neck and shoulder tension, backache or other muscular aches, arthritis, bad circulation, or tiredness, as an aromatherapy massage will the spirits.

So if you are looking for a 'feel good factor' your pendulum will confirm that if you treat yourself it is guaranteed to make you feel very relaxed and pampered, and will release some of the stress and tension from the body.

When you have tried a treatment and enjoyed it, perhaps you will feel that you would like to learn how to give an aromatherapy treatment to your partner or children, and this new skill would certainly raise you in the popularity chart. You can enroll at a local Adult Education Centre as today many courses are being taught at local centres. I attended one of these courses, and as well as learning about oils and enjoying the wonderful massage, it was a great opportunity to practice my technique on class mates, before being let loose on my friends and family!

What exactly are essential oils?

Aromatherapy is a very ancient form of healing, and uses beautiful fragrances. These are all natural ingredients, known as essential oils.

They have come from plants, flowers and fruit, while certain other oils are extracted from resin and tree bark. Nobody really knows the true secret of essential oils – many folks believe it is a magical combination of organic compounds, while others believe and are truly convinced that the wonderful aroma and healing properties come directly from the life force of the flower or bark. Your pendulum will give you an answer to this question.

Dowse:

1. Do healing properties in essential oils come from the life force of the plant?
2. Do the healing properties of essential oils come from the organic compound of the plant?

It has been known for several thousand years that plants contain healing properties, and more confirmation came in the past century from the wonderful work of Dr Bach who gave us flower remedies. I attended a course at his home eighteen years ago, and the house had been kept exactly the same as when he was alive, with old fashioned furnishings and his books on the shelf. His garden still had the same range of plants which he had used in his flower remedies, and it was a truly wonderful experience to visit the home of this amazing man, it was like going on a trip back in time.

It is now a proven fact that flowers and trees have healing powers, and certain plants have the ability to cure specific illnesses. This is the reason why so many biochemists and pharmaceutical companies are investing a lot of money in researching these plant oils. They have succeeded in isolating many of their ingredients, since doing very serious research in the rain forests for cures for illnesses. It is a very slow process as these oils come from different parts of the plants, so biochemists need a lot of patience as they research petals, leaves, seeds, roots, and bark.

If you are interested in learning more about plants used successfully by natives to heal illnesses, I recommend both of Mark J. Plotkin's books *Medicine Quest*[6] and *Tales of a Shaman's Apprentice*.[7]

Today many prescription medicines contain extract from flowers, plants, or trees. Digitalis from the foxglove is used to treat certain heart conditions, and St. John's Wart is used in many hospitals to treat depression. The tea tree, an amazing native of Australia, gives us oil. Tea tree oil is known world wide as a powerful antiseptic which kills germs and harmful bacteria, and many women swear by it as an excellent cure for troublesome thrush.

If you have never used aromatherapy oils, please don't worry that it will be a messy process, with oil getting on the carpet, sheets and your clothes, as these oils are user friendly, and seem to miraculously soak into the skin, so you are not left feeling in need of an instant bath. These treatments can be so much more beneficial if you dowse to find the most effective oil for the occasion. Many patients swear that aromatherapy helps them to reduce their need for medication, as suddenly they find that they don't seem to feel the need for painkilling tablets, or that their erratic sleep pattern has improved dramatically, and they no longer dread going to bed and spending hours desperately trying to get to sleep.

Alzheimer's and Parkinson's disease sufferers report aromatherapy massage and oils relaxes their mind and body, and relations say it stops those who tend to wander off on little journeys, to be peaceful. Aromatherapy helps to release stress, improves arthritis pains, and is comforting to the terminally ill. So with so many different uses it is important to dowse to find the most suitable oil for the patient.

Certain oils are more beneficial than others for improving different ailments, so I have listed some oils for you to dowse. Here are the main categories: floral, green, citrus, and woody. Dowse to ask which category is best for you.

There are many other oils to add to the list, so start dowsing the right oils for you, and then ask if you would benefit from using a combination of oils. You can then dowse to find the best oil to combine favourably with the first you have dowsed. Once you have found the best combination for you, make a note of the combination for this ailment, so that you do not need to dowse each time you use oils for this ailment, as each health problem responds to different oils. Some illnesses respond

mandarin	sandalwood
jasmine	ylang ylang
lavender	frankinsense
juniper	patchouli
tea tree	cypress
rose	eucalyptus
geranium	clary sage
rosemary	neroli

▲ *Chart of aromatherapy oil*

better to a combination of two or three oils, so it is worth taking the time to find the right oils for the ailment.

To avoid dowsing every oil on the list, start by asking the question:

Is the most suitable oil for this treatment in the first column of oils listed? If the answer is NO, then you know not to waste time dowsing every oil in the first column and go straight to the second column. The list of oils is not complete as it is really only to give you an example, so I recommend you purchase a book on aromatherapy, which will give you details of the oils. If you would like to learn how to use these wonderful oils, I recommend attending a class at your local adult centre as it can be great fun and very beneficial.

Sense of smell

Should you or your child not be receptive to the idea of an aromatherapy massage, then another easy option is to use an oil burner, or an oil burning ring, which sits on the light bulb of a table lamp. Simply place a little relaxing fragrance in the ring and add a teaspoonful of water. The heat of the light bulb enables the soothing aroma to fill the room. This is a subtle and easy way of creating a relaxing atmosphere to reduce stress.

The sense of smell can be a powerful tool to heal stress and anxiety, so burning aromatherapy oils in a room changes the ambience. Many therapists use an oil burner in their therapy room to relax patients, so dowse and ask which is the right oil to use in your burner.

Enjoy a magical bath

A really wonderful way to release stress and anxiety or aches and pains, is to lie in a warm bath with a few drops of lavender or other oil in the water, then relax and feel it soaking into your skin. I always switch off the overhead light, and place a lighted candle in the wash basin where it is safe from accident.

Please believe me, it is a wonderful feeling to lie back and relax in the warm water, and gentle scent of oil in the candlelight, like me you probably won't want to come out of the bath until the water becomes cool!

Are you a person who does not like sweet flowery scents? Then don't worry as aromatherapy oils come in a range of scents so there's an oil to suit everyone's taste. As well as the popular floral scents, you can choose the citrus group for their fresh sharp scent; or the spicy green group, which gives a warm smell of spices; and for those who want a more basic scent, there is the earthy woody group. So dowse and find which group of oils is most beneficial for you. Should aromatherapy not appeal to you then reflexology may be the answer, and you will enjoy exploring this ancient therapy.

Reflexology is another very relaxing complementary therapy ideal for those who enjoy having their feet massaged. It is a great therapy for aiding the release of stress and tension, and an excellent tool to unblock any buildup of toxins, and to release negative energy in the body.

How does reflexology work? The principle of reflexology is that the feet are a map of the body, and each part of each foot represents a section of the body. Should you have a problem in a specific area, then massaging the corresponding area of the foot will often release the problem.

All reflexologists are trained to clear energy blockages so if you suspect that you have any energy blockages in your body, then dowse and ask if reflexology treatment can release them.

The reflexologist applies pressure to various points on the foot which effectively releases energy from blocked channels, and this in turn allows energy to circulate to organs and glands, so starting a healing process.

Reflexology is an excellent treatment for anyone who is suffering from ADHD, anxiety, or emotional problems, as it releases tension. This non-invasive holistic therapy treats every organ, endocrine system, muscles, and the skeletal system, indeed every single part of the body.

Reflexology can be done anywhere and as well as being done on the feet, this treatment can be effective when done on the hands. It is certainly relaxing to lie back and have someone work on your feet, but if you do not enjoy having your feet touched, then hand treatment is the answer. I recently attended a hand reflexology course and soon realized it is an ideal treatment to be carried out when there is a shortage of space. There's no longer any need to worry if you get a severe pain, or feel ill when visiting the theatre or a nice restaurant, since this treatment can be carried out without others realizing what's going on. Simply by discreetly holding the person's hand, treatment can be given, so if a member of your family suffers aches and pains, perhaps you would like to learn this method of giving relief. You can dowse to confirm if reflexology will benefit their condition. It is well worth attending a short course in this treatment as knowing the basics can benefit the family.

Next I want to tell you a few facts about the ancient therapy shiatsu.

Shiatsu

Shiatsu is another very ancient therapy which specializes in unblocking meridians and balancing the energy in the body. This Japanese therapy is all about balancing the Yin and Yang (negative and positive) energy and is an excellent treatment to create tranquility, and reduces ADHD symptoms. It is also effective in releasing tension, and relieving backache or digestive problems.

You do not need to remove your clothing other than outer garments – you simply lie on the floor or therapy bed while the therapist works her fingers on various pressure points on the body. It is a similar treatment to acupuncture, but the big advantage with shiatsu is that no needles are used, as fingers do the work.

Dowse:

1. Does your body have any blocked meridians?
2. Would your body benefit from shiatsu treatment?

Perhaps you would prefer acupuncture treatment, so read on to find out about this ancient and well tried treatment.

Acupuncture

This very ancient treatment has been practiced in the East for a great many centuries and is based on balancing the Yin and Yang energy in the body. This unusual therapy is an effective treatment for emotional and behavioural problems, including fatigue, anxiety, and depression. Equally it is often successful in treating sports injuries, arthritic pains, and gynecological problems.

During a treatment the therapist inserts fine needles into the skin to stimulate certain acupuncture points, and to bring the body back into harmony. Before starting a treatment, the therapist asks many questions about health problems, and looks closely at the patient, taking into consideration the colour of the skin, eyes, and tongue.

Don't be too surprised if a Chinese acupuncturist gives you a bag of Chinese herbs to take home, with instructions to boil the herbs and drink the tea. A word of warning – it smells awful, I assure you!

Dowse:

1. Will acupuncture treatment improve the symptoms?
2. Will drinking the prescribed Chinese herbal potion improve my condition?

Acupuncture is an effective treatment to stop addiction to tobacco, and is now accepted in the western world by many doctors, as an effective therapy for both physical and emotional illnesses.

Perhaps you will prefer a much gentler alternative therapy like crystal healing?

Crystal healing

Crystals have long been recognized as holding mystical and healing powers, and are an exciting tool to treat young children and teenagers, whether suffering from emotional or physical illnesses. These natural stones have been shown to give good results when treating ADHD, anxiety, and emotional problems. Each crystal can be programmed to give out healing energy to the sufferer, so if you do not know a crystal therapist, or it is difficult to get a child to their clinic, then the child can wear the programmed crystal.

Would your child refuse point blank to wear the crystal? Then don't worry as all is not lost! You can get around the problem by programming a crystal to send healing energy to the child, and place it in the child's bedroom.

Dowse:

1. Would crystal therapy help to reduce the symptoms?
2. Will a crystal programmed to give healing, help to reduce symptoms?
3. Dowse to ask if a rose quartz is the right crystal to use for the treatment.

If you receive a 'No' answer, then dowse and ask if a clear quartz is the right crystal to use for this treatment. Another option is the beautiful amethyst, so again you can dowse and ask if it is the right crystal to use for this particular treatment.

Should you decide to use a crystal to heal a member of your family, it is important to regularly cleanse the crystal, as they collect negative energy. There are several different ways to cleanse a crystal, and the easiest method is to mentally run white light or healing energy through the stone for a few seconds. Washing in water containing sea salt is a popular method but some therapists disapprove of this treatment! In the end it is all about intent and positive thought, so whatever method you use to cleanse the energy of the crystal, it will work.

Crystals can be used to give healing to sick animals, so if your dog suffers from arthritis or is of a very nervous disposition, then program a small crystal and attach it to the animal's collar, also place one in his bed.

To program a crystal to give healing or protection, whether clear quartz, rose quartz, amethyst, moonstone, or amber, simply hold the crystal in the palm of your hand, and mentally talk to it. Sounds daft I agree, but as we are all made of energy, the crystals pick up our message. Ask the crystal to please channel healing energy to the patient, and the crystal will then start to beam out healing energy. It's important to remember to say 'Thank you' to the crystal as it builds up a good relationship with the crystal!

Following on from crystals I would like to talk about another natural tool given to us by our Creator, and that is the healing power of light.

Light therapy

Light therapy is rapidly becoming recognized as a powerful healing treatment and is suitable for everyone. Physicists have been telling us for a long time that light is constantly surrounding all of us, and every living thing, as it is an important part of the electromagnetic spectrum.

The powerful vibration of light is the basis of all living beings from the beginning of time. We can all live a few days without food, as has often been proved when survivors of disasters have been found alive many days later. We cannot survive long without light, as light is needed to create oxygen, and the human body is designed to function with both light and darkness.

Light is a powerful natural healer and, as well as healing humans, it quite naturally gives plants the energy needed to grow, and to convert carbon dioxide to oxygen, which is necessary for their survival. Light is something we seldom think about, and most of us underrate its power, but a shortage of light in our life can result in depression and seasonal affective disorder (SAD). Both daylight and sunlight have healing energy, so take advantage of this free therapy when possible, and ensure the living rooms in your home get maximum light. Feng shui appreciates the benefits of mirrors as a tool to create light in the home, particularly rooms facing north. If any of your living rooms or office lack sunlight, dowse and ask if a mirror placed to reflect light would benefit heath.

Jacob Liberman, a very well respected pioneer of light therapy, in his book *Light, Medicine of the Future*, states that light is indeed the medicine of the future, and in years to come, will become accepted by the medical profession as a respected healing tool.[8] Today many healers use light in their work, whether beams of pure white light, rays of coloured light or gold light. A great many healers use light as a form of protection from negative energy, by visualizing a white light surrounding their body, or by placing themselves in a bubble or ball of white light.

Light therapy – the light box

Scientist Dr Harry Oldfield has invented a light box which is an effective and gentle healing tool. This therapy allows the patient to sit in front of the light, and let their body absorb the rays. It is an ideal therapy to relieve symptoms of depression, anxiety stress, or behaviour problems, as well as almost all other illnesses.

This gifted scientist has lectured in many parts of the world, and runs the Harry Oldfield Clinic and School of Electro Crystal

Healing, where therapists come to train in light box and crystal therapy.[9]

Dowse:

1. Would light therapy help to relieve your painful symptoms?
2. Is light a medicine of the future?
3. Would more sunlight be beneficial to my health problem?

I have only mentioned a few of the many alternative therapies available, so please explore all the therapies that your gut feeling tells you may help to reduce your health problem. When you read about a specific treatment, dowse and ask your pendulum if this treatment would improve your illness or injury? You can vary the wording by asking if it would speed up the healing process, or if it would reduce inflammation. There are many different ways to word the question, so please use the words which seem right to you, and don't be afraid to follow your instincts and explore several therapies.

You will find books on most therapies in new-age shops, and you will find that associations linked to most therapies have an informative website on the internet. These web pages usually give an address when you can obtain the name of a local therapist.

Never underestimate the benefits of dowsing for health, since this gift is a 'must' at the scene of an accident, as it will confirm if the patient should be kept still, whether any bones have been broken, and whether nearby plants can be used as a medication.

Dowsing will tell you if the ions in your home or office are badly out of balance, and confirm if a patient's ions need to be rebalanced and, even better, it will do the job of balancing the ions when requested to do so. This little tool can also be used to check that a person's aura is healthy and, when asked, it will cleanse or repair damage.

You will find your pendulum helpful when you suffer backache, as it will guide you to the correct treatment. If in doubt whether to visit a chiropractor, osteopath, or physiotherapist, it will tell you which would be the most beneficial treatment for the injury, so speeding up recovery time and saving money.

Would you like to try an alternative therapy to give your health a boost but don't know which therapy to choose, as it is a minefield with so many different therapies available? When you choose a therapist, please check that they are a member of an organization and work to a Code of Conduct.

There are many therapies available to release stress and replenish your missing 'feel good factor'. If you want to get a friend or partner to give you an aromatherapy massage, then dowse and ask which essential oil would be most beneficial for your present condition. As this will ensure you get the maximum benefit.

Once you become a confident dowser, you'll find that it will save you money by discouraging you from purchasing the wrong oils or creams, and you'll wonder how you managed before you discovered dowsing!

Endnotes

1. Zenion Industries, Health Report. http://www.zenion.com
2. *Nexus New Times*, March 2003, p. 6. Global News. 'Negative Ions Wipe Out Hospital Infections'. Source – *The New Scientist*, January 3 2002. http://www.newscientist.com/news/news.jsp?id=ns99993228
3. Herzberg, Inge Eileen, *Know Your Complementary Therapies*, ICM Poll on behalf of BBC, August 99. Source – Foundation for Integrated Medicine, Evidence to the House of Lords. Science & Technology Committee 111. Complementary & Alternative Medicine. CAM.
4. Plotkin, Mark J., PhD, *Tales of a Shaman's Apprentice, An Ethnobotonist's Search for New Medicine in the Rain Forest*. Penguin Books, USA, 1993. ISBN 0-1401-2991-X.
5. Plotkin, Mark J., PhD, *Medicine Quest, In Search of Nature's Healing Secrets*. Virgin/Penguin. 2001 ISBN 0140262105.
6. Oldfield, Dr Harry, The Harry Oldfield Clinic and School of Electro Crystal Healing, London.
7. Liberman, Jacob, OD. PhD, *Light, Medicine of the Future*. Bear & Company, New Mexico, 1991. ISBN 0-879181-01-0.

3

Dowsing illness

It is now time to talk about a few of the illnesses which can be helped by dowsing to find out which minerals, vitamins, and amino acids are deficient in the body.

Arthritis

Arthritis is a painful complaint which seems to strike all ages, and the number of sufferers is increasing each year. There are many minerals and plants which help some sufferers, but none of them suits all sufferers, so dowse to find which ones are right for you or your patient.

1. Do any of the deadly nightshade family aggravate my arthritis? These include tomatoes, potatoes and aubergines, so ask the pendulum each one in turn.
2. Is the body short of histamine? Then ask, Is there excess?
3. Would copper relieve pain? (It helps inflammatory conditions.) Also ask, Is your body short of copper?
4. Would glucosamine help to relieve symptoms?
5. Would the body benefit from extra boron? (Boron heals bones, skin, and mental performance.)
6. Ask if Devil's Claw would relieve symptoms. Research in China found 90% of patients experienced reduction in inflammation and joint pain.
7. Many sufferers swear by alfalfa. Ask if it would relieve pain and symptoms.

8. Germanium is a trace mineral. Ask if it would improve symptoms and pain level.
9. Sulfur is excellent for cleaning the blood. Ask if the patient would benefit from it.
10. Dowse if the patient is sleeping or working over geopathic stress, as this weakens the immune system, and stops the body from healing itself.
11. Dowse to ask if the parathyroid gland is balanced? If 'No' then use the pendulum to balance it.
12. Dowse to ask if the level of ions is balanced? If 'No' then use the pendulum to balance.
13. Dowse for live rubella vaccine in the body. (Often present in arthritis sufferers.)
14. Is the duodenum balanced?
15. Ask the pendulum to balance energies if not balanced.

When you dowse you will almost certainly find that several items on the above list will all reduce pain, but as you do not want to take too many different pills, you can write down the names of all the minerals or plants which will reduce pain, then dowse.

Ask the pendulum which are the most effective to reduce pain, which are the most effective to reduce symptoms, and then dowse to find which mineral or plant can effectively benefit both symptoms.

Once you have found which of those on the list would improve the symptoms, you can use the pendulum to channel the ingredient to the person. Ask the pendulum to please channel e.g. germanium to the person, and show you the 'Yes' sign when completed.

Irritable bowel syndrome

Irritable bowel syndrome (IBS) is a rapidly increasing health problem which strikes all ages from the young to the old and completely disrupts the sufferer's quality of life. The thought of being on medication for the rest of your life is depressing, so many of those people inflicted with this uncomfortable illness are turning to alternative remedies in their search for a cure.

I have treated many people over the years who have suffered with this complaint, and found that their problem often responds to an increase of chromium in their diet, and brewer's yeast. Also clearing geopathic stress from their home will help. Below I have listed some of the minerals and amino acids which in many cases are known to reduce this problem.

Dowse and ask if the irritable bowel symptoms would be reduced by including any of those on the following list:

1. Would the irritable bowel symptoms be reduced by having more chromium in my diet?
2. Would a course of brewer's yeast reduce the IBS?
3. Would Omega 3 improve the IBS?
4. Would glutamine help to repair the gut damage?
5. Would the amino acid cystine improve the IBS symptoms?
6. Would including more molybdenum in the diet help the IBS?
7. Ask individual questions – Is the body short of zinc, magnesium, selenium, etc?

Many people who suffer from IBS are sleeping over geopathic stress which is weakening their immune system, so ask the pendulum if they are sleeping over any of these rays, and then ask the pendulum to clear the geopathic stress from the building.

Ulcerated colitis

Ulcerated colitis causes a lot of pain and frustration and also falls into the category of distressing illnesses. Many sufferers have found their body is short of the mineral boron so if any of your family suffer from this painful affliction, it's time to dowse for assistance.

1. Dowse the question – Is their body short of boron?
2. Would extra boron in their diet improve symptoms of this illness?

3. Is their body short of chromium?
4. Ask if any of the following would improve symptoms: manganese, mathake, Pan d'Arco, aloe vera, colloidal silver, molybdenum. If you get a 'Yes' to any of these items, you can use the pendulum to channel the ingredient.

Ask it to please top up their body with the correct amount. Also check for the presence of geopathic stress.

Manganese plays a big part in healing as it is one of the vital minerals. These include magnesium, chromium, copper, zinc, and selenium. Manganese works to protect cells and to heal injuries and inflammation. It is an antioxidant and also does the important job of working in conjunction with copper and zinc, so taking a course of zinc without manganese can upset the balance. If you would like to know more information about this important mineral, I recommend Dr Atkins's book *Dr Atkins' Vita-Nutrient Solution.*[1]

Schizophrenia

Schizophrenia is a most distressing illness which affects the family as well as the patient, and the number of sufferers of this dreadful illness is increasing rapidly, to the extent that it is now the commonest serious mental illness in the West. In the United States alone, 24%, that's almost a quarter of all mental patients, admitted to mental hospitals suffer from schizophrenia.[2]
What is responsible for the alarming increase in this distressing illness? So far the medical profession has not found the cause so perhaps dowsing will identify the culprit.

To dowse the cause of the increase in this illness ask:

1. Is schizophrenia caused by a biochemical problem?
2. Dopamine is often linked to brain illnesses so dowse – Is the body short of dopamine? If 'No', then dowse – Does the body have excess dopamine?[3]
3. Is schizophrenia a genetic disorder? 50% of patients who suffer this agonizing illness, come from families with this

disorder. It cannot always be genetic, as this would not account for the other 50% and the reported increase in cases, so perhaps some cases are linked to genetic disorder, while other are caused by another factor.[4]

4. Ask – Is there more than one cause of schizophrenia?

5. Countries where this illness is treated by fasting show noticeable improvement in symptoms, thus suggesting a reduction in intake of certain foods, including cows' milk, is beneficial to the sufferers.[5] Dowse and ask if the patient suffers an allergic reaction to cows' milk? If you receive a 'Yes', then ask if the allergy is to the hormones injected into the cow to increase milk yield? Also dowse – Would the schizophrenic symptoms be reduced by eliminating cows' milk from the diet?

6. As wheat intake would also have been reduced during fasting, dowse and ask if the patient is allergic to wheat. If you receive a 'Yes', then ask if the illness is linked to pesticides or organophosphates. Unless the patient has been on an organic diet, they will be eating residues of those chemicals in their diet. Ask – Would the schizophrenic symptoms be reduced by eliminating wheat from their diet?

7. Research study of a group of patients suffering from schizophrenia showed a substantial depletion of fatty acids Omega 3, and further studies confirmed a deficiency of these important fats in their diet, so patients were given a supplement of fish oil for a six week period. This simple act led to a noticeable clinical improvement in symptoms, so if a member of your family or a friend suffers from this distressing illness, then it is worth considering a supplement of Omega 3, as they could well benefit from this fish oil in their diet. Dowse and ask – Is the patient's body short of Omega 3? Would any of the person's schizophrenic symptoms by improved by a supplement of Omega 3 in their diet?[6]

To heal the symptoms ask the following questions:

1. Does the patient have a negative attachment? It can be a negative entity or earthbound spirit. If you get a 'Yes' answer, ask – Is it influencing their behaviour? Doctors have found that many sufferers have an attachment which influences their behaviour, and when this has been removed, the symptoms improve dramatically.

2. Many schizophrenia patients have a copper imbalance, so dowse the question: Does the patient have too high a level of copper in their body? If the answer is 'No', then dowse – Is the patient's body short of copper? You can then use the pendulum to balance the level of copper in their body.

3. Ask if the histamine level in their body is too high. If you receive a 'No', then ask if the histamine level in their body is too low. The histamine level is linked to the copper level, so disruption there affects the histamine level. Use the pendulum to balance the copper level, then again repeat the exercise to balance the histamine level in their body.

4. Ask if B6 and B12 vitamins would improve symptoms? Swedish research showed B12 beneficial.

5. Dowse separate questions – Is their body short of zinc, molybdenum, manganese, calcium, cystine, glutamine, or selenium.

6. Ask – Would their symptoms be reduced by taking a course of any of them?

Also ask these questions to check

1. Are their chakras balanced?
2. Is their aura healthy?
3. Are they sleeping over geopathic stress?

When you receive a 'Yes' to any of these problems, you can then use the pendulum to balance the energy, or clear negative energy. By balancing the sufferer's energies, you will help them to feel better and hopefully reduce the symptoms.

4. Dowse and ask if their body has a parasite infestation? If you receive a 'Yes' answer to parasites, then ask the pendulum to

remove them, and show you the 'Yes' sign when accomplished. Dr Hulda Clark writes that parasites are the root cause of many illnesses (see Dr Clark's website for treatment of parasites – www.drclark.com).

5. Dowse – Is their thyroid gland out of balance? If 'Yes', then use the pendulum to balance.

This may seem a lot of questions to dowse, but the cause of this illness is elusive, and the fewer powerful drugs taken the better. It is well worth spending a little time checking to find any imbalances in energy and any minerals which will improve the unpleasant symptoms.

Parkinson's disease

Parkinson's disease is another illness which affects the family as well as the patient, so anything we can find which will improve symptoms has to be a great bonus for these sufferers.

1. Dopamine is recognized as being part of the problem, so start by asking: Does the patient's brain have too much dopamine? L. dopa comes from the *Vicia fava* plant.
2. If you receive a 'No' answer, then ask if the patient's brain is short of dopamine?
3. Dowse and ask – Is their body short of the amino acid tyrosine? Ask if it will improve their symptoms? If the answer is 'Yes', you can ask the pendulum to top up the level in their body to the correct level of this amino acid.
4. There are several minerals and vitamins which can improve symptoms, so ask which ones suit your friend or patient, as everyone reacts differently to illness. Some sufferers may be short of one mineral, while other sufferers with the same illness may be short of a different one. Dowse – Would any of the following minerals or vitamins improve the symptoms of Parkinson's disease? Ginkgo bilobo, Cat's Claw, selenium, zinc, copper, vitamin C, vitamin E. If you receive a 'Yes' answer, then you can dowse each one individually,

and ask if they would improve symptoms. Once you have established which substances would be helpful, you can ask the pendulum to top up their body to the correct level.

5. You should also dowse to check their chakras are balanced,
6. Are the levels of their negative and positive ions balanced? Also ask if they are sleeping over geopathic stress.
7. The symptoms of this illness can be linked to deficiency of melatonin, so dowse and ask if the body is receiving the right amount of melatonin.
8. If 'No', then ask if the pineal gland is functioning efficiently.
9. Ask if healing energy would help the pineal gland to work more efficiently. If the answer is 'Yes', then ask the pendulum to please channel healing energy to the pineal gland and show you the 'Yes' sign when done.

Diabetes

The illness diabetes is on the increase, and is now responsible for many deaths each year. In 2001 it claimed 934,550 lives and the numbers have increased since then, so diabetes is a disease not to be taken lightly[7]

There has been a lot of publicity recently about the possibility of margarine being linked to diabetes, so we will start by dowsing this question.

1. Does margarine in the diet aggravate the sufferer's diabetes?
2. Does regularly eating margarine cause a form of diabetes?
3. Is the patient's diabetes linked to certain cooking oils?
4. Has a reaction to cows' milk caused the diabetes? If 'Yes', ask – Is the allergy to the protein in cows' milk?
5. Would the patient benefit from a course of the mineral vanadium? (Vanadium controls insulin.)
6. Is the patient's body short of chromium?
7. Would the patient's health benefit from a course of taurine amino acid?

8. Ask if the solar plexus chakra is out of balance? This is often out of balance in diabetes sufferers. If 'Yes', then ask the pendulum to please balance the chakra.
9. Would the patient benefit from a course of pfaffia, a rain forest medicine?

Patients who have recently been diagnosed with diabetes may be interested to learn of an exercise recommended by Thomas Haberle in his book *Helping and Healing*.[8] He suggests that patients who have only recently been diagnosed with diabetes may find it can be cured by doing deep trunk bending five times each morning.

The action of bending over to touch your toes causes the stomach to press against the pancreas and to stimulate the weakened pancreas! Sounds too simple, but often the simple explanation is the one which works. Dowse and ask if the patient's diabetes would be improved by regularly doing deep trunk bending exercises?

Can I remind you to check the chakras are balanced, check the ions, and whether the person is sleeping over geopathic stress. Next we are going to dowse treatments for depression.

Depression

Depression is a nightmare illness, as so many sufferers receive very little sympathy, or understanding of their illness, and families and workmates cannot begin to comprehend the inner agonies experienced by sufferers of this illness.

If anyone in your family suffers from depression, there are some basic questions you can dowse which may relieve their symptoms. It is important to get to the root of the cause, and often it can be related to a shortage of vitamins, minerals, or sleeping over geopathic stress lines, so first ask the all important questions:

1. Is the person sleeping over a geopathic stress line?
2. Are they sleeping over a negative ley line?

3. Are they sitting over a negative energy line at work?

Any sufferer who is exposed to geopathic stress for several hours each day or night will not respond to treatment for this illness until the energy has been balanced, as exposure to this energy is fuelling their depression symptoms.

Now dowse and ask the pendulum the following questions:

1. Would a course of cobalt help to improve depression symptoms?
2. Would more B12 in their diet improve their health?
3. Is their body short of serotonin?
4. Is their thyroid gland depressed?
5. Is the pituitary gland out of balance?
6. Is the hypothalamus gland out of balance?
7. Depression and mood swings are often linked to an imbalance of melatonin and serotonin, so dowse and ask if the person's serotonin (one of the body's chemical messengers) level is wrong? If the answer is 'Yes', then ask the pendulum to adjust to the correct level.
8. Then dowse and ask if they have a low level of melatonin in their body. Again if the answer is 'Yes', ask the pendulum to please raise the level of melatonin to the correct level (needs to be done regularly).

If the person's levels of either of these two important hormones is wrong, then it suggests their pineal gland may not be working effectively, so please ask if their pineal gland is out of balance? Then ask if it would benefit from receiving healing? You will almost certainly receive a 'Yes' sign to some of the above questions, so ask your pendulum to please balance the level of the missing chemical minerals or vitamins, to the correct level. For more information on serotonin I recommend Oliver James's book *Britain on the Couch*.[9]

Next ask the pendulum to please balance all the glands in the body and, when this has been done, ask the pendulum to clear the person of negative energy.

Then ask your pendulum to check if the person has a strong energy link with the earth; after that question has been answered, ask if their chakras are balanced.

Once you have made a list of all the shortages and problems, ask the pendulum to clear each problem as a separate exercise, and to show you the 'Yes' sign when it has been done.

Now on to the imbalance in energies. Start by asking the pendulum to balance the sufferer's energies in their body, and now it is time to clear the energies of the house, so ask the pendulum to please clear all geopathic stress and negative energies from the house. This could take five minutes, so please be patient!

You may find that the person feels better after your dowsing session, or comments that they are having better quality of sleep, so check their body regularly for shortages, and if you can find time to sit down and ask the pendulum to give them healing each week, they will hopefully feel better.

If the person does not seem to feel any improvement in their symptoms, after your dowsing sessions, then you have to look elsewhere for the cause of the problem. Perhaps they are exposed to powerful electromagnetic fields, from overhead cables or from a cordless phone in the next room. Electromagnetic fields can travel through walks, and if your pillow is against a wall and one of these cordless phones is on the other side of the wall, then it could be the culprit.

Depression can occasionally be caused when an earthbound spirit becomes attached to a person, as, if the spirit suffered depression in its own life, it brings these symptoms with it, so you can then dowse to find if the sufferer has a negative spirit attached. I can hear you saying 'How on earth do you get rid of a spirit attachment?'

Often the pendulum can remove the spirit, so dowse and ask the pendulum to please remove the spirit attachment, and take it to where it will be helped.

Should the pendulum be unable to remove the attachment, then either ask mentally, or ask the pendulum to ask the services of Archangel Michael to remove the spirit, as he is the expert in this field. Do not ever attempt to remove a negative entity from a person, unless you are experienced in this work, and have checked you have a cloak of protection around you.

Now I want to tell you a few suggestions which may help reduce heart problems.

The heart problems

Heart problems are blamed for a high number of deaths in the USA, and for 45% of adult deaths in the UK, so what is the cause of these problems, and what can we do about it?

When a heart disease is caused by a digestive problem, dowse and ask if the patient's body has excess of homocysteine. If the answer is 'Yes', then ask the pendulum to balance the level. Heart disease caused by stress creates a breakdown of the natural amino acid homocysteine. Dowse to check the level of this amino acid is correct in the patient's body.

As there are several different causes of heart problems, depending on whether the fault is in an artery, a chamber, a valve, or a vein, so there are a range of plants, amino acids, and minerals, which help some problems but not others.

Below I have given you a list of amino acids, plants, and minerals which are known to improve symptoms in certain patients.

Ask if any of the sufferer's symptoms would be improved by taking a course of any of the following items, and if you receive a 'Yes' sign, please ask the pendulum to channel the correct amount to them.

Ask your pendulum how often you should do this exercise, as one amount may be sufficient of one amino acid, but perhaps there is a real shortage of another, and it will require three or four separate channeled amounts.

1. Amino acid L. carnitine.
2. Amino acid lysine (it is reported to be able to strip plaque from blocked arteries).
3. Cat's claw (stops clots forming.)

4. Dowse – Would hawthorn help the heart problem? (German research showed it increases the flow of blood to the heart).

5. A shortage of folic acid is linked to heart problems. Dowse – Is patient's body short of folic acid?

6. Vanadium is thought to be helpful to cardiovascular illnesses, so dowse – Would the patient benefit from a course of vanadium?

7. Dowse – Is the patient's body short of copper?

8. Dowse – Would extra testosterone benefit a coronary artery problem? Is patient's body short of it?

Does Cat's Claw sound a strange name for a medicine? This vine found in South America and parts of Asia grows up to 100 ft. high, and is recognized as a beneficial treatment for Crohn's disease, cancerous tumours, lupus, diabetes, rheumatoid arthritis, and other immune system illnesses.

You could also ask separate questions – Would patient benefit from more potassium, or ginkgo biloba? Check if the patient is sleeping over geopathic stress, as almost all heart and cancer patients are found to be, or working at a desk over these negative energy lines. If the answer is 'Yes', ask the pendulum to clear all geopathic stress and negative energies and fill the house with white light.

It's now time to say a few words about cancer.

Cancer

The number of cancer cases is rising steadily, and the media tell us that today one in every three people can expect to be diagnosed at some time in their life with a form of cancer, which is not a cheering thought. A great deal of money is spent each year on research, trying to find a cure for this dreadful illness, but perhaps some of the millions of pounds would be better spent finding the causes and eliminating them.

The big problem with cancer is that it is an immune illness, in that it strikes when the immune system is low, and it can be triggered off by a great number of different things.

Electromagnetic energy from pylons and overhead power lines seems to be a cause in some areas, while pollution is a cause in another area. Then there are many food colourants which are suspects – in fact today's newspapers are full of the story that a harmful illegal red colourant has been found in food on sale in supermarkets. Certain chemicals and organophosphates in the food chain have been shown to be carcinogens, and these are sprayed on the fruit we eat.

Dowse and ask:

1. Can cancer be caused by certain food in the diet?
2. Can cancer be caused by pollution in the environment?
3. Can cancer be caused by colourants in food?
4. Can the cancer be caused by electromagnetic energy from overhead power lines?
5. Can cancer be triggered off by a bereavement or other emotional upset?

I feel certain that cancer can often be caused by a combination of things so dowse and ask if there is more than one factor which caused the cancer to grow.

These are some of the causes. I am sure you can think of many more possibilities to dowse.

Check for the presence of geopathic stress, as it is usually present in the home or workplace of all cancer sufferers.

There are many different minerals and plants which have helped to kill tumours but, as there are so many different types of cancer, certain minerals or plants are only helpful to some types of cancer and not others.

As I mentioned earlier, when you dowse to establish if a person's body is short of a particular mineral, vitamin, amino acid, or plant residue, when you receive a 'Yes' sign, you can use the pendulum to channel the correct level for their needs, and ask how often it is required. Alternatively you can probably purchase it at your local health shop.

1. Vitamin B17 amygdalin has helped many sufferers, so dowse and ask – Would a course of B17 reduce the tumour? If 'Yes',

then ask pendulum to channel it, and then ask how often it needs to be channeled? How many days, weeks, or months?

2. Dowse and ask – Is the patient's body short of melatonin? If 'Yes', as the pineal gland is linked to the action of melatonin, ask if the pineal gland is functioning properly? If 'No', then channel healing to balance the gland.

3. Would the tumour be reduced in size by taking a course of any of the following: echinacea, coenzyme Q10, lapacho, pfaffia, selenium, mistletoe, willow, Pacific yew, Madagascan periwinkle, germanium, lithium, or Cat's Claw. If you receive a 'Yes' answer, ask if more than one of this group would be beneficial? You can then dowse each one separately to find those which would improve health. Also ask: Would any of the following strengthen the immune system?

All of the above are known to help certain cancers, and strengthen the immune system.

Breast cancer sufferers are often short of iodine, also the hormone DHEA. Both Pacific yew and willow have been found helpful by some cancer patients, so dowse and ask the pendulum for answers.

The rain forest gives us many miraculous cures, but sadly greed has meant that so many of the forests have been cut, and burned, and insects killed, thus these cures are in short supply. So although scientists may have the knowledge, there are not sufficient ingredients available to manufacture treatments, but this is where using the pendulum to channel a cure is invaluable.

Venom from the copper headed viper effectively puts the tumour to sleep by choking off its ability to feed and grow. The venom stops cancerous cells sticking to healthy cells, so stops them growing blood cells to feed on. I agree it sounds a bit risky to channel venom to a loved one, but dowse and ask if this particular venom would reduce the tumour, and also dowse and ask if it would damage the health of the patient! Ask the pendulum how many times the serum needs to be channeled to the patient to be beneficial. Research is still being carried out on this venom, but results on mice and rats showed a 70% reduction on breast tumours, and a 90% reduction on lung tumours. Food for thought!

Ecteinascidin from the Caribbean squid is reported to treats melanoma and breast cancer,[10] so dowse and ask if this serum would benefit your patient, and ask if it will have an adverse effect on their health. Nature gives us some wonderful cures and they come from the most unexpected places.

An alkaloid found in the bark and needles of the Pacific yew tree attacks harmful microtubules, and has been used by several tribes to treat other major illnesses. If you would like to know more about the amazing rain forest medicines, again I recommend the books of Mark J. Plotkin, *Medicine Quest*[10] and *Tales of a Shaman's Apprentice*.[11]

Cancer is a serious health problem, which today is affecting so many young children, as well as adults, so it is vital to fight this illness with every conceivable tool we can find, and there are some pretty unusual tools available, if we have the courage to try to use them.

For those of you who are not too keen to channel snake's venom to a loved one, how about Raymond Grace's method of mentally shrinking the tumour? In his book *The Future is Yours, Do Something About It*,[12] he describes how we can shrink cancerous tumours or other illnesses, by regularly changing the energy frequency. I recommend this method, as I have used a similar method for many years with success. He recommends holding the pendulum and mentally asking it to scramble the frequency of the tumour or other illness, and visualize it shrinking. Then ask the pendulum to reprogram the tumour to the frequency of healthy cells.

As I said earlier, we are all energy, so this is simply another case of our energy being used, to alter the frequency of another energy! Sounds simple when you say it like that! This is a book worth reading, as when you have mastered the technique, and feel confident to scramble energies, you can treat all sorts of illnesses from headaches to tumours.

Again I say 'Remember we are all made of energy', so by channeling energy to a sick person, we are simply exchanging energy, and the same applies with scrambling the frequency of energy of an illness: we are simply using our energy to change another energy. The only point I must repeat is, please make sure you have placed some form of protection around your aura before you attempt this work.

Any healer who works on a very high vibration can do this work effectively, without using a pendulum, since by channeling white light instead of the pendulum to do the work, you could achieve the same results.

Once you have checked the patient's body for medication, always ask the pendulum to check the body polarity of a cancer patient, as this is often reversed when the patient has been exposed to the geopathic stress energy. This can make the person feel a bit distant, and lack motivation to do certain tasks. The pendulum will balance the polarity if asked.

I have found that all patients I have ever treated who suffered from any form of cancer, other than skin cancer, had each been sleeping over a geopathic stress line, which had weakened their immune system. This is confirmed in Gustav Freiherr von Pohl's book *Earth Currents, Causative Factor of Cancer and Other Diseases.*[13]

This amazing man dowsed every house in the small market town of Vilsbiburg in Bavaria, and was able to detect every property where geopathic stress was present, and where residents had suffered from cancer. This work was carried out in 1929, and geopathic energy has been recognized as a health hazard in parts of Europe for many years, but is still not accepted by the medical profession in either the United States or Great Britain.

I have been a guest on many BBC radio programmes talking about geopathic stress, and received enormous interest in the subject. One Saturday morning programme stirred up so much reaction that the studio had to send a van to deliver the sacks of mail. So many listeners wrote saying I had described their symptoms, and asked where could they find more information on this subject. As well as the BBC, I have done many local radio programmes, and given talks to groups, and each time I get the same reaction of 'Please tell us where we can find more information about geopathic stress'.

Please remember to check both the home and workplace for geopathic stress of anyone who suffers from cancer, also check the person has a good strong link with the earth, as we all have an invisible link which comes from our Creator. This energy link comes down from the source, through our head, and down through our body, into the ground, keeping us well earthed, but this invisible energy link can be severed when exposed to geopathic stress energy.

You can renew the link, by visualizing a beam of energy coming down from the Creator, or the universal energy, through the person's head and body, and deep down into the earth. An alternative is to hold the pendulum and ask it to please renew the person's earth link and show you the 'Yes' sign when completed. Then you should check it has been done, by dowsing to ask if the patient now has a good earth link. Unless the person's energies are balanced, their body will not respond quickly to treatment, so please check them regularly.

Skin cancer

Cases of skin cancer are becoming more common so it is necessary to take all possible precautions to prevent this menace. So 'Think pendulum' and 'Think ultraviolet' while you lie back in your sun lounger, or stretch out on the sand to enjoy the luxurious feeling of well being that comes from the heat of the sun's rays soaking into your body. Regularly dowse to ensure you have not been over exposed to ultraviolet rays. Beware of excess exposure, and always use a sun screen, as almost every time you are outdoors your body is exposed to ultraviolet radiation. Whether in the shade or direct sunshine, the sun's rays penetrate through mist and light cloud.

Your trusty pendulum will confirm when your body has had sufficient exposure for that day, so if in doubt, keep your pendulum handy in your beach bag! Please don't be fooled into thinking you are only vulnerable on a beautiful day, as your body is receiving ultraviolet rays on cloudy days, and the bad news is that these rays are ageing!

Ultraviolet radiation is an electromagnetic radiation which is an important component of sunlight, and is able to penetrate the ozone layer over three separate wavelengths, and doctors tell us it is a known cause of skin cancer and skin ageing.

Sadly global warming is here and the increase in the ozone layer means that long hours of sunbathing are no longer safe. The 'Everything in Moderation' rule now applies, as ultraviolet rays stimulate the production of melatonin, and this produces vitamin D in our skin. Over exposure can do serious harm as excess ultraviolet rays can block the action of vitamin D in your body.

Don't hibernate when the sun shines since the sun's rays are very helpful in small doses, as the body needs vitamin D, which is essential to create healthy bone growth.

Dowse:

1. Has your child already received the safe amount of sun exposure for the day?
2. Ask your pendulum how many minutes is the safe time for exposure to the sun on that day.
3. Ask if regular use of sunscreens which contain certain chemicals can damage health.
4. When sunscreens are on the skin, can they become carcinogenic when cell chromosomes interact with light and chemicals?

The ultraviolet rays are also germicidal and known to be helpful in clearing some cases of childhood eczema rashes. Several decades ago, before the days of global warming, mothers left their babies in their prams, with the nappy rash exposed to the sun's rays, as it killed the bacteria.

Don't risk getting skin cancer as it can strike anyone. Melanoma is a tumour which can be either benign or malignant. It's a pigment-producing cell type, and the malignant tumour is particularly nasty and virile. This type of tumour must be treated early to avoid rapid spread. It can often develop from an existing mole, and most often seems to develop in fair skinned people.

Should you be unfortunate enough to suffer from this form of cancer, the one treatment I know which has very good results, and no side effects, is to soak a small pad in fresh urine, and place it on the tumour. Urine therapy can be very effective in treating this and other illnesses. It has no side effects, it is natural, sterile and gentle, and a little cologne on the pad disguises any smell! When you are desperate you'll try any treatment!

Dowse:

1. Can urine therapy reduce skin cancer?
2. Can covering skin cancer with a pad soaked in fresh urine reduce the cancer?

However, no remedy that I suggest should be taken without advising your doctor. Should you already be receiving treatment, you should inform your doctor of your intention to resort to this therapy in addition to your treatment. Please, please do not stop treatment prescribed by your doctor or hospital, and don't be too upset if they scoff at my suggested treatment!

Ultraviolet rays are natural and they are essential for good health, so enjoy them and always 'Be Aware' and keep your pendulum handy! But go easy on the sunscreens.

There is mounting evidence that certain brands of sunscreen contain chemicals which penetrate the skin. Dr Lita Lee[14] states the rise in cases of skin cancer coincides with the increased use of sunscreens. Is this a coincidence? The chemical ingredients in certain brands of commercial sunscreens cause mutations, when the cells' chromosomes interact with light and chemicals. These facts suggest it is wise to use organic sunscreens or brands low in chemicals.

And remember, your pendulum will confirm which are the right creams to use.

Female infertility

Infertility is a very distressing problem which faces a high number of couples today, and there can be many different causes. In the case where the woman seems to be unable to conceive, and yet there is no apparent medical reason, then this can be caused by her sleeping over geopathic stress energy.

If you know of anyone who is having problems conceiving a baby, and who has been told by medical specialists that there is no obvious medical cause for the problem, then please dowse her home and workplace, as it is very likely that her problem could be linked to exposure to this powerful negative energy.

I have cleared several homes of geopathic stress, where the woman was trying desperately to conceive, and when I had rebalanced her energies and given her healing, she then conceived, and gave birth to a healthy baby. Please dowse and ask the following questions:

1. Is the woman sleeping over a geopathic stress line?
2. Is her body short of copper? (This is common after having been on 'the Pill'.) (Copper enhances fertility.)
3. Would a course of agnus castus help resolve the infertility problem?
4. Is her body short of molybdenum?
5. Is her body short of manganese?

Please dowse the above questions, and if you get a 'Yes' sign to any of them, then please ask the pendulum to channel the right amount to the patient, then dowse and ask how often it is required?

As I mentioned earlier, please also check her energy levels are balanced, and that she has a powerful link with the earth, as often when people have been sleeping over these geopathic stress lines, their link is cut by this powerful energy.

Male infertility

Male infertility has always been present in a very small number of men, but it has escalated and is now a serious twenty-first century problem. A high number of cases are caused by stress of work, exposure to electromagnetic fields, pollution, organophosphates, and other chemicals.

First dowse and ask the pendulum if the man is sleeping or working over a geopathic stress line, since if he is sitting at a desk for eight hours a day over a geopathic stress line, or his bed is sited over a geopathic stress line, so that he is exposed to the negative energy while he sleeps, it can have a serious effect on his sperm count.

Dowse and ask:

1. Will the man's fertility be improved by taking a course of vanadium?
2. Will his fertility be enhanced by taking Saw Palmetto (North American Indian medicine)?
3. Ask if his body is short of copper.

If you receive a 'Yes' answer to any of these questions, please ask the pendulum to channel the necessary amount to them, and show you the 'Yes' sign when completed.

It may seem a bit time consuming to sit down with your pendulum to channel minerals or plants to an infertile couple, but helping them to conceive is indescribably rewarding, I can assure you.

Next I am going to tell you how to track the cause of bad sleep patterns and insomnia, as these complaints disrupt so many lives.

Insomnia and bad sleep patterns

When you have problems getting a good night's sound sleep, your life is disrupted as nerves get on edge and life becomes very strained as tolerance levels drop! There are so many different causes of insomnia. It's all very well being told to avoid a cat nap in the afternoon or early evening, or cut out alcohol and coffee in the late evening, or have your dinner early rather than later, but often the problem goes way beyond these simple suggestions. Perhaps dowsing will locate the root of the problem, so start by asking the following questions:

1. Are you sleeping over a geopathic stress energy line?
2. Are electromagnetic fields (emfs) from the cordless telephone point near the headboard of the bed disrupting sleep?
3. If a computer is in your room, is it unplugged? They give off emfs when plugged in to the socket, even when switched off. This can disrupt your pineal gland and supply of melatonin. Ask if the emfs from the computer are disrupting your sleep. Are ions unbalanced in the room?
4. Do you suffer anxiety? Ask your pendulum if this is the cause of the problem?
5. Is a mirror hanging on the wall opposite your bed? Bad feng shui! Ask if mirror energy is disrupting sleep patterns.

Mirrors are water energy, so too much of this energy in a room can upset the energy balance.

There are many herbs and plants available that help the body to relax and create good quality sleep. Dowse the following plants to find the right one for you.

Ask if chamomile as a drink, or as a tablet, will improve your sleep quality. Chamomile is well recognized as an effective relaxant, and in Germany is found in many medications. This plant can also be taken as a tea and has a pleasant taste, but if you really don't like the flavour, then add a spoonful of honey to the drink – and the bonus is that honey offers beneficial healing qualities.

Valerian and vervain are both excellent herbs to instigate relaxation and improve the quality of your sleep. They can be bought separately or as a combination tablet, so dowse and ask if taking a course of these plant would help to improve your sleep pattern.

Dowse and ask if hawthorn or passion flower would improve your sleep. And then as a last resort if all else fails, ask if potassium would improve your sleep. If the answer is 'Yes', then a banana eaten before bedtime may do the trick!

A shortage of melatonin can cause sleeping problems and this can affect people who spend a lot of time indoors, so their body does not get melatonin from sunshine. Alternatively perhaps their pineal gland is sluggish, so disrupting the supply of melatonin in the body. You can purchase melatonin in drug stores in the US, but it is not available in the UK other than on the internet.

Should the sleep problem remain after treating with herbs or plants, then it is time to ask the pendulum if the problem is linked to the environment. If 'No' to that question, then ask if it is linked to something in your diet.

If you get a positive reply to this question, you then have to look for the source of the problem, so start by asking if it is linked to aspartame. If 'No' then ask if it is linked to fluoride. If 'No', keep asking other possibilities and you will eventually find the culprit. Perhaps a colourant or food preservative is at the root of your sleep problem.

There are many illnesses which I have not mentioned, but I hope that the examples I have given, of how the pendulum can be used to find the best treatment for an illness, and the possible benefits of certain minerals, amino acids, plants, and vitamins will give you confidence to use the pendulum to explore this field, since whatever the illness or symptoms, by dowsing you will be able to establish if a certain product will reduce pain or relieve symptoms.

There are many plants and shrubs known today to be effective medicine for certain illnesses, but my experience is that pfaffia is one of the most versatile. This shrub from the Amazon Basin, sometimes known as suma or Brazilian ginseng, has been found to inhibit certain cancers, fights the Epstein–Barr virus, improves diabetes and cardiovascular disease. This amazing shrub also helps to resolve hormone problems, rejuvenates sexual desires, fights depression and is an anti-inflammatory treatment so useful to treat rheumatic aches. I find when I am giving healing, I am asked by my spirit helpers to channel pfaffia to a person, more than any other plant. Have a look on the internet as there are a great many websites extolling the virtues of this amazing plant. By dowsing you will be able to establish if it will benefit your patient or friend.

The benefits of dowsing for health can never be measured, whether to give healing to a person or animal or to diagnose an ailment.

Summary

Radiesthesia is the name for medical dowsing, and many alternative therapists use a pendulum to diagnose their patient's illness, so the accuracy of this form of medical diagnosis is well respected in this field. By asking your pendulum a few simple questions, it is often possible to diagnose an illness and to find the cause. Once you have located the culprit, it is sometimes possible to remove it from your diet or lifestyle. Your pendulum will confirm if your body is short of certain minerals, plants, amino acids, or metals, so don't be afraid to ask important questions, as your gut feeling will tell you if the answer is correct. To check the accuracy of the answer, it is wise to rephrase the question and you should get the same answer.

Arthritis is a cruel complaint which restricts movement and causes pain, so anything which can improve symptoms is welcome. Dowsing will confirm if this complaint is linked to a reaction to any of the deadly nightshade group of foods, which includes our much loved potatoes, and tomatoes. Also check for an imbalance of copper, and if you are sleeping or sitting over geopathic stress energy.

Young and old today are being affected by irritable bowel syndrome, which causes discomfort and affects both social life and work. Often this complaint can be caused by a weak immune system linked to geopathic stress, and a shortage of certain ingredients.

Your pendulum will confirm if symptoms would improve by taking a course of brewer's yeast or chromium, and balancing the level of the amino acid cystine.

The number of schizophrenia sufferers is increasing, and this is an alarming fact as this illness can cause distress to both patient and family, so try dowsing to locate the root cause of the problem. I have suggested several possible causes so please dowse, and if you are not confident about doing it properly, then ask a friend to dowse, as it is important to help the patient reduce symptoms of this frustrating illness. Dowse and ask if the histamine level is wrong, and another option is to dowse and ask if the person has a negative attachment.

Cancer is becoming uncomfortably common as experts tell us that one in three of us will at one time in our life develop this vicious illness. There are so many different causes of cancer, although all stem from a weak immune system, usually linked to exposure to geopathic stress.

Dowsing will confirm if the cancer is linked to pollutants, chemicals, food colourants, or exposure to electromagnetic fields, and whether the patient would benefit from a course of pfaffia, B17 or having their pineal gland balanced. I have given you many options to dowse including serum from a snake, so by using your pendulum to search my suggestions plus any other possible cures you may hear about, you may be able to find a treatment which will reduce the cancer.

You can dowse to help find relief for those members of your family or friends who suffer from heart disease, diabetes, depression, lupus, Parkinson's disease, or any other health problems. Perhaps you have read about a cure in a magazine or heard about it on a radio programme, so use your pendulum to dowse, and ask if it would be an effective treatment for the illness.

Your trusty pendulum will give you answers to all medical problems, whether it is to ask about a new brand of pills advertised, or to locate the cause of a knee problem, so trust your pendulum and get dowsing!

Endnotes

1. Atkins, Robert C., M.D. *Dr Atkins' Vita-Nutrient Solution, Nature's Answer to Drugs.* A Fireside Book. Simon and Schuster, New York, 1999. ISBN 0-684-81849-5

2. *Nexus New Times*, Vol. 11 No. 2, May 2004. Foster, Harold D., PhD., Prof. Dept. of Geography.

3. *Nexus New Times*, Myers, D. G., 1992. *Psychology.* Worth Publication, NY.

4. *Nexus New Times*, Vissodes, D. N., Venulet, A., and Jenner, F. A., 1986. 'A Double Gluten Free–Gluten Gluten/Loaded Controlled Trial in a Secure Ward Population'.

5. *British Journal of Psychiatry*, Vol. 148, pp. 447—452.

6. The Fish Foundation. Ref. 3. *Fatty Acids and Schizophrenia*, Lipids 1996. 31: Supplement S163–S165. Laugharne, J. D. E., Mellor, J. E., and Peet, M., *www.fish-foundation.org.uk*

7. The National Center for Health Statistics. *Fast Stats*, Death/Mortality. Preliminary 2001 data. Smith, Thomas, *Nexus New Times*, 'Our Deadly Diabetes Deception', Vol. 11 No. 3, July 2004.

8. Haberle, Thomas, *Helping and Healing*, Sheldon Press, London, 1984. ISBN 0-85969-528-X.

9. James, Oliver, *Britain on the Couch*, Century/Random House, London, 1997. ISBN 0-7126-7885-9.

10. Plotkin, Mark J., PhD, *Medicine Quest. In Search of Nature's Healing Secrets*, Virgin/Penguin, 2001. ISBN 0-1402-6210-5.

11. Plotkin, Mark J., PhD, *Tales of a Shaman's Apprentice, An Ethnobotonist's Search for New Medicine in the Amazon Rainforest.* Penguin Books, 1993. ISBN 0-1401-2991-X.

12. Grace, Raymond, *The Future is Yours, Do Something About It*, Hampton Roads Publishing Co., 2003. ISBN 1571743901

13. Freiherr von Pohl, Gustav, *Earth Currents, Causative Factor of Cancer and Other Diseases*, Frech-Verlag, 1987. ISBN 3-7724-9402-1 Topp *Healthy Living* 9402.

14. Hattersley, Joseph G., *Nexus New Times*, Vol. 8 No. 4, p. 31, July 2001. '*The Healing Power of Full Spectrum Light. L. L. Lee. Your Health*. July 1999, Vol. 4(3), p. 3.

4

Dowsing for life

There are so many separate factors which can govern our good health, and each one can be diagnosed by the pendulum for the best choice of treatment and remedies, so let's start by talking about dowsing your medication.

Dowsing your medication

Dowsing is an excellent way to check that you are taking the right measure of medication, and if you are concerned that your medication is creating unpleasant side effects, or is not reducing the symptoms, then you can dowse to get confirmation, but please **do not stop taking medication without consulting your doctor.**

Start by making a list of the dose of medication. Ask the questions:

Is one pill taken three times per day the correct level of this medication?
Are two pills taken three times a day the correct level of medication?

Change the numbers around, depending if the pills are to be taken once each day, or after meals etc. You can also check liquid medication by asking:

Is one spoon measure the correct amount each day?
Is one spoon measure after each meal the correct amount?

By asking a variation of questions you will be able to establish the correct level of medication.

Fifteen years ago I visited a homeopathic doctor for treatment of a shoulder injury, and the first question this doctor asked was 'Do you dowse?'. I looked at her in astonishment, and asked why she asked this question, as it is probably the last question I would expect a doctor to ask me.

She explained that with all her patients who dowsed, she gave them three different medications, to dowse each morning, to ask which was the right medication for that particular day. She went on to explain that the body's needs were slightly different each day, and so it was wrong to keep taking the same medicine day in day out for years. This information felt right to me, and made me realize dowsing is an invaluable tool to establish the body's medication needs.

Does your body need that supplement or a course of minerals?

Are you like me, a sucker for glossy supplement brochures which paint a glowing picture of improved health and vitality? I regularly fall into this trap, and purchase supplements which end up sitting in a drawer, and never being used. There's no excuse as I am a dowser! But I do forget to dowse, when confronted with an advertisement telling me how fit I will become if I take the pills. Please don't fall into this trap, and so before you purchase any minerals, vitamins, amino acids or supplements, always dowse to ask if your body is short of them, then ask if your body will benefit from a course of them?

Minerals and trace minerals all have a job to do in the body, and a shortage of one of these vital ingredients can have a ripple on effect on health. They act as a catalyst for a great many different biological reactions within our body, including production of hormones, digestion, muscle response, and even the transmission of messages through our nervous system, so have a look at the following list of minerals, and dowse to ask if your body is short of any of them.

Minerals	
Potassium	Boron
Selenium	Chromium
Iodine	Iron
Copper	Magnesium
Calcium	Zinc
Manganese	Molybdenum

Start by asking if your body is short of any of the minerals in the table. If the answer is 'Yes', ask if your body is short of more than one mineral. If 'Yes', then ask if your body is short of any of the first six listed.

If the answer is 'No', then you know the shortage is within the next six listed, so you have two options: you can either dowse all six individually, or to speed up the exercise, you can ask if your body is short of any of the next three on the list and if 'No', then you know the missing minerals are in the last three listed.

A good practice is to dowse one or two weeks after starting to take the pills or capsules, to establish if your body still requires the same dose, as by then your body will have built up a reserve, so may only require a lower dose. Dowse again in one month's time, and again in three months' time, to check that your body is still benefiting from the pills.

Dowse your child's health problems

As well as dowsing for your medication, you can dowse to ask if your child is poorly. We parents have all known days when our kids complain of feeling ill, and we wonder whether or not to send them to school. Are they really ill or are they trying to avoid going to school on a specific day, to avoid a lesson they dislike? Now if you suspect your child is faking symptoms, you don't need to feel guilty about sending them to school when they may just be poorly. You can dowse and ask the following questions:

1. Does my child feel unwell?
2. Is my child trying to avoid attending school today?
3. Is my child starting an illness?

Change the question around and use the child's name to get answers. Perhaps the child is genuinely feeling ill, in which case you don't want to send him to school, then have the school phoning you and asking you to collect him, so a few moments spent dowsing the question will be well spent.

You can also use your pendulum to diagnose a rash which suddenly appeared:

1. Is it a heat rash?
2. Is it German measles?
3. Is it an allergic reaction?

By a process of elimination you can dowse every possible cause of a rash, and then establish if it is infectious, contagious, or simply an allergic reaction.

If your child has been diagnosed as suffering from ADHD you can ask the pendulum if it is the correct diagnosis, and if the child is on the correct medication. You can ask if the drug Ritalin is beneficial to your child.

Dowsing for allergies

Symptoms of allergic reaction to a food are different from those created by food intolerance, as an allergic reaction is often almost instantaneous, and symptoms can by quite violent, whereas food intolerance reaction is often mild, and can occur a few days after contact with the food. This intolerance is often recognized by symptoms which include the feeling of a bloated stomach, or migraine.

Sufferers will all tell you that trying to diagnose the cause of their allergies has been a nightmare, as it is a process of elimination which takes a very long time, and in the meantime, they continue to suffer.

Dowsing enables you to find the root cause of allergies, whether food intolerance, soy, colourants, additives, dairy produce, chemicals, insects, dust, preservatives, animal fur, or pollen, as these plus a wide range of other items can cause the body's allergic reaction.

Start by dowsing the question:

'Is my body's allergic reaction caused by a certain food?'
If the answer is 'Yes', then ask:

'Is my body allergic to any dairy produce?'
If the answer is 'Yes', then ask:

'Is my body allergic to cows' milk?'
If the answer is 'Yes', you can then ask:

'Am I allergic to organic cows' milk?'
'Am I allergic to goats' milk?'
'Am I allergic to soy milk?'

Once you have established which category of food or other group is responsible for the allergic reaction, please dowse to check if they are also allergic to another group, as many people suffer from multiple allergies. When you have discovered the culprit, please remember that when you exclude it from your diet, you are also excluding the minerals and vitamins it supplies, so always ensure that when you exclude it from your diet, you replace the missing minerals and vitamins which you would have received from the food.

Today there are many different milk products available, so it is possible to be allergic to one, and not to another. If you are not allergic to milk, then list other dairy products and get asking!

Make a list of all the dairy products in your diet, then dowse each one individually, to find which to exclude from your diet. If dairy products are not the culprits, then dowse meats, including meat in pies, fresh meat, tinned meat, packets of cold meat, and sausages.

When dairy products or meat are not the culprits, dowse fruit, vegetables, wheat and pulses, and if you get a 'Yes' to any of these groups, then make a list of those items you have eaten in this group, and your pendulum will give you the answer.

Many people today are unaware that they have an allergic reaction to soy, which is found in many dishes, so dowse and ask if you or your child is allergic to soy, and if the answer is 'Yes,' then dowse to ask if the margarine you purchase contains soy. Finnish research found children who ate more butter than margarine did not develop a soy allergy. Is this because a very high number of commercially marketed margarines are made with soy oil?

Infants allergic to dairy formula are often also allergic to soy formula, so please tell any of your friends whose baby is suffering from allergy problems to check for soy allergy.

Please dowse to find if the allergic reaction is linked to soy, as this ingredient is found in so many foods including canned tuna, certain chocolate, luncheon meat, most breads, and chocolate. Soy has many names, so may be listed as textured vegetable protein or vegetable protein concentrate. Checking the list of ingredients for soy content is not sufficient, it is really important to dowse if the food contains soy, as it may be listed under a variety of names.[1] Once you have found the cause of your allergy, you can then ask if you are allergic to other brands of this food, since it could be that this particular brand contains an ingredient not in other brands. Manufacturers can sometimes use slightly different ingredients, or the same ingredients but from different sources. It is a complex business trying to find the cause of allergies, but although dowsing may sound a lengthy process, it is still a much quicker route, to track down the cause of the allergy, than spending weeks trying certain foods and waiting for reactions.

If your allergy is not caused by food, try dowsing preservatives or colourants as many of these additives are known to create health problems. It is also important to dowse to ask if the sufferer is sleeping over a geopathic stress energy line, as this weakens the immune system, and makes them more susceptible to allergies. Often folks who don't know very much about dowsing as a tool to find allergies think of it as a real 'off the wall' type of treatment, but are soon converted when they find the pendulum has successfully diagnosed the root of the problem.

Checking beauty products

Are you concerned about the number of chemicals in your hair shampoos, face creams, or lotions and, when you look at the label, the list of ingredients contains all sorts of strange chemical names which mean very little to you? Perhaps it's time to check them out, and you may get a surprise at some of the contents of your products.

Certain brands of deodorants contain aluminium, which some researchers suggests is thought to be linked to Alzheimer's disease, so aluminium-free deodorants are on sale at health shops.

Dowse and ask the pendulum if the deodorant you use contains aluminium. An excellent alternative available from many health shops is a salt stone, which is rubbed under your armpit each morning, and it works very effectively all day long. Dowse and ask if this stone would be better for your health than your present deodorant?

Many popular brands of shampoos, face creams, and body lotions all contain chemicals, and a high percentage of all chemicals which go on our skin are soaked through into the bloodstream. Do we really want more chemicals than necessary in our blood?

Dowse and ask if your face cream contains any harmful chemicals, then dowse and ask if it contains any chemicals used as industrial anti-freeze. Also ask if the cream contains a chemical used as an engine de-greaser. You can ask the same questions of shampoos. Check the suitability of the products, and ask if they are suitable for your hair or skin.

Next I want to tell you about your body's acid/alkali levels.

Check your body's acid/alkali level

Certain digestive problems are created or aggravated by an imbalance in the body's acid/alkali level. Your body will often give you warning symptoms by creating strange rumbling noises, or your tummy swells up so that it feels distended, after you have eaten certain foods.

If your body's acid/alkali level is out of balance, you may sometimes find symptoms like indigestion make their presence felt, when your body is trying to tell you this food is too acidic for you. Do you find that every time you eat certain foods, your body complains strongly, and you know it disagrees with you, but as you really like this food, you continue to eat it. How often do you hear someone saying 'I love it but it disagrees with me' or 'I'll suffer later' Now you know how to dowse, you can check the acid/alkali levels of food.

Dowse the question:
'Is the acid/alkali level in my blood balanced?' If the answer is 'No', it's time to find the problem.
Start the search by asking:
'Please show me the acid/alkali level on a 1–10 scale'. You can either write the numbers 1–10 down and dowse over them, or mentally ask the question.
'Is the acid level in my body above 5 on a 1–10 scale?' If the answer is No, then ask:
'Is the acid level above 3 on a 1–10 scale?
Your body needs 70% alkali and 30% acid, so on a 1–10 scale your acid level should not be higher than 3. You can phrase the questions in several different ways to check the answers are the same, so ask the questions
'Is the acid level in my body too high? or
'Is the alkali level in my body too low?
When you have established the level, you will then be able to solve some digestive problems by balancing your diet, which should contain more fruit and vegetables than meat, as they are alkali forming.

Protein foods are acid forming.

Most fruit and vegetables are alkali forming.

Once you have checked your body's acid/alkali level, if it is out of balance, you can ask the pendulum to please balance your body's acid/alkali level, and show you the 'Yes' sign when completed. Now it is time to check your body's energy levels.

Your body's energy levels

If you constantly feel drained of energy, ask a friend to dowse your physical energy level on a 1–10 scale, and if it is below 6 then you urgently need to improve the level.

Dowse to ask if your body is short of iron, as this is often linked to tiredness, or perhaps you are sleeping over a negative geopathic stress line. As well as checking the levels of your energies, you can also dowse your family and friends.

Do you regularly feel depressed, and lack concentration and motivation to get jobs done? Perhaps your mental energy is low, so again ask a friend to dowse it on the 1–10 scale. Please don't try to dowse when you are feeling low, as when you have a lot of negative energy in your body, it will influence the working of the pendulum.

You can also dowse your emotional energy on a 1–10 scale, as the body's emotional energy can be low if you have been experiencing a lot of emotional upsets, stress, aggravation, or even subconscious memories of traumatic experiences as an adult or in childhood.

Amino acids – the building blocks

Amino acids are the building blocks in the body, whose job is to repair tissue and build cells. They also form important antibodies in the body. These will combat invading bacteria and discourage harmful viruses. Never underestimate the importance of amino acids, as they are an important part of the body's hormone and enzyme systems, since they carry oxygen through the body, and are involved in muscle activity.

Amino acids work naturally in our body by enabling our system to do the job of keeping us healthy, so these nutrients are essential to keep the smooth running of health, and an imbalance can create problems. Below I have listed some of the most commonly used amino acids, so if you have a problem linked to one of them, then dowsing could resolve this health issue.

When your body's digestive system breaks down protein in the body, the 20 known amino acids are formed. Eight are known as essential amino acids, as these cannot be manufactured by the body, whereas the other 12 can be manufactured in the body.[1]

Here are a few examples of illnesses where the body is often short of an amino acid: Parkinson's disease and depression sufferers are often short of tyrosine, infertility can be linked to arginine, IBS and liver problems can be a shortage of cystine. Epilepsy, Alzheimer's and blood pressure can often be helped by taurine. Dowse and ask if your or a relative's illness is linked to a shortage of an amino acid, then ask if an amino acid would improve the symptoms.

Colour and your body

Do you ever wonder why you have a strong urge to wear a certain colour, when you had intended to wear a completely different outfit? This is your body telling you that it needs the energy of a particular colour, so go with it. Colour has the power to motivate and inspire us, and to lift our energy to a higher level, or have a negative effect, so dowsing colours can be a beneficial exercise.

Dowse the colours of your bedroom, and ask the pendulum if your stress levels would benefit from a more relaxing colour scheme? The colour in your bedroom can affect your sleep pattern so get dowsing!

Are you considering redecorating your lounge, and can't decide on a colour scheme? Then write down a list of colours and dowse to find which end result would make you happiest? If you can't decide which curtain material you like best, then you can dowse over samples of curtain materials, to ask which would create the best results. You can also dowse over tins of different coloured paints for best results, as the pendulum will confirm which results would make you most satisfied. Dowsing for the right colours in your interior design can help you to create a peaceful ambience, so experiment with your pendulum.

Colour plays a big part in our emotional and mental levels, so anyone suffering from hypertension, anxiety problems, depression, or insomnia will usually benefit from having peaceful colours around them. By having the right colours in your home, it enables the body to relax and release stress, which helps the body to heal itself.

When I am going to give a talk to a group, I often find I reach for a red or tomato coloured jacket in the wardrobe, and realize that my body is telling me I need the red energy to boost my energy level. On other occasions I am compelled to wear a restful jade green colour, and know I need the peaceful energy of green, so dowse the colours to find out what colour would improve your energy level. You can also dowse for the best colour for curtains, carpet or furniture, as you will be amazed the difference you feel in the presence of certain colours.

Never doubt the importance of colour, as colour has the power to motivate, energize or deflate you. It can bring passion and inspiration into your life, and when you become aware of how you can use colour to an advantage, it opens up a whole new world. Colour can be used to create a peaceful atmosphere or to give healing energy to the sick, so use your pendulum to find the best colours for certain situations.

We talk about people 'power dressing' and that's exactly the effect you get when you wear bold colours, as they energize and can have an unbelievable influence on our mood as well as make a statement.

There are situations when bold colours are wrong for a person, and I found one such example when I was recently asked to feng shui a family home, where the little six year old son suffered from ADHD. On entering his bedroom I nearly turned around and went out again, as the energy in the room was unbelievably angry. The room was a small box room, and all four walls were painted a bright vibrant red, and the only other colour in the room was white, so the energy in the room was fire energy, and a noticeable lack of earth energy. It was no surprise to learn that this little lad was on Ritalin medication and behaved in a disruptive angry manner, as I would have felt the same had I slept in this room.

I explained to his mother that the energies in the room were out of balance and a change of colour scheme was necessary, whereupon she assured me that her son insisted on having red walls as this was his favourite colour! I suggested painting the walls white and hanging large football posters on the walls, as I knew instinctively that this child's behaviour problems would not improve while he slept and played in this room where the energies were disruptive.

If your child or teenager suffers from behaviour problems, have a close look at the décor in their bedroom, and dowse to ask if the colour scheme is affecting their behaviour. Feng shui experts tell you to clear the clutter, but youngsters resent being told to tidy their room, so rather than have constant rows, forget the clutter and untidiness, and concentrate on the colour as it could pay dividends!

If you don't have confidence to be guided by your gut feeling about which colours to choose for bedspreads, curtains or décor, try dowsing! To dowse for beneficial colours compatible with your body's energy, simply hold the pendulum over a piece of fabric or a colour chart, and ask the question 'Is this colour compatible with the vibrational frequency of my body?'

As you know, the human brain has two separate sides, the analytical and the creative, and colour is linked to the feelings, intuition, artistic ability and sentiments, and so plays an important part in our life. Never underestimate the power of colour.

Checking the levels of metals in your body

Are you surprised to learn that the human body has traces of several metals, and certain symptoms occur when these stocks are depleted?

I have often found that when the body is short of copper, for example, aches start to appear; and when we are short of iron, we often feel tired. A chromium shortage is common in IBS patients, and those with colon problems, and it is also present when folks have a craving for sweet cakes and biscuits.

Dowse to ask if your body is short of any of the following metals excluding lead and aluminium, and then dowse to ask if it has excess of any on the list: copper, mercury, silver, gold, aluminium, lead, zinc, iron. Questions to ask:

'Is my body short of copper?'

'Please show me the "Yes" sign if my body is short of copper'.

Ask these questions for each metal on the list, and any others you may like to add to it. When you have dowsed all the metals for a shortage, it is time to ask for excess. Questions to ask:

'Does my body have excess copper?'

'Please show me the "Yes" sign if my body has excess copper'.

You can then ask the pendulum to remove the excess metal, by swinging it back and forward to get movement started, and then ask it to show the 'Yes' sign when it has been done.

Excess of certain metals can cause severe illness, and as it is a slow process, you don't realize there is a problem until symptoms are established.

How does mercury get into your body? Mercury can leak from amalgam fillings in your teeth, and is also found in fish and seafood.

Lead is found in old paintwork, water passing through lead pipes, and automobile fuel.

Chemicals in the environment are one of today's problems, so you can dowse to find if they are affecting your health.

Harmful chemicals in the environment

Scorecard[3] advise us that over 4 billion pounds of toxic chemicals are released each year into the environment in the United States, which includes 72 million pounds of known carcinogens. These are only the figures based on chemical releases, and transfers reported by industrial facilities to the Toxic Release Inventory (TRI), and do not include major sources of pollution or toxic chemicals that are not covered by the TRI.

You can dowse and ask if there are harmful chemicals in the atmosphere where you live and, if you get a positive reply, then you can get accurate information from the Scorecard website. Once you have established the answer to your questions, you can dowse to check the answers.

If you would like to know the level of toxic chemicals released in your locality, then have a look at Scorecard, the Pollution Information Centre's website, as they list details of 11,200 chemicals, so by typing in the name of the chemical, and your Zip code, you will receive figures for your area.

Which diet to choose?

Do you keep reminding yourself that you are overweight, and that you really must go on a weight loss diet? Every time you try on a favourite dress or skirt, you struggle with the zip fastener, and a little voice is telling you what you already know, and that it is time to do something about those extra pounds – but which diet do you choose?

There are so many different diets available, all promising that you will lose weight, but not every diet is effective for everyone, as our bodies each have different needs, temperament, and metabolism.

Are you the sort of person who will benefit from the strict regime of attending a weekly group, and if so, which is the best group for you? Perhaps you have a demanding job, with long hours, or which involves a lot of travel, so are unable to commit to a class. Again the big question is 'Which diet fits into your lifestyle?'.

If you are a mum, and want to find a diet which will fit in with food purchased for the family meals, as you don't want to be cooking meals especially for you, then your weight watching needs require a flexible diet.

84

You can dowse the most suitable diet for your body. Start by asking the pendulum: 'Is the Atkins diet the right weight loss diet for my metabolism?' This is a great diet for those who enjoy lots of protein, but if you really enjoy your fruit, then it may be wrong for your body. There are several different blood groups, and depending on your particular blood group, your body is happier on a certain type of diet, so it is important to ensure that your diet includes the needs of your blood group.

Dieting is a demoralizing exercise, so it is much easier to discipline yourself to follow the diet if you have friends who are also on a weight loss diet, and it is fun to go along with friends to a slimming group, as you do not feel self conscious, and you are more likely to keep on the diet, if you have support. Sorry to say 'Doing something about your diet is great, but you will also have to do some form of exercise to firm up your body!'

Dowse the best exercise to suit your body

Are you reminded every time you look in a long mirror that your body is out of condition, and badly in need of exercise? Are you aware that each time you climb up a flight of stairs, you feel tired or breathless, and no way can you run 50 yards to catch a bus, and you are resigned to waiting for the next one?

It's all very well getting these little reminders, and also having your subconscious telling you to do something about it, but where do you start? There are so many different exercises, sports and keep fit groups, so the big question you must ask yourself is, do you only want gentle exercise, or could you honestly make the commitment to regularly attend the local gym if you join? Do you enjoy a gentle swim? Then water aerobics may be right for you.

Have a look in the newspaper and magazines for ideas, and make a list of all the options available. You'll find yoga classes to relieve your stress, and an amazing range of exercise groups or sports available. If you are uneasy about going alone, then ask a neighbour or friend to come along – the main thing is to do something! Once you have started your new fitness regime, you will soon start to feel the benefit, as your energy levels rise, and you no longer find it a great effort to do certain thing, so get dowsing and ask the right exercise group or sport for you. By dowsing the list, and learning what they have to offer, you will find the most suitable exercise for your body, Good Luck!

Dowsing the best exercise for my body

Tai chi	Golf	Yoga
Walking	Pilates	Cycling
Join a gym!	Exercise bike	Swimming
Croquet	Water aerobics	Bowls
Squash	Horse riding	Table tennis
Trampoline	Toning tables	Weight training

Perhaps a weakness left by an old injury in your ankle, back or wrist, will govern the choice, we all have a different level of fitness, and all have different wear and tear on our body, so exercise or sport which suits one person could be a nightmare to another. Don't rush out and join the first club you see advertised. Dowse to find which of the above are suitable, explore what they have to offer, then when you have made a short list of possibilities, dowse each one to find which is the most suitable.

Once you have decided on the exercise or sport, make a list of possible clubs, as one will offer better facilities, or have better energy than another, or you may find one instructor more helpful than another. If there are several instructors to choose from, ask the pendulum which one will be more compatible with you. Getting your waistline in shape is important, but it is also important to ensure that you body is balanced and energy is flowing smoothly.

Many treatments and cures have been handed down from generation to generation in such countries as China and Africa, and in North American Indian tribes, and most of these treatments are quick and effective, with few or no side effects.

So how did they find these unlikely cures, often surprisingly close to the problem. Was it a process of elimination, or did they stumble across the cure by accident? Or did their spirit guides and helpers lead them to the right plant or tree?

The Chinese people centuries ago discovered that most forms of illness are usually linked to the yin and yang, and it is only now, in this new century, that therapists are able to spread the message that illness is an imbalance of the body's energies.

Today alternative therapies and alternative medicine wear many hats, and are often called holistic medicine, and many of those therapists who work with energy call their work Energy Medicine, but please don't be confused by the name, as this is a form of alternative and complementary medicine; whichever energy therapy you choose, it will work discreetly to balance the energy in your body. Energy balancing is the basis of several therapies and the benefits are enormous, so if you are feeling tired or below par, perhaps you need to treat your body to a complementary therapy.

Eastern therapies which work to balance the body's meridians are working to balance the Chi, sometimes called the Ki, Prana or Shen, depending on the therapist and the source of the treatment, so don't be confused by any of these names, as it's all energy!

As well as working on the patient's body energies, the therapist will often work with energy from the Creator, or the Universal energy, to assist in the healing process, so dowsing will enable you to select the therapist most able to tune into your body's energy system.

Today there's an amazing number of complementary therapies available to suit everyone's taste and needs, so dowse to ask how many sessions are required to treat your aches or balance your energy.

Dowsing is also the gardener's best friend as it will confirm any drainage problems in your garden, tell you when is the best time to prune shrubs and your favourite rose bushes. For those folks who are keen to keep their lawn looking green and lush, the pendulum will confirm when your grass is in need of a fertilizer dressing or answer any other questions about your lawn.

Are you wondering if it's time to replace the soil in your flower beds or in the large pots on your patio or yard? Dowse to ask if the soil is tired and if most of the goodness is no longer in the soil?

Often we need a treatment because we have been over enthusiastic when doing gardening, You only intend to stay out for a short time, but don't realize how long you have been bending or digging, until your back tells you it is time to stop. Dowsing can't take much of the backache out of gardening, but it can give you a few answers on how to keep your plants happy, so let me tell you how it can help your plants to grow bigger and better!

Dowse your plants' needs

Plants, just like us, have their likes and dislikes, and are happier and thrive in certain parts of the garden more than others, so the pendulum will tell you the best place in the garden to plant an unhappy or sad looking shrub or plant.

Before purchasing a plant feed for the soil. You can dowse and ask:

1. Is the soil healthy?
2. Is the soil too acidic?
3. Is the soil too alkaline?
4. Is the soil missing a trace element?
5. When purchasing plant food, ask your pendulum if this is most suitable brand in the shop.
6. Does the plant prefer to be planted when the moon is waxing?
7. Does the plant prefer to be planted when the moon is waning?

As well as establishing the right balance of the soil, you can also dowse various fertilizers to learn which is most beneficial for your plants. Dowse and ask if your plants would like extra magnesium, potash, boron, phosphorous or manganese.

If you are planning a herb garden, you can ask the pendulum to show you the best area in the garden for the project, and which herbs will thrive there.

Once you get used to thinking 'Dowse' you will find all sorts of questions to ask your pendulum, and soon realize it takes the headaches out of gardening, as it will tell you the best time to plant, and answer many other gardening questions! Perhaps the plant roots or foliage are short of food.

Are your animals healthy?

Is your dog looking fed up and his coat is dull, or his nose is dry? Then you can dowse to find if his diet is short of important minerals or vitamins. You can also establish if he is feeling lonely, has fleas, or if he is infested with worms.

Dowse and ask if he has any aches or pains, or is he sleeping in his bed which is over geopathic stress rays or on a negative energy line? You can also dowse his diet, to find out if he enjoys his present brand of dog food, or if he prefers a different brand! Make a list of all the various brands you purchase and their contents, and dowse to ask his favourite brand. Also dowse to ask if his favourite food is beef, chicken, rabbit, lamb, or turkey. After all, when you are purchasing your dog's food, it is as easy to buy one brand as another, so it makes a lot of sense to buy the one he will enjoy most!

You can apply the same dowsing technique to your horse, cat, rabbit, bird, mouse, hamster, guinea pig etc. Dowse and ask the following questions or similar wording:

1. Is my dog's energy level low? (If you have more than one dog, be specific, say his name and breed.)
2. Is the animal suffering pain?
3. Would the animal enjoy receiving healing energy? (All animals usually enjoy it.)

4. Is the animal short of any minerals? You can then ask the pendulum to channel the missing minerals to him, or include them in his dinner.
5. You can also ask separate questions: (a) Does he have an infection?; (b) Would he be happier to have more exercise? etc.

Does your pet suffer from stiff joints due to arthritis or wear and tear? then you can dowse for the most beneficial medication to give relief, but please remember to cleanse your pendulum!

Use the pendulum to balance the yin and yang energy in his body, then ask if his body is low in any of the following: zinc, calcium, boron, glucosamine, or magnesium. If 'Yes', you can dowse each one to find the shortage, then use the pendulum to channel the correct amount to him. Please consult your vet before taking my advice, as I am not qualified to give medical advice, but I do talk from experience.

Once you have checked these minerals, you can ask if he would benefit from regularly having alfalfa in his diet, as this is an excellent ingredient to improve arthritic symptoms. Dowse and ask if a piece of rock sulfur in his drinking water bowl would cleanse his blood. And also ask the pendulum if his parathyroid gland is balanced, as this gland is often out of balance in arthritis sufferers.

Again I say, if you establish your pet's energy is low, then you can use the pendulum to balance his energy levels; and if he requires healing, and you are not confident to give it to him, then hold the pendulum, and ask it to please channel healing energy to your pet. Don't worry, you won't 'freak him out' as animals all enjoy receiving healing energy, and as they are psychic, they recognize the good energy, just as they recognize anyone who has bad energy.

Summary

In this chapter I have tried to demonstrate the enormous number of uses for the pendulum, so you will know that this tool is always there to confirm your doubts, and inspire you to find the right diet or exercise class to suit you, or perhaps help you decide on a colour scheme in your home!

Are you aware that you can measure your body's energy level? So if you experience a few days of feeling flat and lacking in energy, you can dowse to check that your energy levels are at a healthy level, and if not, then it's time to grab your pendulum, and ask it to please balance your body's energy. You can now dowse your body's acid/alkali levels, and any of your friends who complain of feeling bloated can also have the treat of being dowsed!

I have covered many different uses for your pendulum, and not all of them will be relevant to you, but if you benefit from one of the uses I have suggested, then you have been rewarded for taking the time to read this chapter! Please remember that as well as using the pendulum to dowse for your health, you can dowse for your family, friends, and animals. How about teaching your husband to dowse so that he can keep his plants happy?

Teaching your children to dowse is a source of great entertainment as they can spend hours using the pendulum to search for sweets or 'goodies' you have hidden in the garden, so you see the uses for the pendulum go on and on!

Endnotes

1. *Nexus New Times*, Vol. 11 No. 5, 2005. 'The Hidden Dangers of Soy Allergens'.
   Kaayla, T. Daniel, PhD, CCN, 2004. 'The Whole Soy Story, The Dark Side of America's Favorite Health Food' (a) 'Margarine' Dunder, T., Kuikka. L., *et al*. 'Diet Serum Fatty Acids and Atopic Disease in Childhood'. The Margarine Connection, Allerg. 2001, Vol. 56(5), pp. 425–428.
2. Austin Nutritional Research, 'Amino Acids', www.anrvitamins.com or www.austin.com
3. Scorecard. The Pollution Information Site, Environmental Defense, Pollution Locator. www.scorecard.org

5

Dowsing – your home
and family

Dowsing can be a very useful tool to solve all sorts of problems in your home or workplace, ranging from tracking a burst pipe to finding an electrical fault. It can also be a wonderful way to entertain the children, by organizing a 'Dowse to find the Hidden Object game' and guaranteed to keep the family amused for hours. As children usually master the skill of dowsing very quickly, all that is required is to supply them with rods or a pendulum, and then hide a few sweets or items around the garden. Here are a few uses for dowsing in your home or office:

1. Finding electromagnetic energy lines in the home.
2. Locating geopathic stress energy lines.
3. Checking if your microwave oven is leaking electromagnetic fields.
4. Tracing missing objects.
5. Checking the air conditioning for harmful bacteria.
6. Locating the crack in a burst pipe.
7. Dowsing to see if carpets give off formaldehyde.
8. Locating a well in the garden.

From the above list you will realize that other possibilities are endless, and perhaps the most difficult problem is remembering to use the pendulum to dowse. It is amazing how often when I have asked a person if they dowsed a problem, they will say in surprise, 'Oh I didn't think' or 'I forgot to dowse' so when any problems occur in your home or work place, then Think Dowsing, and you will get some free help.

Locating a blocked or cracked drain

As well as the above list of uses in your home, dowsing can be a valuable help when urgently trying to locate a broken or blocked drain, and this can be 'panic stations' if the blockage is linked to the toilet or kitchen sink! To find the offending blockage or crack, simply walk over the area, or down the path or driveway, and mentally ask your pendulum or rods to show you the 'Yes' sign when they pass over the cracked drain. You will be forever grateful to your rods or pendulum, as they will have saved you the cost of the mammoth job of digging up the entire area to search for the damage.

Finding concealed electrical wiring

When doing some DIY work, are you ever concerned about your safety when drilling a hole in the wall of the room you are decorating, to hang a picture or mirror on a wall? Do you have an uneasy feeling that there may be an electric wire sunk in the wall, and are not happy about the thought of drilling through a power supply? Then it's another case of 'pendulum to the rescue' as by asking the pendulum if there is a live wire hidden in that part of the wall, you will be able to establish an area of wall free from this hazard.

Pendulum to the rescue!

When you are cooking a meal, do you ever have a moment's panic and think 'Did I salt the potatoes before the phone rang?' or forget what time it was when you put a dish in the oven? Now you can dowse to check if you have salted the potatoes, or check how many minutes food has been in the oven.

Do you ever experience the feeling of worry when entertaining guests for dinner, and you are not sure if the meat has cooked right through to the middle of the meat? You can dowse and ask the pendulum: 'Is the food in the oven thoroughly cooked?' Be sure to be specific about the name of the food, if you have more than one dish in the oven. Also don't make the mistake of asking if the dish is cooked! You must say the name of the content!

Most busy housewives or bachelors go by their gut feeling or guesswork when cooking, and if we don't have a recipe with specific instructions, then dowsing takes the guessing out of cooking. Yes, charcoal is excellent for digestion problems, but we don't want our meal to become a charcoal offering!

Life in the kitchen will become much easier when you get into the habit of using the pendulum to answer questions, whether it's concerning food, drink, or electrical equipment.

Washday blues!

When about to load washing into the washing machine, do you ever look at an item and wonder if it is colour fast? Or will the colour run, and discolour the other contents of the machine? Most of us at one time can remember a washday disaster, when our husband's best shirt came out of the machine a delicate shade of pink!

If in doubt that an item is colourfast, dowse and ask the pendulum if the colour will run from this garment if washed at a temperature of 50 degrees? Or at Regulo 6 on the program. You can dowse to get the correct temperature or program for the garment to be colourfast. Dowse 'Will garment be colourfast in a 30 degrees wash?' If 'Yes', you can then ask it will be colourfast at 40 degrees etc. If you ask if the colours will run, if washed in the washing machine, you will get a different answer, as washing in the machine is no different from washing in the sink, the problem being the temperature of the water. This is a case when the wording of the question is important.

Dowsing the seating for a dinner party

Have you ever worried yourself sick about how best to arrange the seating at a family or business dinner party? Is there one difficult guest who talks too much, or is a thoroughly boring person? Then by dowsing you answer your question. This tool is particularly useful to arrange seating for a family wedding, when you have not met some of the in-laws, and are keen for the seating to be a success, so that guests will have things in common, and enjoy each other's company.

Dowse and ask the following question regarding layout of the room. 'What is the best number of tables?' 6, or 8, or 10, dowse each number. Once you have found the right number of tables, you can then dowse to ask which is the most beneficial direction for tables to face? The shape of the room and the lighting can have a positive or negative effect on the event, so although it may seem daft to ask this question, you can ask 'Is north/south the best direction for the tables?' If 'No', then ask if east/west is the most beneficial direction for tables to face.

Once you have established the right number of tables and the best direction for them to face, you can then dowse for the most beneficial number of guests at each table, to help make the event a success. You can start by asking if eight people at each table is the best number of people at each table; if you get a 'No', then ask if 12 people is the right number. You could also dowse if, at this event, it would be more beneficial to have long tables running the length or width of the room. Once you know your venue, you can phrase the questions according to the number of people attending the event, and the shape of the venue.

When these technicalities have been sorted out, it is time to get down to the really important job of sorting out the energies of the venue, since if the energies are wrong, then no amount of preparation will lift the energies.

Another option is to make a list of the names of the guests and give each one a number, then draw a layout of the tables, and dowse which numbers are most beneficial at each table, then if you want to get the mix exactly right, you can dowse the best seating position for each person.

Don't ask 'What is the best seat for each person?' as you will probably get wrong answers, as some people may prefer hard or soft seats, or leather or upholstery, so you see it is important to stop and think, before you ask a question, to ensure it is very specific!

If the event is an important board or committee meeting, you can use this system of questions to ensure the meeting goes smoothly. Dowse and ask the best layout to get the desired decision on an important issue, and make sure the energies are balanced, as negativity will affect performance and decisions.

Checking the energies of the venue

1. Start by asking your pendulum 'Does the building have negative energy?'
2. Then ask 'Will it influence the mood of the event?'
3. If you receive a 'Yes' to both questions, then sit down quietly, take a deep breath, let it out and then relax, and ask your pendulum to please remove the negative energy from the building, and fill it with bright white light and positive energy. Then check the energies again by asking if the energies in the building are balanced? If 'No', then ask the pendulum to balance the energies and don't forget to ask it to show you the 'Yes' sign when it has completed the task.
4. Now ask the pendulum if there are any Dark Ley Lines present? As these are powerful dark energy, it is important to neutralize them, so ask the pendulum to please change them to positive energy.

Dowsing for staff

Dowsing has so many different uses that there are many occasions when we simply don't think to ask its assistance. One time it can be a great friend is when you are trying to recruit staff. Whether it is a man to look after the garden and cut the lawn, a lady to do some light domestic housework, a dog walker, or a babysitter for the children, the pendulum will confirm if the person will behave responsibly, and be conscientious in doing the work.

As well as using your pendulum to assist in finding help in the home, you can also use it very successfully to check you are employing the right staff. Yes, it sounds a bit unprofessional as a good manager should be able to know who are the right people and who are wrong for the job, but it is easy to be wrong and that's where the pendulum comes into its own.

A friend of mine told me, much to my surprise, that for many years he had used the pendulum to select new staff when a vacancy occurred. This man, who held a senior position in one of the service industries, said that when he advertised in a news-paper or business magazine for a staff vacancy, he always dowsed the application letters received from hopeful applicants, and let the pendulum make the decision of choosing the right person for the job, before he had carried out the interviews.

He told me that he had used this system of staff selection for many years, and each time the pendulum had been highly successful, as the applicant chosen by the pendulum had always fitted well into the team, was a good worker, very healthy and conscientious. I found it highly amusing to visualize the reaction of those applicants who had not been successful, if they had known that they had lost the opportunity on the strength of the swinging of a pendulum! Can you imagine their reaction and the language

Dowsing for a family doctor and a dentist

Have you recently moved home and need to register with another doctor or medical centre? Do you want to find a specific practice? Perhaps a patient-friendly doctor, who has a nice bedside manner, and who gives you their attention, one who listens to your problems? Your pendulum will confirm which of the local doctors or centres will be most suitable for your needs. Perhaps you, or one of your children, suffer from a specific problem, so you want to find a doctor who is sympathetic to this illness, or one who is knowledgeable on this subject. Your pendulum will be able to help, and you will probably find that if you call at several centres or practices, your gut feeling will be the same as the answer from the pendulum!

Once you have made a decision on the choice of a new doctor, it is time to locate a nice dentist. It's no good waiting until toothache occurs, so make a list of local dentists, and ask which ones like children. Once you have identified those who like children, dowse and ask which dentist your children would prefer to visit. You can also ask if this is the best local dentist to treat your children's teeth. Phrase the questions in different ways depending on your specific needs.

Locating a veterinary surgeon for your animals

Moving involves so many changes, and one important one to get settled quickly before their services are required is a choice of veterinary surgeons. Choosing a vet for your animals requires a bit of thought, as animals are very psychic and know which vets they like, and which make them uneasy.

It is a good idea to write down a list of local veterinary surgeries and ask the pendulum to locate a vet who has healing energy, as animals love this energy, and it will help them to relax and be less afraid of their visit.

You can also ask the pendulum to please help find a vet whom your dog or cat will like. If you own a horse, then ask the pendulum to help locate a vet who is knowledgeable with horses, also one who likes horses. You could also ask it to locate one whom your horse would like.

Choosing a school or playgroup

It is not always easy to find the right school or playgroup for your child, as different children have very different needs and temperament, so what one likes another may hate. If your child has a specific health problem, or is shy or sensitive, you can dowse for the most suitable school for their needs, as they would prefer a small quieter school than a child who is full of energy and wants lots of activity and sport, and would benefit from being at a large school. You can also dowse for academic results, and quality of teachers.

As your child's school plays an important part in influencing their adult life, it is important to ensure that they are in the school which is best suited for their particular needs. You can make a long list of all the things you require from a school to benefit your child: perhaps the child is artistic so you want a school with a strong art department, or your child has a very high IQ, so you want a school where he will be encouraged to use this gift, and not suffer frustration by having this ability stifled.

Once you have made a list of your choice of requirements, then make a list of schools available, and dowse to find the most beneficial school for the child. When you have made your choice, go and visit the available schools on the list, and you will find that you will almost certainly agree with the pendulum's choice.

A really big problem which can raise its ugly head is if a child has been adopted. At what stage in its life do you explain that they have been adopted, and is it better to keep quiet and hope they never find out?

Adoption – who are my real parents?

It is a horrific dilemma which faces many thousands of parents who adopt a child, as it is frightening to have to choose the right time to break the news to the child you love, that you are not her natural parents. Every year there are adoptive parents making themselves ill with worry about this subject, and the pendulum can help in this delicate matter, by asking the pendulum if the child is emotionally ready to accept the facts.

If the answer is 'No', then ask separate questions: will they be emotionally ready in two years' time, or five or ten years' time?

The next problem which raises its head is that the adopted child, teenager or adult will start to experience uncontrollable, unsettling urges to find their real parents. Some will leave no stone unturned in their desperate search for the parent they never knew.

If you have tried the usual sources of the internet, voters' roll, adoption agencies etc. and are feeling sick with frustration, and don't know which other avenue to explore, then the pendulum is the next option.

The first fact which must be established is 'Are either of my parents still alive?' and once you know if they are alive, you know whether to proceed with a further search. Start dowsing the following questions:

1. Is my natural mother alive?
2. Is my natural father alive?
3. Do they live together?
4. Would my natural mother like to meet me?
5. Would my natural father like to meet me?

You can also dowse to ask if you have any brothers or sisters or half brothers or sisters, and even dowse their age. You can ask the pendulum if your mother has a job or ask if she has good health.

To locate real parents or a missing person

The pendulum will enable you to locate which part of the world is your parents' home, but as your parents may not be living together, you have to first ask if your parents live at the same address, as it is possible they have not lived together for many years. Once you have established if they are together or alone, you can dowse and ask if he or she lives in the USA. If the answer is 'No', then ask separate questions, such as whether they live in Canada, UK, Europe, etc., and once you get a 'Yes' sign you can then divide the country into areas and dowse each area.

If they live in the USA, you can ask if they live in the northern half of the country, and if the answer is 'No', then you do not need to waste time asking about each state in that half of the country, as you know they don't live there. Then ask if they live in the southern half of the country, and when you get a 'Yes', you can then ask if they live on the western side of the southern half, and if the answer is 'No', then you know they live on the eastern side of southern half of the country, so you then dowse each state in that region until you get a 'Yes'.

Once you find the correct State, you can draw a square representing the State, and divide it into quarters, you then dowse each quarter asking if this is in the region of their home, until you get a 'Yes' sign, so you have narrowed your search down to a smaller area. The area can be more accurately defined, by dividing the area confirmed by the pendulum into four sections, and again dowsing the area. To find the exact location, you can dowse over a street map of the towns in the area, and ask the pendulum to show you the 'Yes' sign when you are in the area of their home.

An alternative, instead of dowsing, is to move your dowsing rods slowly over a map of the USA, and ask the rods to show you a 'Yes' sign when they pass over the area of your parents' home. You can then get a street map enlarged, so that you can see details, and slowly move the dowsing rods over the street map, asking them to show you the 'Yes' sign when they pass over the road where your parents live.

If you know their surname, you will be able to search the telephone directory or voters' roll, but if you don't know their surname, then you have to keep dowsing to refine the search further.

Dowsers have been used by the police on many occasions, to find missing climbers, or bodies of missing persons, so think positively as dowsing is an effective way to locate a person.

Missing animals

If your animal who normally never wanders far from your garden becomes missing, you start to worry if they don't come rushing up the garden when called, and you get a sick feeling that they are in trouble.

Your pendulum can put your mind at rest, as it can confirm if your pet is sleeping in next door's garden shed, or if he has been shut accidentally in their garage. Often when a dog or cat goes missing, it can be the call of nature, and they have gone off on a jaunt to find a mate.

Dowsing will confirm if your pet has had an accident, or if it is perfectly happy, and it will also tell you how many days before he will return home, as sometimes an amorous animal will sit outside a house for several days waiting patiently in the hope of meeting his lady love.

They're late! Where are they?

When you have arranged to meet a person and they don't turn up on time, it is easy to start worrying that something has happened to them. Has their car been involved in an accident? Have they forgotten they had arranged to meet me? All these thoughts go through your head, as you sit in a restaurant patiently waiting for them to arrive. Now you can dowse to ask if the person has been delayed, whom you had perhaps arranged to meet for lunch or go to a show, fails to turn up, and you are constantly watching out of the window for them, or perhaps even worse, standing outside a theatre, or in a busy rail station.

As you now know how to dowse, you can put your mind at rest by asking several questions.

1. Is the person on their way to meet me?
2. Have they already left their home?
3. Has the train been delayed?
4. Have they mistaken the time of our meeting?

102

5. Have they experienced car problems?
6. Have they remembered they have arranged to meet me?

You can phrase the questions in any manner depending on the answer to the first question. Dowsing has got to be better than sitting feeling agitated, or constantly looking both ways scanning crowds as you hope to recognize them in the distance.

Don't worry if you don't have your pendulum with you, as you can improvise by using a door key on a piece of string or a chain.

Finding a house number

Have you ever gone to keep an appointment at a person's home or office and, when you get to the area, you realize to your horror that you have left the address at home. Or perhaps you remember the name of the road, but cannot, no matter how hard you try, remember the number of the building.

Dowsing is a great help in this situation as you can dowse and ask if the forgotten number is an odd number, and if you receive a 'No' answer, you know the building is an even number, so this narrows down the number of possibilities by 50% immediately.

You can then ask if it on the right hand side of the road. Once you know which side of the road to search, you can ask the pendulum if the number is higher than 20, and if the answer is 'Yes', then you can ask if the number if higher than 30. If you then get a 'No' sign you know that the number is between 20 and 30, and you know it is even or odd, so you only have a handful of numbers to dowse. This is a quick way to find a house number as if you can get to within 50 yards of the house, you can always ask at a nearby house for assistance.

Sometimes the number is not the problem but the name causes confusion, did they say Castle Road, or was it Castle Road East or Castle Road West? The more you try to remember the instructions, the more confused you become, so once again you can dowse, and find the correct road.

Mislaid or missing items

How often have you mislaid the front door keys or your car keys when you are in a hurry to keep an appointment, or you can't remember where you filed an important document? We have all at times suffered this frustration of searching frantically. You start in the obvious places then, as you get more impatient, you find yourself becoming irrational, and looking in places where you know it won't be found.

The most annoying thing about this situation is that it never seems to happen when you have plenty time to spare – it is always when you are about to leave your home or office that you discover the loss. The good news is that next time you discover you have mislaid your keys or any other object, you can take a deep breath to help you relax, then allow your pendulum to help locate the missing item.

When you dowse to locate your missing purse, spectacles, keys etc., it is essential to phrase the question accurately, otherwise you will get the wrong answer. I know, as I have made this mistake! I had an experience many years ago when a friend telephoned me in an agitated state, to ask me to dowse as she had mislaid her spectacles, and was in a hurry to find them, as she was due to go by train to London for an important appointment.

I agreed to assist and dowsed to ask my pendulum if the spectacles were upstairs, and was shown the 'No' sign so I knew they were somewhere in a downstairs room. I asked if they were in the lounge, dining room or cloakroom but got a negative answer, but when I asked if they were in the kitchen, I got a lovely big 'Yes' swing from the pendulum. Success, or so I thought, but when I spoke to my friend, she assured me she had not found the missing spectacles.

I was puzzled and confused by this result as I had been very confident that there would not be any problem locating them, but when I told my friend they were definitely in the kitchen, she said 'Oh yes. But these are my everyday ones, and not the ones I mislaid!' this taught me a lesson always to ask the person if they have more that one of the missing item.

Always remember when asking the pendulum to locate an item, you must be specific about the details, e.g. the spectacles in the red case, or blue case etc. This applies to purses or wallets, as we often have old ones which we keep as spares, or a non-practical one for special occasions, so state clearly the appearance of the missing one.

When asking for missing keys, it is important to be very specific about their description, as we often have several sets of keys in the house so, for example, ask for help to locate keys on the key ring with the green fob, or amethyst stone.

Finding a lost item

To find a lost item in your home or office, draw a map of the layout of the rooms, and mark the name of each room, and number the bedrooms No. 1, No. 2, No. 3 etc.; also bathrooms and toilets should be numbered No. 1, No. 2. etc. so the pendulum knows which one we are talking about. Start by asking:

1. Is the missing item in an upstairs room? If answer is 'No' then ask:
2. Is the missing item in a downstairs room? If 'No', then ask:
3. Is the missing item in the loft, basement, garage, garden shed, or car?

If you get a 'Yes', then you can ask a separate question about each place. Once you have found the right area to search for the missing object, if it is a small object like a ring, then you can narrow down the area by dividing the room into four parts and asking if it is part No. 1, then ask No. 2 etc. and so you only have to look in one quarter of the room.

You can also ask if it is in a drawer. Or has it been accidentally covered by newspaper or other item? By a process of elimination you will find the object. It is also well worth asking the angelic kingdom to assist in your search, and ask the assistance of

St Anthony who is the saint who assists those who have lost articles. Good Luck!

Ever lost your car in the car park?

Losing your purse or keys is frustrating, but losing your car in a large multilevel car park, airport or other venue, is one of our worst nightmares. You get back to the car park, feeling tired after a day's shopping or an important meeting, and suddenly you realize you can't remember on which floor you parked your car. You wander along the car park floors frantically looking for your car, and you simply cannot find it, so you immediately think 'Has it been stolen?' and this is a case of Pendulum to the Rescue! You can dowse the following questions:

1. Has my car been stolen?
2. Is my car parked in this car park?
3. Is the car parked on a floor above level 6?

You can dowse to find which floor, and don't forget that some multilevel car parks also have half floor levels.

It may seem a stupid question, but it is always worth asking if your car is parked in that car park, as in airports car parks often look alike so it is easy to become disoriented. It is also wise to dowse the correct car park before you contact the police, as I know of a young man who reported to the police that his car had been stolen, then found it the next day in a nearby car park. Yes it sounds daft, but is an easy mistake to make, if you've gone into other car parks to try to find a space, or perhaps you are in the habit of using another nearby, so out of habit you look for your car there.

Time of birth

Have you ever visited an astrologer and the first questions they have asked you are 'What is you place, date, and time of birth?' Panic! Most of us know the town of our birth, and the date, but how do you find the exact time of birth. This is an important fact needed to give an accurate astrology chart reading, so big problems arise if your mother has passed to spirit, and nobody else alive knew the time of birth. It's okay if you were born in Scotland, as it has always been registered on the birth certificate, but until recently this fact was not deemed necessary on the birth certificate in England.

The pendulum will give you an accurate answer, so start by asking if you were born in the morning, and if the answer is 'Yes', then you do not need to check the afternoon hours. To narrow down the search, you can ask if you were born between midnight and 6 a.m. If 'Yes', you can then dowse each hour until you find the correct hour.

Once you have established the correct hour of birth, you can then dowse to find the minutes of the hour, as the astrologer wants to know the minutes as well as the hour. Start by asking if you were born in the first 30 minutes after the hour. If 'Yes', you can then ask if you were born within the first 15 minutes after the hour, and if you get another 'Yes', you know the birth was between the hour and 15 minutes past, so you can either dowse all 15 minutes until you get the correct answer, or dowse 5, 10 and 15 minutes as separate questions.

You may prefer to dowse over the chart, over the page, which can be used as a.m. or p.m.

Birthday date

Most of us know some folks who take their birthday very seriously, and would be most upset if you forget to send them a card, so what happens when you simply cannot remember the date? You know it's around this time of year, but can't remember if it is July or August – all you know is that it's a summer birthday. But perhaps you have mislaid your diary or address book, which lists birthdays, so again it's a case of using the pendulum. It is so easy to forget dates of birthdays, unless

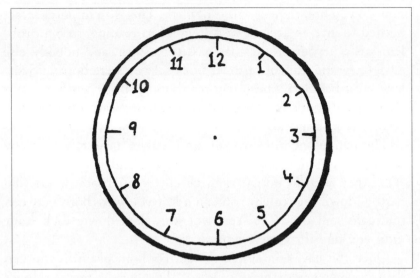

▲ *Chart of hours and chart of 5 minute intervals*

you are a very organized person, so stop feeling guilty, as dowsing can help.

You can dowse to establish the correct month, and once that has been done, ask if the birthday is in the first half of the month, and if you receive a 'No' then you know it is in the latter half of the month, so either dowse each date, or ask if it is in the third week of the month; if 'No', you then know it is during the last week, so you can dowse the last seven days. Alternatively you can send the card, knowing the birthday wishes will arrive around birthday time and, after all, it is the thought that counts!

Dowsing to track down a computer fault

Most of us feel out of our depth when our computer develops problems, and it always seems to occur at the most inconvenient time, and usually when you are in a hurry to finish some work. One of the most annoying facts about this sudden lack of communication is that tracking down the fault can be costly.

The first instinct is to call the assistance of an expert, but before contacting an engineer to locate the problem, think 'Pendulum' as dowsing will almost certainly diagnose the trouble, provided you ask the right questions.

Start by looking at the handbook, and making a list of all possibilities. You can then dowse and ask any questions you think will help to track down the problem area. For example ask:

1. Is the problem caused by a virus?
2. Is the problem in the hard drive?
3. Is the problem in the CD Rom?
4. Is the problem the server?

When you have located the root of the problem you can then instruct the engineer to look at this section first. If you are using an engineer from an advertisement in the Yellow Pages or other trade directory, you can dowse and find the most suitable or reliable engineer for the job.

Your printer

Printers can be temperamental, but the same dowsing methods applies to your printer as to your computer, so any printer problems can be dowsed before returning it to the supplier, and by dowsing and asking similar questions to those listed below, you will track down the fault.

1. Is paper jammed in the printer?
2. Is there a problem with the ink cartridge?
3. Is the problem electrical?

Once you have located the problem, you then have to choose a specialist to repair the fault, and again the pendulum will assist in finding a reliable repair person. Simply make a list of the names of firms who service printers, and dowse over each name, and ask if they are reliable and knowledgeable, and also conscientious. This system can also be used for finding a reliable car repair specialist when your car develops problems.

Dowsing to find car problems

Dowsing is an excellent way to track down the root of car problems. Do you sometimes worry about a strange noise coming from your car when travelling at a certain speed, or you feel a slight vibration which you know should not be there? Even worse is the day when you are in a hurry to keep an appointment and your car refuses to start.

When the car engine refuses to start, before rushing to call the garage, make a list of possible causes of the problem and then ask your pendulum to assist in finding the fault. Dowse:

1. Has the starter motor jammed?
2. Is the battery flat?
3. Are the points dirty?

It is so often something very simple which causes the car to have difficulty in starting the engine, so by dowsing to find the fault it can then be resolved quickly.

If you are concerned that your car engine is making a strange noise, or you hear a sound of metal rubbing on metal, then make a list from the handbook of all the possibilities.

You can dowse and ask if the problem is in the engine, electrics, fuel system, or ignition, and when you know which section has the problem, you can then list all the items in that part of the car, and so diagnose the exact problem. This exercise will save time and money as you can ask the mechanic to look at that section first, so eliminate time spent searching in the wrong part of the car for the problem.

Dowsing will also confirm if your car tyres are at the correct pressure, and if they are in need of balancing by the garage, so when you have car problems, remember your pendulum will be able to assist in diagnosing the problem.

Summary

This chapter covers some of the many situations when dowsing can be an invaluable tool in the home as it can assist you in locating blocked drains, concealed wiring or the cause of a washing machine problem. It can also be helpful when you want to choose the most suitable school or college for your child or the best family doctor, or a veterinary surgeon for the family pets.

Your pendulum will help you to choose the best value carpets if purchasing new carpets, and will confirm if a high level of formaldehyde is in the carpet.

In the kitchen the pendulum will confirm if food is still edible and for the gardener if will confirm if the plants are short of minerals or if the soil is too acid or alkaline.

When you have built up a good working relationship with your pendulum, so that you are in tune with it's energy, you will find you can get reliable answers to all sorts of everyday questions and. you'll be amazed at how many different questions you will find to ask your pendulum.

Dowsing cuts corners and speeds up the lengthy route for adopted children and adults to find their natural parents, and is an invaluable help when trying to find a missing teenager, who perhaps left home abruptly after a family row. You can also use dowsing to locate a missing cat or dog, as it will confirm if the animal is shut in a neighbour's garage, or has gone off on a romantic journey!

So whether your car or washing machine are making a strange noise, or your computer is being temperamental, before calling in an expert 'Think Dowsing'.

6

ADHD, emotional and behaviour problems

Attention Deficit Hyperactive Disorder (ADHD) is a modern day illness which causes unbelievable misery and frustration to both parents and children, and any parent whose child is diagnosed as suffering from this nightmare illness will tell you that it creates havoc in the home. Life becomes a never ending strain on the nerves, and gone are the peaceful family meals and pleasant family outings, as every day is a battle. The International Control Board (INCB), a World Health Organization agency, in 1995 stated 10–12% of children between 6 and 14 years in the USA were diagnosed with ADHD.[22]

The treatment options

So what is ADHD and can it be cured by drugs or alternative therapies? Parents have two options.

1. Those who are aware of the far reaching benefits of healing and natural treatments will take this route, and explore the many therapies including sound healing, reiki and spiritual healing, Thoughfield therapy, NLP, aromatherapy, the Tomatis method, and many other well tried therapies, before considering the conventional medical route.
2. The route for parents who have no knowledge of alternative therapies, or are sceptical about their benefits. This route involves the child being on a program of regular

medication, with psycho-stimulant or antidepressant type drugs.

Dowsing is a helpful tool in dealing with this distressing condition as it will confirm which is the right therapy for the child, which is the right treatment and which foods aggravate the situation. Start by cleansing your pendulum of negative energy then dowse the following questions: Is ADHD an incurable illness? Is ADHD hereditary?

Is ADHD an illness?

There are two very separate schools of thought about the diagnosis and cause of ADHD. The medical profession in general believe it is an incurable illness which is hereditary, a genetic risk factor, and they claim their research results show it is usually found in one or both of the child's parents, a fact anxious parents deny strongly!

I question the fact that it is hereditary, as I have treated children suffering from this behaviour problem, whose parents were well balanced, and had none of these symptoms when a child. According to figures from the National Institute of Mental Health (NIH) publication No. 96–3572, the number of children diagnosed as suffering from ADHS in the United States is roughly 2 million,[1] and the number of sufferers in Great Britain is also rising steadily. The USA has approximately 90% of the world's Ritalin patients![22]

In Australia there are roughly 50,000 children being prescribed drugs for ADHD. So do the medical experts really and truly believe that one parent of each of these children suffered from ADHD? More confirmation of this growing behaviour problem in Australia is the fact that prescriptions for Ritalin, over an eight year period, have increased by a mammoth 620%.[2]

The most common drugs used for ADHD are pharmaceutically very similar to cocaine, and these drugs have significant side effects.

Clearly it must be a great relief to enjoy a few moments of peace and quiet, but do we really want our children to become docile and compliant? Remember these children are tomorrow's adults, they will become leaders, businessmen and the teachers of our grandchildren, so it is essential that their personality is not suffocated, as they need to develop their personality. Parents and teachers cannot fail to notice that children on regular medication for behaviour problems seem to develop a 'zombiefied look' and there is a noticeable lack of sparkle in their eyes, and lively expressions are missing from their face, so are we inhibiting their creativity?

It is so much better if possible to find the root cause of the child's ADHD symptoms, since by eliminating food colourants, aspartame (the artificial sweetener) and monosodium glutamate from their diet there is a strong possibility that, in many children, their symptoms will be dramatically reduced, so eliminating the need for medical drugs such as Cylert. Dowse:

1. Are the child's symptoms linked to food colourants in their diet?
2. Are the child's symptoms linked to aspartame artificial sweetener in their diet?
3. Are the symptoms linked to food preservatives in their diet?

The Public Citizen Organization has petitioned the US Food and Drug Administration (FDA) to remove Pemoline (Cylert) from the market. This central nervous system stimulant is prescribed to treat ADHD, but Public Citizen are rightly concerned, as they report it is known to have caused a number of liver failure cases.[3]

It is interesting to note that several studies have shown another possible culprit, as certain behavioural changes experienced by ADHD sufferers can in some cases be caused by exposure to fluoride.

In 1999 the US Environmental Protection Agency (EPA) released results of a study showing a link between silicofluoride and high levels of lead in children's blood, so it is hardly surprising, since as we know lead is linked to behaviour problems, that researchers found many children diagnosed with ADHD had dangerously high levels of lead in their blood.[20]

Lead has been recognized as a killer poison for many decades, since even minute amounts will accumulate in the brains of young children, and has been shown to damage the brain. It has also been shown to produce abnormal behaviour in laboratory animals, in conjunction with deficiencies of certain minerals and vitamins.

Another very good reason to choose the alternative route for your child's treatment is that reliable evidence shows certain stimulant medication can affect growth hormone production, which is an extremely alarming fact, as it could affect all of the body's organs including the brain.

A worrisome report confirming research results on laboratory rats at the University of Buffalo showed Ritalin produces changes in the brain, similar to the effects of cocaine.[2] I agree that rats are different from humans, but are you happy about your child receiving medication which showed harmful effects on rats? Dowse:

1. Can stimulant drugs have any harmful effects on the child?
2. Can stimulant drugs reduce the overall blood flow to the child's brain?

In the USA, Dr Peter Breggin MD, in his book *Talking Back to Ritalin*, has also reported that these stimulant drugs have a harmful effect on the brain, as they reduce overall blood flow, disturb glucose metabolism, and may cause permanent shrinkage or atrophy of the brain.[5]

It is not surprising that, after reading this doctor's comments, there are over 3 million websites on Ritalin, and many of these web pages on this particular drug make alarming reading.

Looking back on my school days, I do not recall any children in the school who suffered these violent and disruptive symptoms, which raises the question, 'Are these behaviour problems linked to diet, allergic reaction, or lack of discipline?'

Many parents and alternative therapists believe strongly that ADHD is a curable condition, and are quick to tell about the success of a particular diet or treatment, so who do you believe?

Could the answer simply be that some children diagnosed by their doctor as suffering from ADHD do not in fact suffer from this illness, and are simply having a very violent reaction to additives, colourants, artificial sweeteners or negative surroundings, while other children are correctly diagnosed with this illness.

So what is the cause of this violent and anti-social behaviour? Dowse:

1. Is the child desperately trying to seek attention?
2. Does the child have a violent allergic reaction to colourants in food or sweets?
3. Is this unhappiness an allergy to cows' milk?
4. Is the child sleeping over a geopathic stress or black ley line?
5. Does the child want the security of parental discipline?
6. Is the child's body short of essential fatty acids.

A wise parent will look closely at the above questions and have the child's bedroom checked for harmful energy lines, and also have the child tested for allergies, before taking the drug route.

ADHD is described by the medical profession as a neurobiological disorder which affects a small percentage of school-age children and adults. The symptoms vary from child to child, and can include inability to pay attention,[4] hyperactive behaviour, irrational outbursts, difficulty listening to conversation, very easily distracted, and constantly losing things which are often close by. Certain sufferers are easily recognized as they are consistent fidgets, unable to stay still, seem to talk incessantly, and have the very annoying habit of interrupting your conversation. These children easily become agitated and seem unable to relax.

Are you really surprised that children suffering from any level of ADHD become frustrated in the classroom, as their outbursts and rowdy behaviour is probably a way of covering up how wretched they feel. Lets face it, constantly being told off for daydreaming, or for not paying attention, when in fact you are

116

doing your best, must make life hard. I sympathize with them, as I can well remember at school my teachers regularly telling me to stop grinning, when I should have been serious, and I am still grinning!

It is quite natural for children to have 'off days' when they display this form of bad behaviour, but it's everything in moderation, and when it happens with uncomfortable regularity, then it is time to take a closer look the situation.

Most children suffering from ADHD start to show the symptoms in early childhood, rather than in their teens, so please don't think that your rebelling teenager is suffering from ADHD when they seem to change almost over night from a sweet child to a rebel. This is all part of growing up.

I know it is very easy to say 'don't feel guilty', but doctors generally believe that parents of ADHD children who lack parental discipline skills, or even used too much discipline, should never feel guilty as they are not at fault, since the illness falls into the neurobiological category.

Other therapists ask if it is only a coincidence that the increase in ADHD seems to coincide with introduction of the fashionable attitude that it is right to encourage self expression, and wrong to discipline your child? My mother regularly used the expression 'Intolerant people make the best parents' so perhaps she was right! Today it is an offence to hit a child, but it is quite natural to hit a child lightly, to let them know the boundaries. We regularly see examples of this discipline in films or television programs, when a lion, tiger or bear will gently give their cub a clout with their huge paw, to warn them to behave, so perhaps today we have become too tolerant!

The medical profession does not as yet have a single specific test which can diagnose this illness, due to the fact that there is not one specific symptom which is found in each case of ADHD. So the seriousness of several symptoms have to be considered to rule out other illnesses.

To establish a clear picture of the illness, each case history includes emotional and social behaviour, their academic abilities, and a thorough physical examination which includes the hearing, which can often be the root of many of the problems.

There is a standard evaluation for diagnosing ADHD, so no matter whether it is your local doctor, school psychologist, or pediatrician who makes the final diagnosis, the results should be the same. These health experts firmly believe that this is a hereditary illness, so usually include investigation of the health of parents.

Some different types of medication

There are several different types of medication prescribed for ADHD and psycho-stimulant drugs are the most common medication, although new non-stimulant drugs are coming to the fore. Some children also take anti-depressants, while others are on anti-hypertension medication. The Big Questions are:

1. Are you happy about your child taking prescription drugs for years to come?
2. Do you worry that these medicines may be addictive?
3. Are you concerned about any side effects of these drugs?

Very recently the label of a new anti-stimulant drug Strattera had a bold warning added to the label, as it was found to damage the liver of a very small percentage of children, and practitioners were notified to be aware of any children on this medication whose skin had turned a sallow colour.[21] Strattera is the first of the new non-stimulant type of medication to be approved for the treatment of both children and adults who suffer from ADHD symptoms, so another good reason to avoid medication when at all possible.

Surely the next step must be to find the cause of the rapid escalation of this behaviour problem, as we do not know the long term effect of these drugs, and some experts report that they become addictive, so lets start by considering some obvious ingredients in the diet.

Organic cows' milk

Cows' milk is often linked to allergic reaction due to the hormones injected into cattle to increase milk yield, and the chemicals in their feed. Perhaps it's time to introduce organic cows' milk into your child's diet as this milk is sold in most supermarkets, it is easily available, and can be frozen for a later date. Organic milk is much healthier as the animals have been fed on chemical-free food which includes red clover, so it's not surprising organic milk contains three quarters more of the wonder nutrient Omega 3 than ordinary cows' milk. So it is very beneficial for your children to drink organic milk.[6]

What are the benefits of the ingredient red clover in organic milk? This plant is recognized as an anti-spasmodic, it eases bronchial irritation and coughs, is anti-diarrhetic,[7] and it is also a blood and lymph cleanser, so even if your child is not allergic to cows' milk, they can only benefit from traces of this plant in their diet.

Dowse:

1. Will your child's health have increased benefits from organic milk in the diet containing red clover?
2. Will your child's ADHD type symptoms decrease by including organic milk in his diet?
3. Would your child's health improve by removing cows' milk from their diet?
4. Would soy milk be more beneficial than cows' milk in the diet?

The importance of Omega 3 in the diet

Fatty acids play an extremely important, and often underestimated, role in our health, so it is essential that the body has adequate supplies, as they are a 'must' in the diet of anyone suffering from emotional or behavioural disorders, and are crucial to ensuring normal function of the brain.

Omega 3 oil, as well as being accepted as a preventative of heart disease, it is also thought to improve some levels of depression and behaviour problems. Results of trials recently carried out in Durham, and not yet published, are expected to show a noticeable improvement in level of school performance, in the group of children given the Omega 3 supplement. 40% of the children involved in this trial showed obvious improvement in these trials conducted by Dr Alex Richardson.[8]

A study carried out at Purdue University on the benefits and effects of fatty acid on children's health and behaviour showed that children whose body is low in Omega 3 are more likely to be in the group suffering from behaviour problems.

Research on rats fed a diet of sunflower and peanuts suffered a shortage of Omega 3 in their brain cells and organettes, and showed decreased learning abilities, and a deficiency in nutrients.[9]

Another well documented study on the benefits of fish oil in children's diet showed more confirmation, as a result of this study involving boys in the 6–12 year old age group who suffered a range of behavioural problems. These included learning and health problems, and researchers found that a greater number of the boys suffered sleep problems, temper tantrums and learning difficulties. Those who regularly caught colds and had taken antibiotics had lower levels of oils in their body than the other group who were free from these health and behaviour problems.[10]

It's time to dowse and get some confirmation about the benefits of fish oil.

Dowse:

1. Can Omega 3 in the diet reduce some temper tantrums?
2. Can Omega 3 help to control certain emotional behaviour problems?
3. Can Omega 3 oil in the diet often reduce depression symptoms?

4. Can Omega 3 oil in the diet reduce eczema?
5. Can Omega 3 in the diet reduce cracks in the heels?
6. Can Omega 3 in the diet help to improve the memory?

As yet the root cause of ADHD is unknown but an interesting study reported in the *American Journal of Clinical Nutrition* in 1995 showed 53 children involved in the exercise had a significantly lower concentration of key fatty acids in their blood than the control group.[11]

Again, we only have the word of the researchers of these various studies that a shortage of essential fatty acids is a cause of ADHD problems, but just in case these results are correct, it is well worth including these important fatty acids in children's diet.

To say there is a lot of interest in Omega 3 today is probably an understatement, as there are 7 million websites on Omega 3 (7,610,000 to be exact, at the time of writing), and so it is not really surprising to learn that there have been over 2,000 scientific studies carried out on this subject. Results of these studies demonstrated very clearly that many health and behaviour problems are linked to a serious deficiency of this essential fatty acid, which is very low in the US and UK diet.

A fact to make us stop and think is that researchers report that roughly 60% of the American population has a deficiency of this important fish oil, and 20% appear to have an almost undetectable level in their body.

The British Heart Foundation report one adult in the UK dies every three minutes of heart disease, and advise that these oils help prevent blood clotting, which is a major cause of heart attacks. The American Heart Association's journal of November 19 2002 recommends at least one gram of Omega 3 daily, so as well as giving this important oil to children with attention or behaviour problems, adults should also have a daily dose to avoid heart problems in the future.[12]

Another good reason for including Omega 3 in the diet, as well as discouraging heart problems, and improving behaviour and emotional problems, is that this amazing oil has also been shown to be in short supply in the body of those people suffering from eczema and skin problems including cracked heels.[13]

So what is so magic about this fish oil, and what does it do to create such beneficial effects? To put it simply, it seems to act like a lubricant to the cell membranes of the brain, so the wheels are oiled. You can either include it in your diet by eating oily fish, nuts, leafy green vegetables, or take the easy route, and purchase easy to swallow capsules from your local health store.

You will find an excellent technical explanation on the BBC Science and Nature website.

Gradually word is spreading about the vital part this fish oil plays in our good health, and that it is linked to memory and behaviour problems, so much so that a leading baby food manufacturer is considering adding it to their products. Ironically the importance of Omega 3 has been realized in several countries for many years, including Japan, where fish is a large part of the diet and supplements are taken of this oil which belongs to the family of polyunsaturated fatty acids.

Essential fatty acids and dyslexia

Dyslexia is at last becoming accepted as an existing problem, and not just imagination, and studies of dyslexic children have shown the problem in some cases is due to a deficiency of essential fatty acids in their diet. Research by Dr Alex Richardson involved 41 children who had reading difficulties, and were given a supplement of fish oil or placebo. In the group of children who received fish oil, their reading improved, concentration was better and they experienced less anxiety. This sounds another very good reason to ensure your children have essential fatty acids in their diet.[14]

Dowse:

1. Ask if dyslexia can often be caused by a deficiency of essential fatty acids.
2. Ask if dyslexia is an imaginary problem.

3. Ask if your child's ADHD has been wrongly diagnosed.
4. Are behavioural problems linked to another factor?
5. Can including Omega 3 oil in your child's diet improve his dyslexic symptoms?
6. Is your child's dyslexia linked to an Omega 3 oil shortage?

Emotional behaviour and food colourants

Another question many people are asking today is 'Are many of today's health problems caused by toxins and chemicals in our food chain?' There is such an unexplained increase in certain illness and behaviour problems, and also the high number of adults who suffer from a low immune system illnesses or suffer depression and anxiety. Is there also a link between diet and the increase in violence and crime in the teenage group?

People usually groan or raise their eyebrows when they hear someone say 'When I was young', but that's exactly what I am about to say! When I was a child, the family diet consisted of natural foods, all chemical free, and dairy produce was free from added hormones and antibiotics. Fruit grew in the garden or was local produce, unlike much of today's fruit which is sprayed many times with chemicals before travelling great distances, often from the other side of the world. Plus many brain building fat soluble vitamins and amino acids are missing from today's diet, and these are so important for growth of a healthy mind and body.

Does your child's behaviour pattern change when they have eaten a packet of highly coloured sweets or cakes which contained a high level of food colouring, or preservatives? I have chatted to many mums, who've said they limit the number of sweets their child is allowed to eat at any one time, as their personality seems to change dramatically, after digesting food containing certain colourants or preservatives. For no obvious reason they seem to become noisier, more boisterous and excitable.

Artificial food colouring and preservatives are blamed by many doctors and parents as having a very significant impact on the child's level of hyperactivity. Research has been going on for several years to establish the link between artificial colourants, preservatives, and excitable behaviour. News Medical Net report an article in the *British Medical Journal*, which suggests a very significant improvement in children's hyperactive behaviour could be produced if artificial colourants and sodium benzoate were removed from their diet.

A group of scientists have completed a study on the behaviour of a group of 3 year old children with artificial colourants in their diet. When colourants were removed, the parents reported noticeable changes for the better, particularly in disruptive behaviour and inattentiveness. The study was funded by the Food Standard Agency, and involved both the School of Medicine and the School of Psychology at Southampton University, and the David Hide Asthma and Allergy Centre at St. Mary's Hospital, Isle of Wight.[15]

Further research is being carried out on a grant of £750,000 to investigate these questions in this 'Food and Behavior in Children' (FABIC) study.

Research in Surrey, England, in 1987 involving the Hyperactive Children's Support Group (a national charity founded in 1987) and Dr Neil Ward, involved 357 children all diagnosed as suffering from ADHD; results showed that of these children, 87% had an adverse reaction to artificial colourants and 72% had an adverse reaction to artificial preservatives, more confirmation that when possible these ingredients should be removed from the diet.[16]

Also in 1987, in Scotland, research by Dr Ian Menzies showed great results by removing artificial additives, and more confirmation comes from results of research carried out at the Institute of Child Health in 1993.[17]

It is a matter of urgency that we finally have proof that many cases, where ADHD and ADD have been diagnosed as an illness, are in fact simply the body's reaction to these unnatural toxins in their system. It is criminal for these children and some adults to be on powerful medication like Ritalin, if the root of the problem is easily and fairly painlessly solved, by reducing the number of sweets and preservatives in their diet. Dowse and ask the following questions:

1. Is some of your child's hyperactive behaviour caused by certain food preservatives?
2. Are many cases of ADHD and ADD caused by food colourants in the diet?
3. Can sodium benzoate in the diet trigger hyperactive behaviour?

If you would like more information about the effects of additives on health, have a look at The Hyperactive Children's Support Group's website who are based in England. For readers in the USA, please have a look on the internet and use any search engine to type in hyperactive children's support groups in the USA.

Increase in unruly teenagers and vandalism

We are constantly hearing about teachers in certain schools having to deal with disobedient, foul mouthed teenagers, so are these unpleasant youngsters perhaps perfectly nice youngsters whose behaviour is linked to their diet? So many teenagers drink cans of soft drinks and eat instant foods, many of these containing artificial sweeteners, colourants, and preservatives. Are you concerned about the behaviour of your teenager? Then as a test, try to subtly change their diet for a couple of weeks, and watch for an improvement!

Is there a link between the fact that more and more young children are turning to drugs, and the high level of additives including artificial sweeteners, colourants, and preservatives in their diet? The answer in some cases will be Yes, as many youngsters, whose behaviour problems disappeared after their parents had removed additives from their diet, have reported they feel calmer inside their head.

Maniac car drivers! Road rage!

Is it my imagination or are there many more lunatic car drivers loose on our roads? How often, when driving along a freeway, do you see drivers making inexcusably inconsiderate manoeuvres, and risking lives as they switch from lane to lane at high speed. Have you been on the receiving end of their unjustified frustration, when you can feel their agitation as they drive too close behind your car, trying hard to force you to travel much faster than the speed limit, while flashing their lights at you?

Several people have mentioned their frightening motorway experiences to me recently, and I too have become very aware of a noticeable increase in this lack of courtesy. I can almost feel the anger and frustration coming from these drivers, as their facial expressions give a very clear message to other drivers that they mean business. So is there a link between these drivers who are over-reacting and suffering from a form of 'road rage', and artificial additives in their diet? Dowse the following questions:

1. Are symptoms of road rage often caused by something in the diet?
2. Can road rage be instigated by chemicals in the diet?
3. Can aspartame create aggressive behaviour?
4. Can food preservatives create aggressive behaviour?

Of course, there can be many other factors like money or job worries, which may cause depression, but these worries don't usually cause irrational behaviour. It all seems to fit in with the results of research on children which showed ADHD symptoms improved or vanished when the offending additives were removed from their diet. It seems logical that if it reduces behavioural and anti-social problems in children, then it could also effectively reduce some cases of road rage, as the symptoms of this modern-day problem are very similar to those of ADHD!

Allergies and behaviour problems

The body's immune system develops from the day we are born, and has an amazing ability to distinguish between foods and other items which are either beneficial or harmful to health. An allergic response is usually triggered off by anything which causes an imbalance in the system.

We all recognize certain signs of an allergic reaction and give a heavy sigh when it's hay fever time, or the dreaded pollen count is high, and our eyes become red and itchy, and our nose starts to run, making us feel miserable. At least these reactions don't last for too long, but it's a different story if a child is allergic to something in the atmosphere, or an ingredient in the daily diet. The cause of an allergic reaction is often not the most obvious things. We all know about cats' hair, yeast, dust mites, wheat, soy, and certain food colourants, but it can often be a reaction to a chemical like formaldehyde in the carpet, or chemicals in household cleaners.

Finding the culprit can be a lengthy process of elimination, but by making a list of all possible causes of an allergic reaction it is possible to dowse, to find which foods, medication, chemicals, or circumstances create an allergic reaction, and which trigger off bad behaviour. Children who are cows' milk intolerant often become very hyperactive, suffer muscle weakness or fatigue symptoms, so if you are concerned that the ADHD symptoms may be linked to intolerance to cows' milk, then perhaps it's worth testing an alternative. As I mentioned earlier, I recommend organic cows' milk, but if that causes a reaction, then perhaps it's time to test goats' milk, which is an excellent alternative and it very seldom seems to trigger any allergic reaction. Soya milk is another alternative which is acceptable to most children.

Could it be that a member of your family or someone you know is concerned about undiagnosed allergies? There are many therapists and dowsers who specialize in detecting the source of the problem, so ask in your local health shop or alternative health clinic, as a visit is usually money well spent! Either

Radiesthesia or Kinesiology will often help to pinpoint the source of the allergic reaction. Dowse and ask the following questions:

1. Does the child have an allergic reaction, and to what?
2. Is the allergic reaction caused by a weakened immune system?
3. Is the child allergic to any dairy products?
4. Is the allergic reaction caused by colourant tartrazine E102 in food?

As each one of us is a unique individual vibrating on slightly different energy, we all have different allergies, but some of us go through life without ever being aware of them. Many of us experience different reactions to food, as the balance in some bodies is more acidic, and in some it is more alkaline.

Check foods for colourants

As I mentioned earlier, food colourants are often linked to behaviour problems, and it is not always easy to remove colourants from the diet, as they seem to crop up in the most unexpected places, and it surprises many folks to learn that some hens' eggs contain colourants.

Hens in years gone by were fed on a diet mainly of maize and grass but, in the past twenty five years, many hens have chemical colouring added to their diet to boost the colour of the yolk. When you cook eggs and notice the yoke is a pale yellow colour, then it has probably been laid by a hen on a colourant-free diet, whereas an egg which has a dark yellow yoke may possibly have had colourant added to the hen's diet. In the UK eggs with the lion stamp are colourant free, and eggs sold in health shops and Iceland Frozen Foods stores are free from colourant.[18]

Of the yellow colourants perhaps the worst Yellow Peril comes from tartrazine E102, sometimes referred to as FD&C Yellow Number 5, used to colour certain foods, cosmetics and other products. This unsavoury colour is derived from coal-tar and is an industrial waste which is reputed to be a catalyst in hyperactive and other behaviour problems, as well as asthma, migraine, thyroid cancer, and lupus. In the United States manufacturers of all products whether food, cosmetics, shampoos, or birth control pills, are required to indicate on the label when a product contains tartrazine. In the UK and Europe it is listed as E102, and in both Norway and Austria this colourant is banned.[19]

Another possible cause of hyperactive behaviour is low blood sugar, so let's talk about it now.

Low blood sugar – hypoglycemia

Either a child or adult who regularly consumes high levels of refined carbohydrates in their diet is quite liable to experience behaviour problems, as a sudden raising of the blood sugar upsets the insulin balance in their body, which in turn causes a chain reaction.

When the blood sugar is below the normal level, the body produces hormones to correct the problem, but the symptoms of this upset in level of the blood sugar can often be similar to ADHD. Common symptoms are irrational behaviour, feelings of depression, lifelessness and lack of energy, feelings of nausea, and wobbly legs. If your child suffers from some of these symptoms, please consider low blood sugar as a possible problem, before committing him to a life on medication. Dowse and ask your pendulum:

1. Is your child's behaviour problem linked to low blood sugar?
2. Does your child consume a high level of sugar in his diet?

This problem is a vicious circle, as low blood pressure creates a craving for sweet food, since this is the body's way of trying to correct the sugar level. So an ongoing situation arises as the more sweet food consumed, the more low blood sugar level, and so more craving and more symptoms.

How can this problem be resolved? My answer is chromium tablets! I get terrific cravings for sweet biscuits, and will rush around the kitchen desperately searching for biscuits, and then I realize my problem is a craving for sugar, so I take a chromium tablet. This innocent looking tablet stops me from getting unstoppable urges to eat sweet things, so mums, when you have an urge for sweet goodies, I recommend instead, have a chromium picolinate tablet. It works for me, and can be purchased in any health shop.

Before ending this chapter on children's behavioural problems, I would like to mention the temperamental problems which some teenagers display!

Are you puzzled why your child who has always been good natured, well behaved and smiling, has become a defiant teenager, who takes offence at the slightest thing? It's often a mystery which no medical doctor can unravel, as all teenagers have different problems.

As a concerned parent, where do you start looking for the root of this inexplicable personality change? Again it's dowsing to the rescue! By asking your pendulum a few questions, you will be able to eliminate a number of possible causes, and hopefully diagnose the cause of the unhappiness. Growing up can be a lonely time as young teenagers are in an 'in-between stage' of no longer being a child and almost but not quite fully adult.

Many unexplained changes in moods can possible be due to too much aspartame in their diet from drinking lots of cans of fizzy drinks, or is their body short of Omega 3 oil? Perhaps they are rebelling against home restrictions or even worse, they are worrying about the shape of their body!

Dowse:

1. Is my child's behaviour change caused by aspartame in her diet?
2. Is my child rebelling against restrictions in the home?
3. Is she unhappy at school or college?
4. Is her body short of Omega 3 oil?
5. Is she sleeping over a geopathic stress line?

There are so many different reasons for a change in behaviour, so make a list and start dowsing, as perhaps your child is making a statement, or feels she knows better than you about certain matters!

When I give healing to a patient one of the first things I do is to balance the level of negative and positive ions in their body, as I have found that almost all physical and mental illnesses and ion imbalance seem to go together, so if you are concerned about your child's behaviour or health, then please dowse to check if the ions in their body are balanced. Ask the pendulum if the negative and positive ions are balanced in the child's body, then rephrase the question and ask if there is an ion imbalance. Once you have received confirmation that there is an imbalance, it is time to ask your pendulum to please balance the ions in the child's body. Now ask the pendulum to balance the ions in your home. This exercise should be done every week to sustain the correct level of ions. In chapter one there is more information about ions.

Please sit down and think about the issues I have mentioned which may be the cause ADHD type symptoms, and once you start to make a list to dowse, you will probably find quite a few questions to add to your list, so good luck!

Summary

I cannot possibly begin to do justice in this chapter to the researchers and doctors who have searched for a cause for ADHD and ADD, but in these few pages I hope I have given you inspiration to dowse to find the cause of your child's behaviour problem, and help them to become a happier child and enjoy their schooldays.

Can ADHD be cured? Many doctors tell us that this is a neurobiological disorder which cannot be cured, but I disagree with this diagnosis as there is a great deal of research which points to the fact that behavioural problem of this type can be caused by a range of different chemicals or foods.

Before visiting a doctor about your child's tantrums and anger, please consider the possibility that he or she is being affected by the fluoride in their toothpaste which may be bringing the fluoride level in their blood over the legal limit. Also try to delete as many colourants as possible from the diet as many are known to instigate hyperactive behaviour.

I must stress that all facts mentioned in this chapter are my experience other than those facts referenced and, as I am not a medical doctor, I must emphasize it is important to consult a medical doctor before following any of my suggestions.

Endnotes

1. Elliott Carl, *American Bioscience Meets The American Dream*. 2003. The American Prospect. http://www.prospect.org
2. Jacobs, Bob, *Nexus New Times*, March 2005. Vol. 12. No 2. 'Australia – Prescriptions for Ritalin increase by 620%'. Rosemary Boom Psychologist, *Sun Herald*, Sydney, June 30 2002. Mackaey, P. and Kopras, A., 'Medication for Attention Deficit Hyperactive Disorder', An Analysis by Federal Electorate, Parliament of Australia, Current Issue Brief 11.2000–2002. *The Courier-Mail*, Brisbane, November 13, 2001.
3. Public Citizen website. *www.citizen.org* 'ADHD Drug Should be Removed From Market', Protecting Health, Safety and Democracy.
4. Briggen, Dr Peter, 'What doctors aren't telling you about stimulants for children'. *Talking Back to Ritalin*.
5. News Release 'Psychiatrists Discloses Ritalin, Hidden Danger to Children'. http://www.breggin.com/ritalinpnews.html
6. The Hickman Academy for Spirit Release, 'A Pint of Organic Milk A Day Works Wonders' by Sean Poulter'. *The Daily Mail*, UK, December 8 2004.
7. Grieve, M., edited by Lloyd, C. F., *A Modern Herbal*, Tiger Books International.
8. Richardson, Alex, 2006, *Food and Behaviour.*'Omega-3 fatty acids in ADHD and related neuro-developmental disorders.' http://www.fabresearch.org
9. Stevens, L. *et al.*, 2003, Food and Behavior Research. Purdue University, 'EFA Supplementation in Children with Inattention, Hyperactivity and Other Disruptive Behavior.
10. Mercola, Dr Joseph. 'Does your child have ADHD? Consider fish oil over Ritalin'. http://www.mercola.com
11. Stevens, L. J., Zontell, S. S., Deck, J .L., Abate, M. L., Watkins, B. A., and Lipp, S. R., 1995, *The American Journal of Clinical Nutrition*, Vol. 59(4-4), pp. 915–920, 'Essential Fatty Acid Metabolism in Boys

With Attention Deficit Hyperactive Disorder', The Fish Foundation. www.fish-foundation.org.uk

12. The Omega 3 Information Service. www.omega-3info.com
13. Mercola, Dr Joseph, 'Omega 3 is Essential to the Human Body'. www.mercola.com
14. Greenhealth Watch (7082) 2001 4:2 (18) Chapman, James. *Daily Mirror*, January 24 2001.
15. News Medical Net. Child Health News. 'Food Coloring and Preservatives Making Kids Hyperactive' www.news-medical.net
16. Ward, Dr Neil, Senior Lecturer in chemistry, University of Surrey. The Hyperactive
   Children's Support Group. http://www.hacsg.org.uk
17. Menzies, Dr Ian, 'The Hyperactive Children's Society Support Group. http://www.hacsg.org.uk
18. 'Eggs Show their True Color' http://www.iceland.co.uk
19. 'Tartrazine A Real Yellow Menace' The Practical Hippie. htp://.www.thepracticalhippie.com
20. Boursaw, Jane Louise, *The Kalamazoo Express Weekly*, November 18 1999.
21. Mercola, Dr Joseph, 'ADHD Drug May Harm the Liver – Try These Safe Steps Instead'. www.mercola.com
22. Breggin, Dr Peter R, MD. Testified Before the Subcommittee on Oversight and Investigation, Committee on Education and the Workforce, US House of Representatives. http://www./house.gov/ed_workforce/hearings/106th/oi/ritalin92900/breggin.htm

7

Discover the wonders of
Sound Healing

Healing is more than just laying on of hands or prayers. It comes in many guises and encompasses sound, as this is one of the most powerful healing tools for relieving anxiety, tension, and stress, and creating upliftment. Our ears are our body's vibrational sensors, tuned into every subtle vibration in the earth and atmosphere which affects our health, and creates or disturbs the fine balance in the body. The ears direct soothing sounds to the body to relieve stress, and create balance which is often lost in daily work because of the jangle of traffic and voices in busy places. They are the first sense to develop after birth and are the last sense to leave the body on death.

Dowsing can help you to identify the right music for you, as we are all on very different energy vibrations, so each one of us reacts differently to the various tones of music.

Have you ever been aware of the wonderful sensation of listening to deeply moving musical sounds which carry you off in a lovely daydream when, although it is difficult to explain, you know instinctively that your spirit has been touched by the mystical sound.

When the human body is in perfect health, every organ vibrates in unison as each individual organ has its own frequency vibration. When illness is present, the sensitive vibration is altered and becomes out of sync with the rest of the body.

The healing effects of sound can be used to help rebalance the body's sensitive energy vibrations, as sounds can have a very calming and relaxing effect on the body. Equally the wrong sounds can be guaranteed to get our nerves on edge, by creating disharmony. Every sound which we hear plays a part in our life, although most of us don't spend much time thinking about sounds, as they are part of our surroundings.

Sounds can create a big impact on our mental or emotional state and can certainly play a great part in influencing our spiritual mood. The gentle sound of relaxing music is a powerful and unobtrusive tool which can be used effectively to reduce stress, anxiety, depression, or ADHD symptoms.

The great benefit of using sound to relax a hyperactive child, or one who suffers from any of the ADHD symptoms, is that if the music is played quietly in the background, they will most probably be unaware of its presence and so will not fight the soothing effect, and will become more relaxed. I recommend the gentle sounds of dolphin music with distant sounds of lapping water, as children love dolphins and will not recognize this music as a form of treatment.

One of the greatest benefits of sound healing is that it helps to reduce the amount of medication needed, to relax anyone who is suffering from psychological or behaviour conditions, also it is used in hospices and for palliative care.

Make a list of your favourite music, cleanse your pendulum and then you can dowse to find out which pieces of music can

1. have a healing effect,
2. have a relaxing effect,
3. will release stress.

If you like orchestral music, make a list of classical composers and dowse to ask which one is on the right vibration for you.

You will find that those which are on the right vibration will have a calming effect on your body and, when you listen to the music which is right for you, then you will be aware of being refreshed and stress levels reduced.

Sound therapy has proven to be an effective and flexible hidden helper in cases of pain management, digestive problems, and learning difficulties.[1]

All of us appreciate that different types of music have a different effect on us and we know that soft relaxing music releases tension, but do you know that it can create beneficial changes in the body? It boosts the body's serotonin level and improves sleep pattern and, by increasing the brain's alpha waves, it helps to create a restful relaxed state, which in turn reduces anxiety and releases muscle tension.[2]

Research indicates that practicing relaxation benefits the hypothalamus, as it alters the chemical process, and turns stress responses off. Great! you say. But how do you get a hyperactive child, who never seems to relax or get tired, to sit down and consciously relax? Try soft music!

As I suggested earlier, dolphins are a favourite with children so try playing a CD of music which incorporates their sounds, or alternatively purchase a CD designed by experts in this field. Have a look at the Sound Therapy website, also have a look in new-age shops as they usually have a selection of dolphin music.

Sound and music therapy are well recognized as effective tools to treat both children and adults who suffer from stress or auditory processing problems. Perhaps you already know of the work of French doctor Alfred Tomatis MD, who researched the link between the working of the ear and the brain. Results of his research showed that, without a doubt, there is a strong link between the malfunction of hearing and neurological problems.

If you would like to explore this method of treatment either for your child or yourself, Tomatis Development have 160 centres around the world, and have an excellent website.[3]

Dowse:

1. Do relaxing tones increase your alpha waves?
2. Do relaxing tones boost your body's serotonin level?
3. Does listening to relaxing music benefit your hypothalamus gland?
4. Would any of your family with hearing problems benefit from the Tomatis Development Method?

Modern physics tells us that we are all made of energy, vibrating at our own resonant frequency, and all influenced by sound, although most of us find it difficult to see ourselves as an energy consisting of atoms and particles.

Sound healing falls into a special category of energy medicine, and listening to the relaxing sound of music when you are very stressed or under pressure at work will help to realign the energies in your physical body. This amazing healing tool, which is now being recognized by alternative therapists, is an invaluable and much underestimated tool, in treating both children and adults with behavioural and emotional problems. Sound healing is particularly helpful to people who find visualizing or meditation an impossibility.

Over two decades ago, in 1982, the Sound Healers Association was formed as a non-profit organization, dedicated to researching the benefits of sound healing, and creating awareness of the many uses and benefits of music as a therapeutic tool.[4]

When we are born our sense of sound is already developed, as we have spent several months in our mother's womb, where all sorts of noises are heard. These comforting sounds include gurgling of water, thumping of the mother's heart as it beats, and other body sounds.

Sound is the oldest energy vibration and goes back to the beginning of creation. It is fundamental and the basis of our existence, and once we accept that everything has a vibration and the importance of being in tune with it, life becomes a lot easier.

Sound medicine has been around for a very long time, although only recently becoming known as an alternative therapy. I have been told that Rudolph Steiner, the famous German philosopher, predicted decades ago that 'pure tones' would be used for healing, and that Nostradamus, who has predicted many events which have occurred, also foresaw that pure tones would be used as a healing treatment for cancer.

It has taken many decades for the value of pure sound to be accepted, but at last sound is being rediscovered, as an effective and pain free tool, to treat stress and anxiety. It is being used with great success by many therapists to induce a state of physical and emotional relaxation, and recognized as an effective treatment for certain mental problems.

A number of therapists today are rediscovering that these wonderful soothing tones, whether used in chanting, nature sounds, or music, all have a natural ability to align all of the body's energy fields. How many of us a few years ago would have believed that hospitals and nursing homes would be using sounds to enhance the vitality of their patients.

We know that as yet many members of the medical profession do not acknowledge the benefit of sound healing, but more and more sound therapy courses are becoming available, as people realize it is an effective tool to relieve stress and avoid the need for medication. One of the most beautiful sounds used in healing is the delicate yet powerful vibration of the Tibetan singing bowl.

The Tibetan singing bowls

So how can sound be a form of healing? Perhaps the most delicious musical sound used in healing is the pure tones of Tibetan singing bowls. Little has been written about the history of these amazing bowls, but it is generally accepted that they were never used as begging bowls.

These magical bowls come in a range of sizes and shapes: there are 68 different types of singing bowl and of these 45 bowls are different designs, and 23 varieties of the bowl possess other significant psycho-acoustic features. Most of these bowls, whatever shape or size, give wonderful sounds but there are the odd exceptions, so look out for the bowl which gives a sound on an anger or panic vibration.[5]

Should you decide to treat yourself to one of the wonderful Tibetan bowls, it is important to dowse first, to confirm that you are purchasing a bowl which has the best tone for your energy vibration. Although most of the bowls have a magical tone, there are subtle differences, so cleanse your pendulum, and then ask if the one you are about to purchase has the most beneficial tone for your body's energy vibration.

Healing with Tibetan singing bowls

Once you have become in tune with the energies of your singing bowl, you will be able to use it very successfully to create balance in patients who suffer severe symptoms of stress. This angelic sound is capable of balancing the body's energies, and installing a feeling of peace, similar to the effect received from channeled healing.

When listening to the unique haunting notes, it almost feel as though the sounds have come from another world, as each bowl sings with slightly a different harmony, so creating a deep feeling of relaxation which in modern day living is difficult to find.

The bowls create a form of 'Mind Magic Music' which seems to have a special ability to help in self-transformation, by balancing energies in the body and allowing clearer thinking. Many enthusiasts say that the pure sound of the bowls enables them to recapture a long lost resonance which was so well known and understood by our ancestors, but this truly wonderful sound with the ability to relieve stress from the body is almost lost in today's busy world.

The sound which is like no other music can create great clarity, which enables a person suffering from deep seated anger to see the root of the problem, and clear deep seated anger to release it, and create a feeling of compassion.

It is not difficult to understand why these simple bowls have been used for thousands of years and their benefits recognized as a natural cure for mind illnesses. Their sound is one of the few sounds able to fill an emptiness inside the human body. The strange thing is that it seems to know exactly where to go to let our higher self unfold, and reaches the depth of our being, right to the centre of the soul.

Dowse:

1. Can the sound from this bowl create an altered state of consciousness?
2. Can it awaken your cellular memory?

3. Can the sound from this bowl raise your energy vibration?
4. Can the sound from the bowl help you get into a meditative state?

When you have a few moments to spare, try sitting relaxed in a peaceful room, and listen to the powerful sound of the singing bowls. You will almost certainly feel their rich sonic vibration stirring in the depth of your mind, as you drift off into a peaceful world, quite oblivious of time or surroundings.

Patients relay how they can feel anxieties and tension slip from their body as the sounds wave over them. It's no wonder that many forward thinking hypnotherapists today recognize the benefit to their patients of using the bowls to induce relaxation.

Sound enthusiasts will assure you the sound of the bowls will create an altered state of consciousness, a stirring deep within your mind, and will awaken your cellular memory, so try meditating to this gentle sound.

Whether you use the singing bowls for healing stress or for shamanic work, they will raise the energy on both mental and spiritual levels. This makes a lot of sense, as these very special sound wave patterns given by the bowls are capable of resonating at certain altered brain states, mainly alpha or theta. These are a similar level used in deep meditative state, and as well as meditation, it is also possible to experience astral travel and visual trips to met your guides, family, or other places. An extra bonus if you are lucky is that you may have a conversation with ETs and beings from other planets!

The brain's four separate vibrations

The human brain has two separate sides and each controls different actions.

1. The Left Brain Hemisphere is the side which deals with logical thought and numbers.
2. The Right Brain Hemisphere is the artistic and creative side which is linked to meditation, art and music.

You often hear a person say 'He is too Left Brained' or 'Too Right Brained', which is a description used when a person is too intellectual or very artistic.

Here are the four vibrations of the human brain.

1. Delta which vibrates at 0.5 to 3 vibration.
2. Theta which vibrates at 4 to 7 vibration.
3. Alpha which vibrates at 8 to 14 vibration.
4. Beta which vibrates at 15 vibration upwards.[6]

When a person is described as being in alpha, it usually means they are either in healing mode or in a meditative state, as this is the frequency the body uses in meditation. It is also the vibration used to channel healing energy: it is the vibration of the energy around our earth, which scientists tell us beats at around 10 beats every second.

Being in alpha is a real treat for your brain and your body, as it gives the body an opportunity to relax and recharge itself, and it allows the brain to rest in the quietness which is seldom found in our busy daily life. When your brain is in alpha, you can completely detach yourself from your everyday problems, and afterwards feel refreshed and energized. Listening to the sound of the bowls will help you to drift into an alpha state of mind.

Tibetan singing bowls are blessed with a powerful vibration which, at the same time as being a soft and very spiritual sound, stirs and encourages our awareness of sound and space, and the wonder of real silence, something which few of us every experience. When you are mentally searching for the answer to a problem, and it seems to elude you, try sitting down to listen to the music of the bowls as it will enable you to contemplate the answer to the problem, and guide you to make the right decision.

It's all very well telling you about the wonderful sounds created by singing bowls but what materials are used to make the bowls, and how do they create this special unique sound?

Both the skill and recipe required to make the original bowls is a well kept Tibetan secret, but in an effort to discover the ingredients in these wonderful bowls, the British Museum carried out a metallurgical analysis in London. Results revealed the bowls were made of a combination of 12 different alloys. These ingredients were silver, nickel, copper, zinc, antimony, tin, lead, cobalt, bismuth, arsenic, cadmium, and iron.[7]

That's a pretty interesting list of contents, and you can't help but wonder who thought up this intriguing recipe, and the explanation for the magical sound.

Did previous generations know more about sound and energy than we know today? And is the sound created by this combination of alloys perhaps music from the earth? We are often told that the earth talks to us, and that we humans do not hear the sounds, but animals, birds, and insects are able to hear the earth talk to them. There are so many questions that, unless we can communicate with our spirit guides, we will not learn the answers until we have passed to the spirit world.

Using the bowl

How do you use one of the singing bowls to create haunting sounds? I was taught to hold my hand out flat and place the bowl on the palm of my left hand, and the mallet or wand in the other hand. By running the wand gently around the outside lip of the bowl in a clockwise direction, you will create sound. The movement reminds me of stirring my mother's big china pudding bowl as a child: it is an arm movement rather than a wrist movement.

It takes a few moments to master the correct speed and tone, but once you hear the magical sound you are creating, you feel it going right through your body and the experience is one you won't forget.

For best results always remind yourself to start stirring slowly and gently, and you'll soon get in tune with the vibrations of the bowl, and know which speed is comfortable for you.

Once you have heard the magical sound from the bowl as it builds up to an amazing vibration which stirs your whole being, you will be well and truly hooked on singing bowls! But beware as these dulcet tones can entice your body's chakras to open, so it is essential that you close all except your crown and base chakras when you have ended your session with the bowl. As I mentioned earlier, the awesome power of the energy vibration from the bowls seems to allow you to travel to other places without actually moving from your chair, so take advantage of this treat.

Cleansing the aura

Therapists in tune with energies will often use the sound vibration of a singing bowl to cleanse the aura, as the vibration permeates the body's energy field, the aura, and both cleanses and heals it. It is vitally important to good health that the aura is regularly cleansed and balanced, as all illness starts in the energy field before reaching the body.

Another reason it is essential to keep the aura cleansed and healed is that a damaged aura is an open door for negative spirits to enter, so spending a few moments regularly listening to your bowl and absorbing the special energy of its sound will help to keep you healthy.

Clearing negative energy

With the growing popularity and acceptance of feng shui and space clearing in the West, it is now fashionable to have the energies in the home and workplace both cleansed and balanced. There are many different tools available for this simple task, and some practitioners use the singing bowls to raise the energy in the site, and to create a sacred space, in preference to smudge sticks, clapping, incense sticks, or crystals.

Tibetan singing bowls can be used in many situations to cleanse and raise the energy levels, and when you discover

143

the joy of this wonderful sound, it will open a new door in your life.

Sound therapy incorporates all forms of music and sounds which relax the body, so make use of it as the benefits are enormous and far reaching.

Summary

Sound therapy is rapidly becoming recognized as an effective tool to treat several categories of illness, both physical and emotional. The hearing is the first sense to develop after birth and is a key factor in influencing our sense of peace and tranquility.

Sounds affect our emotional and mental state, so are a tool which should be explored, and used to maximum benefit. Most of us complain that we are short of quality time in our busy life, so it is important to recognize the value of sound therapy. By dowsing to find the right tones of music and most beneficial sounds for you, it is possible to improve your quality of life without cost.

It may sound too easy, but sound healing is recognized as being able to sooth jangled nerves, and help to reduce the need for certain types of medication. Whether the music is love songs, ballads, folk, jazz, or classical, if the vibration feels right, then it is right for you, and can be a great benefit to those suffering from stress, psychological or behavioural conditions.

Stress creates tiredness, so having gentle sounds of music in the room will help the body to relax, and when tension is released you can drift into alpha state, so the body can then get on with the job of healing itself.

I have talked about the magical tones of the Tibetan bowls which create such a unique sound, so should you ever have the opportunity to attend a demonstration of these wonderful bowls, please go along as it will be an awe inspiring experience.

Sound healing is an energy medicine and, as we are all made of energy, it makes a lot of sense to use this simple aid to release stress and help our body to heal.

Endnotes

1. Sound of Music. Heartherapy.com
2. Sound of Music for ADHD. www.soundtherapy.co.uk
3. Tomatis Development. www.tomatis-group.com
4. Morgan, Jeff, Sound Therapy Association. www.soundtherapy.co.uk
5. Perry, Frank, The Singing Bowls of Tibet. frank@frankperry.co.uk
6. Brain Waves and Sound. Educational Coaching UK. http://www.educational-coach.co.uk
7. Bodhisattva Trading Co. Inc. Rain Gray. www.bodhisattva.com

8

Fluoride – is our drinking water being poisoned?

There have been heated disputes regarding the merits of fluoride in drinking water for many decades, and today more and more doctors, scientists and dentists are strongly in disagreement with the addition of this poison to drinking water. Fluoride is an enzyme poison and, although we are not reminded of the fact, this dentist's favourite is in the same class of poison as cyanide![1]

Some dentists are very enthusiastic about the benefits of using fluoride toothpaste, and some governments are keen to add fluoride to drinking water, but many scientists find research results show that fluoride is a serious health hazard, and its use should be discouraged, and dowsing with your pendulum will confirm this fact.

Fluoride is known as an extremely poisonous substance and even at exceptionally low doses has caused a large number of cases of acute poisoning. This is the reason why a 'Poison Warning' is now required on all fluoridated toothpaste sold in the USA.[2]

Dowse:

1. Is fluoride a poison?
2. Is fluoride an enzyme poison?
3. Does fluoride in toothpaste benefit children's teeth?
4. Does fluoride in toothpaste stop tooth decay?

146

Words like 'Poison' and 'Do Not Swallow' are not printed on a product unless it is essential, as no toothpaste manufacturer is going to print this health warning on their product from choice, so rest assured these words were not written in jest!

An obligatory 'Poison' warning will certainly not please the marketing department!

It is so easy to overdose on fluoride, for as well as the fluoride in toothpaste and drinking water, it is also present in water used to cook food, and in the bath water. This is serious cause for concern, as a high percentage of all chemicals getting on to our skin go into the blood stream, so if you take a daily bath or shower, your skin is coming into contact with the poison fluoride.

If fluoride is in drinking water, then each time you drink tea, or coffee, or even enjoy a thirst quenching glass of water, it is adding to the level of fluoride in your system. Fluoride is also around us in the atmosphere, emitted from local industry, and in many pesticide residues, so it is very easy to find you are absorbing a much higher level of fluoride than the government's safe recommended figure.

The problem of excess fluoride intake was some time ago recognized by the well respected *Wall Street Journal*, which published a large article warning their readers that some children get too much fluoride in their diet.[37] Another piece of confirmation came from the US Centers for Disease Control, which published results of a study showing that children are exposed to fluoride from a variety of sources.[5]

Belgium also recognized the possible problem of fluoride levels in the diet and introduced a ban on the sale of fluoride tablets and fluoride chewing gum.[34]

The World Health Organization (WHO) in 1994 issued a statement, declaring that dental and public health administrators should be aware of the total fluoride exposure in the population, before introducing any additional fluoride program for caries prevention.[36] There is no way that water boards, councils or governments can control the level of fluoride consumed by individuals, as they have no technique for measuring how much water we drink each day.

With the medical profession and health therapists constantly reminding us to drink several pints of water each day, even those who are health conscious and follow the advice of the experts will be consuming well above the safe level of fluoride.

Skeletal fluorosis

Skeletal fluorosis is a common complaint today and often misdiagnosed so watch out for early warning symptoms, such as pains in bones and joints, also burning, prickling or tingling sensations. Other symptoms can be chronic fatigue, muscle weakness, lack of appetite, gastrointestinal problems or osteoporosis.

More advanced cases of skeletal fluorosis suffer joint difficulties and patients are often crippled by the vertibrae partially fusing together.[3]

This crippling disease is caused by moderate to high levels of fluoride in drinking water, and there are literally millions of sufferers of this painful disease in India and China.[4] In the US there are roughly 62 million citizens, including 6 million children, who have suffered from skeletal floorosis, caused by excessive consumption of fluoride.[35]

As the early symptoms are similar to arthritis, could this account for the rapid increase in arthritis to epidemic proportions in the US? Fluoride is linked to many research results showing bone damage and arthritis, so it is interesting that figures from Hawaii, which is America's least fluoridated state, also show the least number of arthritis sufferers.

Dowse:

1. Can using fluoride toothpaste ever bring the fluoride level in your body above the safety level?
2. Is skeletal fluorosis caused by excess fluoride in the body?

3. Can fluoride consumption cause bone damage?
4. Can fluoride consumption cause arthritis-type symptoms?

Fluoride and increase in hip fractures

Hip fractures are a major health problem in the US, and are the second most common cause of admission to nursing homes. These injuries cost the country several billion dollars annually, and the Central Disease Control report approximately 340,000 cases each year.[5]

Research carried out to find the cause of these fractures in the elderly population showed a small but very significant increase in the risk of hip fractures in men and women exposed to artificially fluoridation at 1 ppm. This is a very low level and suggests that citizens exposed to higher levels have an increased risk.[6]

Dowse:

1. Does some fluoride from drinking water accumulate in our bones?
2. Can fluoride in drinking water make human bones brittle?
3. Can long term intake of fluoride increase the risk of hip fractures?
4. Can fluoride accumulate in the pineal gland?
5. Can fluoride intake affect the body's level of melatonin?
6. Can regularly drinking fluoridated water lower fertility level?

Some reliable facts

The *Journal of the American Medical Association* (*JAMA*) reports significant increases in the risk of hip fractures in both men and women exposed to artificial fluoridation at 1 ppm.[31] and the *American Journal of Epidemiology* in October 1999 stated fluoride damages bone, even at levels added to drinking water.[32]

Five major epidemiological studies from three countries, USA, UK and France, all show a higher rate of hip fracture in fluoridated regions, reports the *Australian and New Zealand Journal of Public Health*.[33]

Scientists tell us that fluoride accumulates in our bones, and in time can make them brittle, so does this mean that many of us who regularly drink fluoridated water will develop broken bones and require hip replacement joints?

The big question in my mind is 'Will the hospitals be able to cope with the increase in patients suffering hip fractures, knee replacement and broken bones?', not to mention the increase in infertility problems and Alzheimer's patients.

Governments in favour of fluoride in drinking water need to do a lot of forward planning, in anticipation of the mammoth increase in demand for hospital treatment, particularly as there is a shortage of beds in many hospitals.

Fluoride is an insidious poison, which is harmful, toxic and cumulative in its effects, even when ingested in minimal amounts,. It has never been approved by the Food and Drug Administration (FDA) as required by law since 1938, so there is really no proof of the safety of fluoride in our drinking war.[7]

The National Pure Water Association reports there are over 40,000 studies on fluoride published in medical and biochemical journals, and a great many of these report adverse effects on health, including cancers, genetic damage, brain, skin disorders, thyroid dysfunction and behaviour problems.[8] In 1997 the union was formed representing lawyers, scientists and engineers at the US Environmental Protection Agency (EPA), who voted to support a Californian citizen initiative to stop fluoride being added to drinking water.[9] These experts recognized the dangers of overdosing in fluoride, which is confirmed in the largest study done on silicofluoride and tooth decay. It showed the decay rate of permanent teeth was virtually the same in areas with silicofluoride in the water as in those areas where drinking water remained free from fluoride.

Lack of fluoride in drinking water has never been a cause of tooth decay. The cause is poor diet. 'Evidence is quite convincing that the addition of sodium fluoride to the public water supply, at one part per million, is extremely deleterious to the human body' quotes Chief Justice John Flaherty.[5]

The fluoride problems go much farther afield than humans and drinking water, as the US Department of Agriculture's *Agricultural Handbook* states airborne fluorides have caused more damage worldwide to domestic animals than any other air pollutant. Wow! That's a conversation stopper![10]

Another fact to shock you is that there has certainly been more litigation on alleged damage to agriculture by fluoride, than all other pollutants combined.[11]

During the years between 1957 and 1968, fluoride was responsible for more damage claims against industry than all twenty nationally monitored air pollutants combined.[12]

Fluoride and your health

Fluoride is one of forty chemicals used to treat our drinking water, but the sad fact is that fluoride is the only chemical added to our water to treat us, as the rest of the group are added to treat and improve the quality of our drinking water.[13]

This chemical has the ability to disrupt vital enzymes in our body, and so affect the workings of the body's organs and systems, and research has already shown both the thyroid and pineal glands are disrupted.[14]

The smooth running of enzymes is vital for good health, as enzymes are catalysts and a special complex types of protein, produced by living cells in the body, whose job is to activate changes necessary to life within our body. An enormous number of these enzymes live in the body and each has a job to do, so the possibility of the balance of these important enzymes being disrupted by fluoride, is cause for concern.

Dowse:

1. Can airborne fluoride damage the health of any domestic animals?

151

2. Can airborne fluoride damage any agricultural crops?
3. Can fluoride ever disrupt the body's vital enzymes?

Your pineal gland and sleep pattern

Today we are starting to hear more about the pineal gland, which is situated in the brain, but researchers have linked fluoride to a harmful effect on this important gland. This is alarming news, as this gland does the all-important job of secreting melatonin, and if the body's level of this important hormone is out of balance, then sleep problems can occur.

I have found that many cancer patients are also short of melatonin, which ties in with research results showing certain types of cancer developed in laboratory animals fed fluoride in their drinking water.

Research results from Jennifer Luke PhD at Surrey University showed the pineal gland attracts fluoride, which disrupts sleep, and over half of all Americans suffer some level of disturbed sleep.[15] There are many reasons for disturbed sleep, ranging from worrying about debt, relationships, or work, to noise created by neighbours, traffic or snoring, but in many cases the sleep problem is linked to a shortage of melatonin, often caused by excess fluoride in the body. This lowers production of the hormone melatonin and disrupts the biological day and night rhythms.

The thyroid and parathyroid glands

The parathyroid gland is an endocrine gland which works to secrete and regulate the distribution of calcium and phosphorous in the blood, and is very sensitive to excess fluoride. This was shown in research by clinicians in India, who found a close relationship between skeletal fluorosis and hyperparathyroidism.[16]

Are you one of the millions of people who have an underactive thyroid gland? It is known that fluoride can depress the thyroid activity, so does it play havoc with the iodine levels in the body?[17] I find an excellent way to check if my body is short of iodine is to paint a small amount on the inside of my wrist each evening, and if it has gone in the morning then I know I am absorbing it, but if the yellow colour is still there then my body has sufficient iodine. An alternative is to paint the iodine tincture on the inside of the thigh.

Dowse:

1. Can regular fluoride intake disrupt the body's sleep pattern?
2. Can regular fluoride intake disrupt the thyroid gland?
3. Can regular fluoride intake disrupt the body's level of iodine?

Fluoride and the brain

You could say that the fluoride issue is a perennial hot potato which won't go away, as there are so many reliable research results pointing to different illnesses linked to this poison.

The Greater Boston Physicians for Social Responsibility state fluoride exposure experienced by those whose drinking water is fluoridated may have adverse impacts on the developing brain,[5] so does this account for some of today's unexplained behaviour problems?

An alarming report by the Greater Boston Physicians for Social Responsibility showed that fluoride interferes with the brain function of young children, and young animals. These are very serious implications for children in the US, and in other countries, and as these physicians are an extremely reliable source of information, whose opinion is not biased, we need to take heed.[18]

The journal *Brain Research* has published results of a study on rats, which showed that rats drinking 1 ppm (part per million) fluoride in their drinking water, developed histologic lesions in their brain, similar to Alzheimer's disease and dementia. Results also showed possible damage to the blood/brain barrier, due to extended fluoride exposure.[19]

Animal study results show fluoride increases the uptake of aluminium to the brain, so this could answer the unexplained increase in the number of Alzheimer's sufferers.[20]

Dowse:

1. Can regular fluoride intake in our diet cause uptake of aluminium in the brain?
2. Can fluoride residue pass through the blood/brain barrier?
3. Can fluoride in a child's diet create malfunction of the brain?

Fluoride and behavioural changes

Several studies have shown certain behavioural changes can be caused by exposure to fluoride, and this was confirmed when 280,000 children in Massachusetts were found to have high levels of lead in their body, linked to silicofluoride. Researchers in Georgia showed violent behaviour was more frequent in fluoridated areas than in non-fluoridated areas.[27]

In 1999 the US Environmental Protection Agency (EPS) released results of a study showing a link between silicofluoride and high levels of lead in children's blood, so it is hardly surprising that, as we know lead is linked to behaviour problems, researchers found many children diagnosed with ADHD had dangerously high levels of lead in their blood.[28]

Lead has been recognized as a killer for many decades, so it's really alarming to learn that fluoride is more toxic than lead and that, just like lead, even a minute amount will accumulate in the brain of young children, and has been shown to damage the brain. It has also been shown to produce abnormal behaviour in laboratory animals, and in conjunction with deficiencies of certain key nutrients in the adult diet, can reduce IQ, and contribute to certain diseases.[29]

Dowse:

1. Are any behaviour problems linked to fluoride intake?

2. Can fluoride accumulate in a child's brain?
3. Are these symptoms linked to lead in the child's body?
4. Is excess fluoride harmful to children's health?

More confirmation that fluoride is a force to be reckoned with comes from the American Dental Association, whose supplement schedule shows fluoridated water should not be given to children under 6 months age. In the 6 months to 3 year age group, they recommend only one cup of water each day as the controlled dose.[29] So what happens to poor families who don't have money to purchase equipment to purify their water, or purchase supplies of bottled water for their toddler? Even worse for the teeth and for ADHD, is that busy mums well aware they can only give their youngster one cup of water each day, may revert to giving them sweet drinks, which could do more harm to the teeth, and if it contains aspartame, it may affect their health.

The Academy of General Dentistry in the US now also recognize that fluoride is a poison, and recommend non-fluoridated water to prepare infant formula, and infant foods to avoid dental fluorosis.[30]

Fluoride and cancer

There are so many different causes of cancer and one more to add to the list seems to be fluoride, as research has shown some cases of both bone cancer and uterine cancer can be linked with fluoride in drinking water. Cases of bone cancer in male children was between 2 and 7 times greater in areas of New Jersey where water was fluoridated, and more confirmation comes from the EPA researchers, who confirm the bone cancer causing effects of fluoride at low levels in animals.[21]

Japanese researchers are concerned at the results of fluoride studies at the University of the Ryukyus, where scientists studies the relationship between fluoride in drinking water, and deaths from uterine cancer in the area of Okinawa prefecture.

The US government took over administration of this region at the end of the war in 1945, until 1972, and during that period, fluoride was added to the drinking water in many areas. This research studied 20 separate municipalities in Okinawa, and found a positive link between fluoride and the number of deaths from uterine cancer in the region.[22] Details are available on the internet on several study results which show a strong link between fluoride in drinking water and colon cancer.

Dowse:

1. Does regular fluoride intake weaken the immune system?
2. Can a regular fluoride intake cause bone cancer?
3. Is intake of fluoride linked to certain cases of colon cancer?
4. Is intake of fluoride in drinking water linked to certain cases of uterine cancer in Okinawa?

We humans are not the only victims of fluoride poisoning, as the poor elks are at the receiving end of man's interference with their drinking water. Elks who had been drinking the high fluoridated water in Yellowstone Park have been suffering an early death. Many have died 10 years earlier than their normal life span. Is this a warning to we humans?[23]

Dowse and ask your pendulum if your pets would prefer to drink fluoride-free water? Animals can sense when chemicals are present in their food and drink, and will often have a quick smell of their drinking water bowl and walk away.

Perinatal deaths

A perinatal death is a devastating experience for any parent. A toxicologist in the UK found 15% more of these tragic cases occurred in fluoridated water areas than in non-fluoridated areas. Another chilling fact uncovered in this UK research is that the fluoridated area involved had a 30% higher rate of Down syndrome.

These are frightening facts but do tie in with research in Chile, by world renowned researcher Dr Albert Schatz, which showed a link between infant deaths and fluoridation. This resulted in the introduction of a complete ban on fluoride in Chile's water.[24]

Dowse:

1. Were a number of the 15% more perinatal deaths in fluoridated areas in the UK caused by fluoride intake?
2. Were a number of the 15% more perinatal deaths in fluoridated areas in the UK caused by a combination of fluoride intake and sleeping over geopathic stress?
3. Were a number of the 30% increase in Down syndrome births linked to a combination of fluoride and exposure to geopathic stress?

3 ppm or higher level of fluoride in drinking water can lower the fertility rate in animals.[20] Other study results show fluoride in drinking water can have an adverse effect on fertility of women, and in several species of animals.[7] Does this account for some of the high number of couples today requiring fertility treatment? The Food and Agriculture Organization of the United Nations state, from a conservative risk assessment perspective, findings in animal species are assumed to represent potential effects in humans, unless convincing evidence of species specifically is available.[25] So don't listen to anyone who says 'Don't worry about research results done on animals as they are different from humans'. Just quote the words of the United Nations!

Dr Charles Gordon Heyd of the American Medical Association says 'Fluoride is a corrosive poison that will produce serious effects on a long term basis'.[5] His words certainly have an uncomfortable ring of truth, when you realize the results of much reliable research.

Most of us use toothpaste each morning, and don't stop to read the small print on the tube, so are not aware of the warning issued by the manufacturers. Yes toothpaste containing fluoride is a poison, and not meant to be swallowed, so do we really want our children to put this poison in their mouths? Particularly as the warning instructs us to get professional assistance, if your

child swallows more than a brush amount, or to contact the
Poison Control Center!

The fluoride cocktail

The fluoride cocktail is one cocktail to be avoided when possible,
as this combination of chloramines and fluorosilicic acid, which
is used by 91% of US fluoridating communities, is a combination
which can pull health-damaging lead from plumbing systems,
according to research results from the University of North
Carolina.

Somehow this lethal mix succeeds in leaching lead from solder
and plumbing systems, and tests showed the levels of lead to be
three or four times higher in water where combination chemicals
are present.[26]

This fact is truly bad news for homes with children, as no level
of lead is safe for young children, since elevated blood lead levels
are known to be linked to development problems in the fetus and
in pre-school age children, and can have the same effect whether
swallowed or inhaled.

Since fluoride has been banned in drinking water in Finland,
Sweden and Holland, there has been an enormous 92%, 82%
and 72% respectively reduction in tooth decay, so this raises
the question 'Do we really need this poisonous chemical added
to our drinking water?'

If you would like to know more about the adverse effects
of fluoride, have a look on the websites of the New York State
Coalition Opposed to Fluoride (NYSCOF), Citizens for Safe
Drinking Water, Fluoride Debate or Holisticmed, as these
excellent website will answer your question.

I can remember very clearly as a child, playing sweetshops with
my brother, when we squeezed spearmint toothpaste on to a
paper to make sweets, and then ate them. Okay, in those days
fluoride was not yet introduced to the dental industry, but I
am certain some children today, like me, enjoy making sweeties
from their toothpaste. The warning does say to keep all

toothpaste out of reach of children under six years of age, but children like a challenge and, if unsupervised, are quite liable to get a stool and climb up to reach the tube.

Another important point to consider is 'Can you guarantee your child does not swallow any toothpaste?'

How can you help to undo the damage?

When fluoride has accumulated in the body it is essential to encourage it to move out, and alternative therapies are probably the most effective tools. If you are worried that your health is being undermined by fluoride in your body, it may be beneficial to try a course of acupuncture, shiatsu or reflexology to unblock the meridians, as this will enable the energy to flow smoothly around the body, and help it to heal itself. Whatever your health problem from fluoride, it is always well worth having spiritual healing or reiki healing, as this acts as a service to the body, and will tone up the body and balance the energy.

Also sit down and ask your pendulum to please remove fluoride residue from your body, and to show you the 'Yes' sign when it has been done. You have nothing to lose by asking the pendulum for help, so try it and you may be pleasantly surprised.

The most helpful tip I can give you, is to be aware that there is a possibility that fluoride can damage your health, so when possible try to avoid drinking fluoridated water.

Summary

In this chapter I have tried to make you aware of some of the research results which suggest that fluoride is not good news. In fact this chemical is a recognized poison, so how can we guarantee that our children will never swallow the toothpaste?

How can you avoid a build up above the safety level of this poison in your body? According to many research results, it seems that the only certain way to keep the level low is to avoid using toothpaste containing fluoride. If you live in a fluoridated water area you have an added problem, so perhaps it's time to consider purchasing fluoride-free bottled drinking water.

The fact that the World Health Organization recognize that both children and adults can unwittingly acquire an unsafe level of this poison in their body, and that the WHO has felt the need to print a technical report on this subjects, is good reason to seriously consider and dowse for answers on the fluoride health hazard.

Some research results suggest excess fluoride can increase the risk of hip fractures and create brittle bone problems, so perhaps this is the reason that over 40,000 studies on the health effects of fluoride have been published in medical and biochemical journals. This research interest brings to my mind the old saying 'there's no smoke without fire!'.

In short, we have been warned of possible health danger from this enzyme poisoner which is listed in the same category as cyanide. It raises the question 'Can we really risk disrupting the enzymes in the body, and damaging the health of our family by allowing further quantities of fluoride into our body?'. There are very few 'plus marks' for fluoride and a great many 'minus marks' for this poison!

Endnotes

1. Patrick, James B., PhD, former NIH (Nat. Inst. of Health) scientist. Citizens For Safe Drinking Water Opposed to Fluoride. www.nofluoride.com
2. 'Causes Large Number of Acute Poisonings'. Flouridation/Fluoride – Toxic Chemicals in You Water. www.holisticmed.com
3. Newindpress.com NYSCOF 'Death by Fluoride' Sally Stride, Fluoridation Contributing Editor, March 26 2005. www.orgsites.com
4. Jolly. S. S. *et al.*, *Fluoride*. Vol. 4 No. 2, 1971, pp. 64–79, 'Human Fluoride Intoxication in Punjab'.
   Rachel's Environment and Health Weekly. No. 724 May 2001. www.Rachel.org
5. Notable Quotes From Scientists and Medical Organizations Opposing Fluoridation.

Citizens for Safe Drinking Water. www.nofluoride.com

Greater Boston Physicians for Social Responsibility. May 2000.

Dr Ludwig Grosse, Chief of Cancer Research, US Veterans Administration.

Dr Charles Gordon Hyed, Past President of The American Medical Association.

Chief Justice John Flaherty of the Supreme Court of Pennsylvania.

A majority Chairman of the Environmental Resources Committee, Pennsylvania.

House of Representatives. www.nofluoride.com

6. Danielson, Christa, MD, *The Journal of the American Medical Association*, Vol. 268 No. 6, August 12 1992, 'Hip Fractures and Fluoridation in Utah's Elderly Population'.
   Lyon, Joseph L., MD, Egger, Marione, PhD, and Goodenough, Gerald K., MD. www.nofluoride.com

7. *Kalamazoo Express Weekly*, November 18 1999. Bursaw, Jane Louise, ADD Connection. www.nofluoride.com

8. Jones, Jane, The National Pure Water Association. www.npwa.freeserve.co.uk

9. Paul, Ellen, Environmental Research Foundation Home. *Rachel's Environment and Health News*, No. 724, May 10 2001, 'Fluoridation – Time For a Second Look'.
   Also Connett, Michael. http://www.rachel.org

10. US Dept. of Agriculture, *Agriculture Handbook*. No. 380 Revised 1972, p. 109, 'Air Pollution Affecting the Performance of Domestic Animals' www.fluoridealert.org

11. Weinstein, L. H., 1983 'Effects of Fluoride on Plants and Plant Communities. An Overview'. In: Shupe, J. L., Peterson, H. B., and Leone, N. C. (Eds.) *Fluorides: Effects on Vegetables, Animals and Humans*, Paragon Press, Salt Lake City, pp. 53–59. www.fluoridealert.org

12. Groth, E., 1969, *The Peninsula Observer*, 'Air is fluoridated'. www.fluoridealert.org
   Citizens for Safe Drinking Water. www.nofluoride.com

13. 'The Fluoride Debate – Welcome to the Discussion'. www.fluoridedebate.com

14. Dr Anthony D. Fox, *The Lymington Times*, Hants, UK, March 8 2005, Chairman New Forest Safe Water Society.

15. Null, Gary, 'Fluoride and the Pineal Gland' and 'Fluoride The Deadly Legacy'. http://www.garynull.com

16. 'Fluoride. Damning New Evidence' excerpted from 'What Doctors Don't Tell You', March 1999, Researcher Doris Jones.
   Citizens for Safe Drinking Water. www.nofluoride.com

17. Ditkoff, Beth Ann and Lo Gerfo, Paul, *The Thyroid Guide*, York: Harper, 2000, cover notes. ISBN 0060953601.
www.rachel.org. *Rachel's Environment and Health News*, No. 724, May 10 2001.

18. Schettler, Ted *et al.* 'In Harm's Way – Toxic Threat to Child Development', Cambridge, Mass., Greater Boston Physicians for Social Responsibility (GBPSR. May 2000).
http://www.igc.org. *Rachel's Environment and Health Weekly* No. 724. http://www.rachel.org

19. Varner *et al.*, *Brain Research*, 1998, Vol. 784 No. 12, pp. 284–289, 'Fluoridation. Fluoride toxic chemicals in your water'. www.holisticmed. com

20. Spencer, Lee, *Tenterfield Star*, December 14 2004, 'Fluoridation Unsafe and Unethical'. http://tenterfield.yourguide.com

21. The Dept. of Health in New Jersey, The US Environmental Protection Agency, 'Fluoridation/Fluoride toxic chemicals in your water'. www. holisticmed.com

22. *J. Epidemiology* (CL8) December 6 1996, pp. 184–191. Dept. of Preventative Medicine, School of Medicine, University of Ryukyus, Okinawa, Japan. www.holisticmed.com

23. NYSCOF, 'Death by Fluoride', March 26 2005. Sally Stride. Suite 10, Fluoridation Contributing Editor. www.orgsites.com

24. Dr Albert Schatz, 'Causes of Birth Defects and Perinatal Deaths' Fluoridation/Fluoride Toxic Chemicals In Your Water'. www.holisticmed. com

25. The Food and Agriculture Organization of the United Nations. Fluoride Action Network. Pesticide Project.

26. New York State Coalition Opposed to Fluoridation (NYSCOF), 'Fluoride Chemicals Leach Lead in Water!'.
North Carolina News and Observer, 'Water Treatment Process Called Potential Risk. Chemicals Mix with Plumbing Could Put Lead in Tap Water'. http://www.newsobserver.com

27. 'Fluoride: Damning New Evidence', excerpted from 'What Doctors Don't Tell You', March 1999. Researcher Doris Jones. http://www.nofluoride. com. Citizens for Safe Drinking Water.

28. Boursaw, Jane Louise, *Kalamazoo Express Weekly*, November 18 1999. 'ADD Connection'. www.nofluoride.com

29. The Fluoride Debate. 'Welcome to the Discussion' www.fluoridedebate. com

30. The Academy of General Dentistry. www.orgsites.com NYSCOF

31. *The Journal of the American Medical Association*, August 2002. www. nofluoride.com

32. *The American Journal of Epidemiology*, October 1993. www.nofluoride. com
33. *The Australian and New Zealand Journal of Public Health*, Vol. 21 No. 24 1997. www.nofluoride.com
34. BBC News, July 30 2002, 'Belgium – Ban Proposed on Fluoride Supplements'.
    Chris Vermeire and Peter Cremers. www.nofluoride.com
35. newindpress.com
    New York State Coalition Opposed to Fluoridation (NYSCOF), 'Death by Fluoride', Sally Stride, Fluoridation Contributing Editor, March 26 2005. www.orgsites.com
36. The World Health Organization, 'Fluoride and Oral Health' Technical Report Series 846, 1994.
37. Parker-Pope, Tara, *Wall Street Journal*, December 21 1998, 'Some Young Children Get Too Much Fluoride in Caring for Teeth', www.nofluoride. com

9

Dowsing – what's in your food?

You will be amazed how useful dowsing is in the kitchen for checking if food is fresh, contains unhealthy additives or organophosphates, and once you start to think 'Dowse' it will help in the little everyday-hiccups.

1. Perhaps you too forget whether or not you have salted the potatoes? It is such an automatic process that sometimes it is difficult to visualize you have done it, so now you can use your pendulum, to check if the salt has been added.
2. Do you sometimes forget what time it was when you turned on the oven? Has the food cooked long enough? Again pendulum to the rescue.
3. We have all driven down the road, and then suddenly felt our heart give a big leap, as we experience a moment of panic, 'Did I turn off the gas under the cooking pot?' and as we try desperately to remember if we did turn off the gas on the cooker, there is this dreadful feeling in the pit of your stomach that you had better go back and check it out, to be on the safe side.
4. The same situation occurs when you are half way to your destination, and you suddenly have this dreadful thought 'Did I lock the back door?' and the more you try to remember, you just can't convince yourself that you had locked the door, so there's no alternative, although you may be rushing for a train, or have an appointment, but you know for peace of mind you must go home and check the door is

locked. Invariably when you get home you find that you had locked the door, but as these chores are often done when your brain is on automatic pilot, you simply don't remember having done it.

Next time you have a similar situation, park the car, take a deep breath to relax, and then dowse. Ask the pendulum to show you the 'Yes' sign if you locked the back door, and nine times out of ten the task had been done, but the pendulum will put your mind at rest.

So whether it is the house or the car that you are worried about having left unlocked, or doubt if you left the instruction for the milkman, the pendulum will reveal all!

Is food really past its sell-by date?

Today all packaged and tinned food is marked with a sell-by date, and many people automatically throw out any food when it is past the date on the package, but this means good food is often being discarded when it is perfectly edible. My children throw up their hands in horror when they get an item out of my fridge and find it is past its sell-by date, and wonder how I could possibly consider eating it! As my generation were brought up to think 'if food looked all right, smelled all right, then it was all right', so I have always gone by my instinct on most items of food. For those who go strictly by the sell-by date, then by dowsing to ask if the food would be harmful to health if eaten they may not need to dispatch food to the garbage bin! Ask the questions:

1. Is this food edible?
2. Does the food contain harmful bacteria?
3. If eaten, will this food be harmful to health?

How often have you said 'It's a shame to throw it out, but it's past its sell-by date'. So now, by asking these questions, you will be able to enjoy the food and you will save yourself some money.

Wording of the question is important, and remember not just to ask if the food contains bacteria, but if the food has *harmful* bacteria, as all food contains good bacteria, so it's important it should not be removed by the pendulum!

Collecting wild mushrooms

Do you ever go for a country walk and see lovely mushrooms growing in a field, and think 'I'd love to pick them but are they poisonous?' It is sometimes difficult to tell edible mushrooms from poisonous ones, as they all look inviting. Edible varieties often have a delicious mushroom smell, and the skin peels off easily. But unless you know your mushrooms, it is always a risky business to eat wild mushrooms, as you could end up with a very sore tummy!

I used to collect wild mushrooms on the local cliff top and make mushroom and garlic soup, a real treat, but I would dowse the bowl of mushrooms, and ask the pendulum if there were any mushrooms in the bowl which were not edible.

One rule is to avoid varieties growing very close to trees, but again there are exceptions, so if you see any really inviting mushrooms, dowse and ask if they are edible, and take them home and enjoy them. I have in the past found one very large magnificent specimen and thought, 'Ah this would make a wonderful omelette', and quickly dowsed before taking it home, and sure enough it was edible.

To dowse the mushrooms. Hold the pendulum over the bowl or plate of mushrooms, and ask the questions

1. Are all the mushrooms on this plate edible?'
2. Are any of the mushrooms on this plate poisonous?

Once you have confidence in your pendulum and your relationship with it, you can confidently dowse, so allowing you to enjoy the pleasure of eating fresh mushrooms.

Organic food is best!

Organic food is grown in conditions as natural as possible, and organic foods, organic health care products including shampoos, toothpaste and deodorants are usually free from all possible chemicals, and definitely free from any harmful organophosphates.

There are some people who criticize organic produce, so let's dowse to check if specific organic produce is free from organophosphates and chemicals. Dowsing gives you answers to facts which are simply hidden from your view, and will confirm if the organic food in your larder or refrigerator contains unnecessary chemicals.

Dowse to ask the following questions, and if any of the answers seem wrong, then check that you have recently cleansed your pendulum of negative energy.

1. Are the organic carrots free from harmful chemicals? (You should include the word 'harmful' as sometimes chemicals may need to be included for a specific reason, and are not harmful to health.)
2. Are the organic bananas free from harmful chemicals?
3. Does this organic food contain fewer pesticide residues than similar non-organic food?
4. Does this organic food contain fewer food additives than non-organic food?
5. Does this organic food contain any food preservatives?
6. Does this organic food contain fewer toxins than similar non-organic food?
7. Does this organic food contain more vitamins than similar non-organic food
8. Does this organic food contain more minerals than similar non-organic food?
9. Does this organic food contain more anti-oxidants than the non-organic variety?
10. Does this organic food contain less water than the non-organic variety?

11. Is this organic food more nutritious than the non-organic group?

Are you concerned about Genetically Modified foods? If so, you can dowse and ask if the organic food contains any residue of GM food, as GM crops have been known to contaminate crops nearby.

Bovine spongiform encephalopathy (BSE) is a big issue today, so if you are a big meat eater, then you may be concerned about the presence of BSE in the meat you purchase.

12. Dowse and ask your pendulum if the meat is from organically reared cattle?
13. Then ask if the meat is contaminated with BSE?

Organic standards are known to minimize food poisoning risks, but if you are concerned about salmonella in chicken, then dowse the question.

On the subject of salmonella, it is always wise to dowse to check if seafood, particularly prawns, contains this harmful bacteria. Today many fish sold for human consumption are found to contain mercury, which is very harmful to health, so ask your pendulum if the fish contains any mercury, before cooking it.

The questions listed above are simply a sample of suggested questions you may want ask about the food you have purchased, but I am sure you will want to ask different questions, as they come into your mind. Any time you are worried about the risk of food poisoning, or the quality of your food, whether organic or not, then dowse to establish whether there will be any ill effects from eating the food. Your family will thank you for learning how to dowse!

As well as dowsing organic food, you can dowse fresh food from the supermarket or street market, to find if it has organophosphates or harmful chemicals, and here are a few recent examples of unwelcome chemicals found in food.

Check your eggs for chemicals and colourants

The good news is that in the UK alone, millions of eggs are eaten every day, so lots of protein in the diet, but the bad news is that many of these eggs contain harmful chemicals, and colourants to change the colour of the yolk.

You can also dowse the source of the eggs. Dowse these questions:

1. Are these eggs from battery hens?
2. Are these eggs from hens which lived in a barn?
3. Are these eggs free range?
4. Are these eggs organic?

From the answer you will get confirmation that the sales description of the eggs is correct. You can also dowse to find out if the eggs contain any antibodies from lasalocid, as this drug can be legally used in the feed for chickens, turkeys, pheasants and quail, which will all be sold for meat. Lasalocid is not licensed for use in egg laying chickens, but the Soil Association report residue of this drug has been found in some eggs.

Australia recognizes the health effects of lasalocid, and introduced a legal limit of 50 micrograms per kilogram. The levels of this drug found in eggs tested in the UK were an enormous 69 times higher than Australia's limit, so get dowsing, as your health could be at risk! One in eight of the samples tested in UK contained a higher level.[1] Ask the following questions:

1. Do any of these eggs contain the residue of the antibiotic lasalocid? If the answer is 'Yes', then ask as follows:
2. Do any of these eggs contain more than 50 micrograms per kilo of lasalocid?

Lasalocid is a toxic antibiotic used world wide, to control intestinal parasites which cause coccidiosis to be found in poultry farms.[2]

The Soil Association report this antibiotic is too toxic to be used as a medicine, and research showed this antibiotic caused rabbits' hearts to contract when exposed to low levels. Human heart muscles tested back in 1974 showed rapid contractions, still evident one hour later. So if you suffer from any form of heart problem, then be aware of the possibility of the presence of residue of this drug in your eggs at breakfast, or chicken at dinner![3]

Dowse the following questions:

1. Does this chicken contain residues of harmful chemicals?
2. Does this chicken meat contain traces of any antibiotics?
3. Does this pheasant meat contain any harmful antibiotics?
4. Does this quail meat contain any harmful antibiotics?

Cardiomyopathy is one of the most common causes of sudden death in humans, and as rats who accidentally overdosed on lasalocid suffered cardiomyopthy, it is a drug to be taken seriously. If you suffer from rapid heart beat, or other heart problems, perhaps you should consider eating organic eggs, as these should be free from antibiotics.

Unfortunately many crops of fruit and vegetables are sprayed as many as sixteen times with pesticides and so may contain traces of chemicals or organophosphates, so it is wise to check their presence if the fruit or vegetables are not home grown.

An apple a day!

The old saying 'an apple a day keeps the doctor away' could rapidly become a very different story, as the Soil Association confirm that we humans have recently devoured thirty three million apples which could possibly have a residue over the legal limit of organophosphate chlorpyrifos.

This tasty morsel is a class of chemical very toxic to humans and animals, so a very good reason to dowse apples before you eat them. Organophosphates are used by farmers in many parts of the globe on food crops, to kill insects by disrupting their nervous system. Scientists tell us organophosphates are bad news for health, as they are one of the most dangerous chemicals used in farming, and research has linked them to a range of health problems, including cancer, fetal abnormalities, decreasing male fertility and Parkinson's disease. So let's dowse for a few answers to the health effects of these powerful chemicals. Ask the questions:

1. Do these apples contain harmful level of chlorpyrifos?
2. Are organophosphates linked to cancer?
3. Are organophosphates in our food linked to certain cases of decrease in male sperm count?
4. Are organophosphates linked to the increase in infertility?
5. Are organophosphates in our diet linked to the increase in the number of Parkinson's disease sufferers.[4]

Apples are not the only fruit to contain traces of organophosphate as pears are also victims to this treatment. Next time you purchase some pears, remind yourself that they could contain residue of organophosphates, as some crops are treated with carbendazim to control plant disease.

Germany has classified carbendazim as a Hormone Disruption Chemical, and the US Environmental Protection Agency warn it is a possible cancer cause, so next time you buy some nice fresh pears, it's well worth dowsing to ask if they contain carbendazim.[5]

Raspberries

Recently 2.5 million punnets of raspberries destined for the UK were suspect, as samples tested showed residue of chlorothalonil, which the US Environmental Protection Agency state is likely to cause cancer, so please check your raspberries for harmful chemicals before eating them.[5]

Carrots – another victim!

Carrots are also a victim to organophosphates and the United States EPA report 52 million carrots could contain residues of trifluralin, a cancer causing chemical, used to kill weeds around fruit and vegetables and on arable land.

Trifluralin is classified by the US EPA as a possible cause of cancer, and this chemical is banned in some countries, as it is seen as a serious threat to wildlife. Dowse to ask if your carrots contain any residue of trifluralin? Then dowse to ask 'Do these carrots contain any chemicals harmful to health?[5]

It is so important to check food for chemicals, as so many of these modern day chemicals and organophosphates don't have any known antidote, so that once your health has been damaged, it is a very difficult task to return to good health. This was demonstrated by troops exposed to organophosphates in the Vietnam war, who suffered all sorts of unusual and unpleasant health symptoms. I agree that these troops were sometimes sprayed, or among crops which had been sprayed, so their body would have absorbed a lot more chemical than is found in the fruit or vegetables in your diet, but it is a cumulative effect, so it is better to be safe than sorry!

Potato – the family favourite

Our much loved potato is also on the receiving end of chemical treatment, and the Soil Association tell us that 32,000 tons of potatoes may contain residue of aldicarb above the legal limit. So what exactly is aldicarb? This is a chemical which acts as a nerve poison, and its job is killing insects. Any organophosphate which poisons nerves is cause for concern when in the food chain, so it is no wonder that the World Health Organization has classified aldicarb as an extremely hazardous substance![4] Dowse and ask the questions

1. Do these potatoes contain a residue of aldicarb?
2. Do these potatoes contain a residue of any chemicals harmful to health?

I hope by now you are beginning to appreciate just how useful dowsing can be to check the presence of unpleasant chemicals in all sorts of foods.

Check your bread for organophosphates

One of the problems facing farmers is getting crops to grow to the same height, and to be ready for harvesting at the same time, so chlormequat, an organophosphate, is used on crops of wheat, rye, oats, flowers, pears, almonds, and tomatoes.

Great benefit to farmers, but what about those of us who enjoy our daily bread? The Soil Association report that 50% of samples of bread tested were found to contain residue of this toxic chemical. So if your family consumes lots of bread and rolls, it's time to dowse for chlormequat residue, or start buying organic bread![5]

Lettuce

If you are concerned about chemicals in your food, then it's time to dowse lettuce, unless it is organic or home grown, as many lettuce on sale today, contains residue of vinclozolin. This chemical is used on peas, vines, oilseed rape, lettuce, and other fruits and vegetables, and is classified by the International Regulators as a 'Hormone Disrupting Chemical' and a possible cause of cancer. Dowse to ask:

1. Does this lettuce contain residue of vinclozolin?
2. Does this lettuce contain residue of any chemicals harmful to health?
3. Ask your pendulum to please remove the residue, and show you the 'Yes' sign when completed.

You can use the pendulum to check your lettuce for all harmful bacteria as well as chemicals, and this is a wise move, as the Food Standard Agency this month advised that all lettuce should be washed thoroughly before use, as crops of lettuce and tomatoes grown in one part of Spain had been watered with sewage, due to a shortage of water in the area!

Have a look at the Food Standard Agency's website and you will be shocked at the number of food products which have been withdrawn from the market, as they were found to include

173

harmful chemicals. Brands of chorizo sausages contained salmonella, certain rice cakes, ground paprika and pastrami sausages all contained traces of the illegal Red Para Dye.[6]

Which milk is best for you?

Supermarkets today offer a wide variety of milks, and it is often difficult trying to decide which one has highest food value. Cows' milk comes in full cream, semi skimmed or skimmed, so start by asking the pendulum which of these varieties has highest food value? You can then ask if organic cows' milk has higher food value, and you can also ask which contains lowest levels of chemicals?

As well as cows' milk you can purchase goats' milk or soy milk, so dowse and ask if either of them contains higher food value, or ask if they contain less chemicals than cows' milk? For parents· whose children consume a lot of milk each day, it is worth checking them out, as many minor health problems can be related to certain milks, e.g. asthma, wheezing and bronchial problems.

Food colourants

Food colourants are linked to many different allergic reactions, and some colours are banned in many countries, as they have been found in research to be carcinogenic. A recent health scare occurred in the UK when it was discovered that over three hundred food products on sale in many supermarkets had to be withdrawn from sale, as they contained the possible cancer causing colourant Sudan 1, an illegal dye. The UK's *Daily Mail* newspaper reported the operation cost over £100 million – an expensive exercise.

A similar situation has recently been exposed, as yet another illegal dye has been found in a range of food containing spices, so more food hazard warnings. This time the culprit is the colourant Para Red, which is a possible carcinogen, which has been found in many spices, and resulted in another mammoth operation to withdraw more foods from the supermarket shelves,[7] so if you are concerned about food containing harmful colourants, dowse and ask your pendulum the answer.

A quick way to check for colourants is to ask the pendulum if there are any harmful colourants in any of the foods on the bottom shelf of the larder? If you receive a 'Yes', then separate them into two sections, and ask if any of the foods on the right hand side contain harmful colourants? If you receive a 'No' answer, then you know the culprit is in one or more of the foods on the left side of the shelf.

Now dowse and ask if there is more than one item containing harmful colourants.

I suspect that eating one meal which contains harmful colourants will not seriously affect health, but if it is a food that you regularly feed to your family, then it is important to know the contents.

Children's behaviour and additives

Many mothers will be quick to tell you that they limit the number of coloured sweets they give their children, or coloured drinks containing artificial sweeteners, as they noticeably change their children's behaviour pattern.

Children who are normally reasonable, quiet and well behaved, after eating sweets containing certain colourants become noisy, excitable children, showing symptoms of ADHD behaviour. If you are aware that your child becomes noisier after eating certain sweets, then ask the pendulum to dowse whether their change in behaviour pattern is linked to food colourants. If the answer is 'Yes', then get a list of all the food colourants, and dowse to find the culprit.

Start by asking if the cause is in the first 20 on the list? Then ask if it is in the next 20, or alternatively you can ask if it is on the first column, and if 'No' is the answer, ask if it is on the second column. This eliminates the need to dowse every single colourant.

Today there are many foods containing illegal ingredients and chemicals in our food chain, but I have only given a few examples to highlight the fact that we should be aware of the possibility of the presence of unnatural ingredients in our food. Dowsing is a quick and accurate way to check if your food contains any harmful chemicals or colourants. A look at the Food Standard Agency's website will tell you what food has recently been withdrawn from sale due to containing a harmful ingredient. This is a subject which could fill an entire book, so perhaps this will be my next project!

Summary

Dowsing can take a lot of frustration out of cooking, so a pendulum is a useful tool in the kitchen; in fact, to some cooks it is a 'must'! This tiny tool will answer all sorts of questions ranging from whether you have added an ingredient to a dish, the measure required, the oven setting, or the length of time it should be cooked. What other tool can give so many answers and is free?

Your pendulum can confirm if food in your fridge which is past its 'sell-by' date is still fresh and safe to eat, so remember to dowse if it contains harmful bacteria before you banish it to the trash can.

One of the biggest problems facing cooks today is that so many foods contain invisible enemies in the form of organophosphates and other harmful chemicals. Dowsing will confirm if the fruit you've purchased has been sprayed many times with pesticides, as it is alarming how many times some crops are sprayed to kill insects and moulds.

Some researches tell us that organophosphates are used to kill weeds which grow around crops in arable land, so it is easy for these crops to absorb some harmful chemicals, and a worrying fact is that certain of these chemicals used to kill insects act as a nerve agent. I agree that we are only digesting very small amounts of these chemicals, but it is not natural for our body to have to cope with these chemicals, so they are best avoided when possible, as long term effects are not yet known.

Another unknown quantity is genetically modified food, so if you are concerned that any of your food falls into this category, then dowse to check if it is a health hazard. Also dowse to ask if any fruit or vegetables in your kitchen have been sprayed with hormone disrupting chemicals, as it is so important to be aware of the presence of chemicals in our food.

Your pendulum will also confirm if food contains any banned colourants or harmful additives, so if your child is very hyperactive, then it is important to check if colourants or additives are linked to the problem, and if removing them from the diet will reduce symptoms.

I realize this chapter sounds like a horror story, but it is vital to be aware of these unwanted ingredients in the food chain, and to be able to avoid them when possible. Now it is more important than ever before to retain a strong immune system, to help your body's defense against the many immune system illnesses as the number of sufferers is rapidly increasing in all age groups today.

Endnotes

1. The Soil Association, UK. 'Millions of Eggs Contain Drug Residues, shows New Report'. http://www.soilassociation.org
2. The Soil Association, UK, 'Voluntary Ban on Lasalocid Must Be Made Compulsory'. http://www.soilassociation.org
3. The Soil Association, UK, 'Crackdown on Toxic Drug Found in 750,000 Eggs Eaten Every Day'. http://www.soilassociation.org
4. The Soil Association, UK, 'Pesticides In Your Food. New Guide Reveals the Real Problem'. http://www.soilassociation.org
5. The Soil Association, UK, 'What's Your Poison?' April 2005. http://www.soilassociation.org
6. The Food Standard Agency. www.food.gov.uk; also *Daily Mail*, London, July 6 2005. 'Lettuce That's Watered With Raw Sewage'
7. Poulter, Sean, Consumer Affairs Correspondent, *Daily Mail*, London, May 11 2005, 'How Many More Foods Are Unsafe?'.

10

Aspartame – the artificial sweetener researchers say is not so sweet!

To say aspartame is a controversial sweetener is an enormous understatement, and dowsing will confirm this manmade calorie-free sweetener is an ingredient which is used extensively in thousands of food and drink products, and research results link it to a wide range of illnesses. Yes it's hard to believe the facts, but your pendulum will confirm that when your diet contains regular intake of aspartame, your health is at risk!

We all tend to assume that any product approved by the government or FDA is good for health, and those of us who are overweight try to be good and buy sweeteners, in the belief they will help to resolve the weight problem, without any harmful side effects.

All those folks who are conscientious about looking after their teeth purchase sweeteners instead of sugar, but how wrong can they be, as many brands contain aspartame, which has been shown in research results to be the most harmful ingredient added to our food this century. It is found in literally thousands of products on sale in our supermarkets, including certain brands of baked beans, cereal, beverages, soft drinks, sugar free drinks, diet products, flavoured water, yogurt, milk drinks and deserts, and in certain brands of vitamin C tablets. Some researchers refer to aspartame as 'witches' brew' and it is aptly named.

Animals, rodents, insects and birds are all so much wiser than humans when it comes to food, as they know instinctively which foods to avoid, whereas we humans happily eat food as long as it looks nice, tastes nice and smells fresh, even if it contains harmful chemicals and toxins.

How often do you hear someone say 'I am sure my dog is psychic as he knows what's going on!' We regularly get proof that our animals know more than us about certain things, and they are one jump ahead of us, as far as aspartame is concerned. Cats and dogs usually firmly refuse to eat their dinner when it contains aspartame, and flies and wily old cockroaches pass it by. Cunning ants know aspartame is harmful, and fire ants will move away quickly from this poison.[1]

As well as animals recognizing the danger to their health, birds and rodents also avoid it, so how do they all seem to know instinctively which foods to avoid? Our animals often demonstrate that they have psychic abilities and can see spirits, as their fur stands up on their back when there is a spirit present in a room.

I know it sounds a bit dramatic, but I can't help wondering if this gift enables them to see a different energy in food, which contains this artificial sweetener instead of sugar. Perhaps when food contains harmful excitotoxins, the food has a different smell, contains a foreign vibration, or is surrounded by an invisible dark energy? Sadly they cannot tell us the answer.

How does aspartame affect health?

It is what happens to aspartame when digested which is the real health hazard, as methanol is released from the aspartame into the body, which then converts to formic acid, and that's when the health damage becomes serious. So it is not surprising that the Australian Cancer Council state 'There is no safe level of aspartame in the diet'.[1]

According to research results from reliable scientists, formaldehyde from aspartame is recognized as causing gradual damage to the body's nervous system, and the immune system. Would this fact possibly account for the noticeable increase in immune system illnesses such as MS and lupus. Perhaps the most worrying effect is the long term genetic damage shown in research.[5]

Neurosurgeon Russell Blaylock MD advises us aspartame contributes to the formation of formaldehyde in the body.[2] Formaldehyde is a known carcinogen, and so, as more formaldehyde is formed, is it any wonder that cancer is on the rampage? Is it time some of the vast amount of money spent on cancer research is diverted to research the effects of formaldehyde on health?[6] It is around us in our homes and workplace as this carcinogen is present in many carpets and other sources as well as in aspartame.

Another hazard linked to aspartame is that it contains 10% methanol wood alcohol, which is slowly released into the body's system, and Yes it is a poison![5]

Dowse and ask the following questions about aspartame, after you have mentally flushed a beam of white light through your pendulum to cleanse its energy.

1. Does aspartame convert to formic acid when digested in food?
2. Can regularly eating food containing aspartame affect health?
3. Can formic acid from aspartame convert to formaldehyde when digested?
4. Is formaldehyde carcinogenic?
5. Can health be damaged by regularly eating food containing residue of formaldehyde from aspartame?
6. Can regular intake of aspartame in the diet cause seizures?

The World Health Organization (WHO) (Fact Sheet No. 2673, October 2001) list formaldehyde as a probable cancer agent.

The blood/brain barrier

The blood/brain barrier, known as the three Bs, is there to protect the brain from unwelcome intrusion of toxins, chemicals and harmful electromagnetic rays from mobile phones etc. It should protect the body from aspartame and glutamate, but in young children it is not completely developed, so is unable to keep the door tightly closed, and cannot fully protect them from these intruders, and that's the root of many unpleasant symptoms.

Aspartame is recognized by many scientists as the most dangerous food additive of the century, and responsible for 75% of all adverse reactions to food. Hard though it is to believe, there are 90 different symptoms documented, reports Dr Russell L. Blaylock MD, a Professor of Neurosurgery, in his book *Excitotoxins. The Taste that Kills.*[2]

He tells us that these sweeteners are not naturally found in food and drinks, and can cause a range of health problems, both physical and mental, and are shown to increase brain damage.

Alarming health research results

1. Research shows brain tumours in rats

What we must realize is that aspartame is not a natural ingredient, so the human body does not have natural antibodies to fight its invasion. The body simply does not have any countermeasures, except to exclude this chemical completely where possible from the diet.

Research on rats showed that those rats fed aspartame in their diet developed a high incidence of brain tumours, whereas no brain tumours developed in the group of rats on an aspartame-free diet.[3]

Back in 1981 the FDA refused approval to aspartame, as results of research on laboratory animals showed they developed brain tumours and suffered seizures.[4]

2. Research on fibromyalgia

Fibromyalgia, lupus and schizophrenia have in the past twenty years increased to epidemic figures, so is it a coincidence that aspartame was introduced into the diet around that time?

Research in June 2001 showed clearly that when patients suffering from fibromyalgia removed aspartame and monosodium glutamate from their diet, they had relief from painful symptoms.

Fibromyalgia seems to be an increasingly common complaint, and this rheumatologic disorder[7] does not always respond to medication. If the sufferer regularly drinks or eats food sweetened by aspartame, and containing monosodium glutamate (MSG), then as quickly as effects of medication work, they would be cancelled out by the harmful effects of these unnatural substances.

To anyone suffering from this painful illness, I suggest it is well worth trying a diet free from aspartame and MSG for two months, as you may find many of the painful symptoms vanish! Researchers say it is essential to persevere for two months as these poisons are slow to leave the body. (Please check with a medical practitioner before following my advice as I am not a medical doctor.)

As aspartame and MSG are excitotoxins, and can lead to neurotoxicity, I would advise having healing during this period, and using an alternative therapy like acupuncture or shiatsu to clear the meridians and release toxins.

Aspartame disease comes in many forms, including fibromyalgia symptoms, vertigo, tinnitus, depression, blindness, memory loss, and cancer. It is hardly surprising we suffer health effects, as formaldehyde from aspartame is grouped in the same class of deadly poisons as arsenic!

3. Seizures and memory loss

The US Air Force has accepted that aspartame creates a serious risk of pilots experiencing a seizure while flying a plane, so much so that 20 articles have been written in *Flying Safely* and the US Navy's magazine *Navy Physiology* warning pilots of the danger of seizure, vertigo, and delirious effects, and a greater likelihood of birth defects.

This warning is justified, as over 600 pilots have reported suffering Grand Mal seizures when flying a plane. As these pilots are responsible for the lives of crew members on the plane, and the lives of those on the ground, should a plane crash these strong warnings are justified.

A hot line was set up for all pilots suffering acute reactions. These warnings were first published over 20 years ago by the Aerospace Medical Association, and have regularly appeared in a selection of flying magazines since.[2]

More proof that the brain can be affected by aspartame in the diet comes from research results which link this toxin to long term memory loss is reported in *Psychology Today*.[8]

Dowse and find out some more truths about the possible dangers of aspartame to your health.

1. Can regular consumption of aspartame in diet be linked to fibromyalgia symptoms?
2. When digested, does aspartame in our food release methanol?
3. Can regularly eating food containing aspartame be linked to increase in cases of lupus?
4. Can regularly eating food containing aspartame affect memory?
5. Can aspartame pass through the blood/brain barrier of young children? If you are concerned that there is aspartame in your body, it is possible to ask the pendulum to please remove the residue of aspartame, also remove formaldehyde and formic acid. Simply swing the pendulum slightly to get it moving, and then ask it to please show you the 'Yes' sign when the residue has been removed.

Awareness is spreading!

Awareness of the aspartame health hazard is spreading in many countries, and concern over possible health damage is nothing new, as a decade ago a consumer group, directed by scientists and physicians in India, issued a very strong warning to the Indian nation. They followed up the warning with a publication which did not hold back on the dangers of aspartame, in a

Consumers Action in Safety and Health newsletter. In the same year the *Journal of the Diabetic Association of India* (Vol. 35 No. 4, 1995) warned the breakdown products of aspartame are toxic and, a year later, the *Bombay Times* carried a warning article on June 21 1996. Sadly people ignore or forget these warnings, unless the message is regularly televised or reported in the media.[9]

There is so much concern about this hidden health hazard that support groups have been formed in many countries, and the Aspartame Consumer Safety Network Worldwide is fighting a continuous battle to create public awareness of the possible health effects of aspartame in the diet. In the UK the Additive Survivors Network (UK) is doing a great job, and the World Natural Health Organization is working to create awareness of aspartame and promote alternative health care.

Today I checked aspartame on the internet and found 621,000 websites on the subject, and many of them tell of experiences of sufferers, or are groups giving details of the adverse health effects of consuming aspartame. Please ask your pendulum to check if your food and drink contains any aspartame. It's time to listen as research results cannot all be wrong!

Summary

Aspartame is a calorie-free sweetener found in a large number of foods, and in many sugar-free or low calorie brands of food and drinks. Governments and food manufacturers tell us this chemical does not have any harmful effect on health, but many reliable research results tell a very different story! If you have already dowsed the questions on aspartame, you will have received confirmation that it's time to exclude this chemical from your diet.

When well respected scientists or organizations like the Australian Cancer Council state there is no safe level of aspartame in the diet, then it's time to take notice.

As I've explained briefly in this chapter, aspartame converts to formaldehyde which is a known carcinogen. This raises the question 'Why did the FDA refuse approval of aspartame in 1981?'

The research results showed brain tumours and seizures suffered by laboratory rats fed aspartame in their diet? So 'Why did they give approval several years later?'

To any reader suffering from fibromyalgia, lupus or schizophrenia, I suggest it would be a worthwhile exercise to exclude this controversial artificial sweetener from your diet for a period, and watch carefully for any changes or improvements in symptoms.

If you are convinced that your illness is linked to this chemical, and feel very isolated, and don't know where to get support, please contact the Aspartame Consumer Safety Network as they have groups in many parts of the world. Also have a look on the internet, as there is an enormous number of websites all offering an abundance of information, and most of them recognize the health effects of aspartame in the diet.

Endnotes

1. Relfe, Stephanie, 'Aspartame. 92 symptoms Linked by the FDA Including Death'. www.relfe.com
2. Extracted from *Blazing Tattles*, Vol. 4. Nos 4, 5, 6, April/June 95, with permission.
   Source Mark Gold. *Nexus New Times*, October 1995.
   (a) Dr Russell L. Blaylock, MD., *Excitotoxins. The Taste That Kills*.
   (b) Dept. of Health and Human Services Report on all Adverse Reaction Monitoring Systems, February 25 and 28 1994.
3. Some studies on aspartame:
   The Feingold Association of the United States, 'Increasing Brain Tumors in Rats, Is There a Link to Aspartame?'.
   Olnet, J. W., Farber, N. B., Spitznagel, E., and Robins, L. N., *Journal of Neuropathic Exp. Neurol.*, Vol. 55 No. 11, pp. 1115–1123, November 1996. http://www.diet-studies.com http://www.feingold.org
4. Article by courtesy of Mark Gold, Researcher, 'Aspartame: the Bad News' www.dorway.com
5. Mark Gold, 'Aspartame Summary'. www.holisticmed.com
6. Trocho C., *et al.*, 'Aspartame Ingestion Causes Formaldehyde Accumulation in the Body'. 'Formaldehyde Derived From Dietary Aspartame Binds

185

to Tissue Components in Vitro' *Life Science*, Vol. 63 No .5, p. 337. www.holisticmed.com

7. 'Aspartame and MSG Cause to Painful Fibromyalgia Symptoms', *Ann Pharmacother.*, 35 (6) 702–70 6, June 2001.
   Smith, J. D., Terpening, C. M., Schmidt, S. O., and Gums, J. G., 'Relief of Fibromyalgia Symptoms Following Discontinuation of Dietary Excitotoxins'. Malcolm Randall Veterans Affairs Medicine Center, PMID: 1140898

8. Rebhahn, Peter, 'Dangerous Diet Drinks, Aspartame Causes Memory Loss', *Psychology Today*, Vol. 34. No. 2, p. 20, March/April. www.holisticmed. com

9. 'India Warns of Aspartame' News Report. www.holisticmed.com
   Dr J. Barua, Ophthalmologist and Dr Arun Bal, Surgeon, *Journal of the Diabetic Association of India*, Vol. 35 No. 4 1955.

11

Microwave ovens – friend or foe?

Does your gut feeling ring warning bells when you use your microwave oven? Well it could be right, as a number of research projects have shown this method of cooking or heating food destroys the molecular structure of food, and creates new chemicals. Your pendulum will confirm these facts.

You may think the microwave is one of your best friends in the kitchen, but is it your family's best friend? Are these modern day ovens really safe? Ask your pendulum if these innocent looking ovens are perhaps a lot more harmful than they look? Dowsing will tell you if this form of cooking can be much more dangerous to your family's health than most of us imagine.

While many millions of families around the world use their microwave oven daily, some scientists are telling us the microwave oven is bad news, so is it time to listen to these warnings? Research has consistently shown that the microwave oven can upset the immune system, create carcinogenic free radicals, reduce nutrients in food, and cause changes in the blood. More about the evidence later.

Science has shown microwave ovens can damage health as they have two very different forms of attack. The first is by the electromagnetic fields released from the door seal, and the second, and by far the worst, is the damage the cooking process does to food, which creates harmful free radicals and new toxins, some of which are carcinogenic.

Dowse:

1. Can microwave cooking destroy the molecular structure of food?
2. Can microwave cooking create new chemicals in the food?
3. Are any of the new chemicals created by microwave cooking carcinogenic?
4. Can microwave cooking create free radicals?
5. Can microwave cookery reduce valuable nutrients in food?

How do microwave ovens work?

The microwaves from the oven are short waves of electromagnetic fields (emfs) and have the amazing ability to travel at the speed of light, so these much favoured ovens heat food rapidly at a frequency of 2450 MHz, and give off a high level of electromagnetic fields. The legal limit of leakage in the West is 5 milliwatts, but that's not the end of the emissions, as your microwave oven, like your computer screen, gives off fields, whether switched off or not. When ovens are not in use, they give off 20 milligauss, and when in use, the emissions from the microwave oven are 250 milligauss during cooking time.

You can argue that the oven is often switched on for no more than a few minutes, but there are a lot of research results from emf exposure, which shows that continuous levels of exposure to 3 milligauss is linked to serious health problems. So if your oven is not in use, it is a wise move to unplug it from the power supply, or you'll constantly be zapped by 20 milligauss – a very good reason to make sure you always unplug your oven when not in use.[11]

Do microwave ovens leak radiation?

So do microwave ovens really leak radiation from the door? The answer is Yes! according to reliable research carried out in several different countries over a period of years. Modern microwave ovens usually have a safe seal on the doors, but some older models are a serious health hazard.

In America alone, 90% of families use a microwave oven to prepare meals, so we are talking about a lot of people, and many have used a microwave oven for over a decade, not realizing it creates new chemicals in food and could slowly be damaging to health.

Alarming research results

How many housewives in the western world know about research studies in 1973 in the US by scientists P. Czerski and W. M. Leach, whose research results proved microwaves cause cancer in animals. This was followed in the late 1980s by the American National Council for Radiation Protection (NCRP) announcing children of mothers exposed to emissions from microwave ovens were found to have an increased rate of malformed babies.[13] This is an alarming fact with enormous implications, so dowse and ask your pendulum if regular exposure to emissions from a microwave oven may be linked to the birth of any malformed babies.

We don't yet know the long term effect on health of exposure to microwave emissions, so is it a slow drip effect which builds up? Only time will tell! In the meantime, it's a wise move to follow the advice of scientists who say Beware of These Ovens.

In America the federal guidelines are 5 milliwatts per square centimetre, at a distance of 5 cm, but Russia's acceptable leakage level is considerably lower.[5]

Russia stand firm on such a low rate of emissions, which makes us wonder why did the Russian government in 1976 introduce a complete 20 year ban on the use of microwave ovens, following research done by scientists using very sophisticated equipment at the Institute of Radio Technology at Klinsk?

This team proved emissions from the microwave oven have a negative effect on the general biological welfare of humans, without ingesting any food cooked in the microwave oven. Simply entering the energy field of the food causes harmful side effects, so its not surprising the Soviet Union introduced the ban, and tried to warn the world of these dangers.[10]

Robert O. Becker's excellent book *The Body Electric* describes this microwave illness, and how microwave cookery can be linked to several health problems including blood disorder, nervous system problems, distortion to alpha, theta and delta brain waves, inability to concentrate, anxiety and many other serious illnesses, each caused by a breakdown of the body's system. I recommend this book to anyone who wants to learn more about this serious subject.[8]

So let's dowse and ask if exposure to microwave emissions, or eating a diet of microwaved food, can damage health, and does food cooked in this manner lose nutritional value? These answers are priority for several reasons. The cook's health could be at risk, and medical facilities in many countries are not equipped to cope with an increase in illness.

Dowse:

1. Can exposure to emissions leaked from a microwave oven distort brain waves?
2. Can exposure to emissions from a microwave oven create a blood disorder?

The German Foundation for Product Tests (the Berliner Stiftung Warentest) back in 1990 carried out a programme testing emissions from various ovens, while they were in the process of cooking food. Their results showed that all of these ovens emitted radiation, but modern ovens have a better safety record. The basic facts are that the same violent damage that occurs in the human body when exposed to microwaves, also occurs in the molecules of food when exposed to these same rays.[12]

Molecular changes in food

Let's now talk about the possible damage caused to health by the molecular changes in the food, which occur during this method of cooking.

190

Not everyone who is exposed regularly to emissions will suffer from the same symptoms, as these negative energies tend to find the weak area in the body, and that's where the troubles will take root! It can be a very long term effect, depending on the strength of the immune system, but is it worth taking any chances with good health?

The problems start when food is cooked in the microwave oven, as radiation hits cells, which are torn apart and reformed into new compounds, and that's when structural damage occurs. So its no wonder food molecules are damaged! With each cycle of energy, the polarity changes from negative to positive. This process is known to occur millions of times every second when the oven is heating food. To put it simply, the radiation causes ionization and decay, so it appears that we are feeding our family damaged food!

Germany reveals all!

All was revealed two decades ago when the Institute of Radiation Hygiene of the German Federal Office of Public Health (BGA) announced the results of 16 separate studies comparatively evaluated, regarding both the thermal and non-thermal effects of microwave radiation.

Serious influence occurred on the working of the thyroid and adrenal glands, and their hormones.

Both the adrenal and thyroid glands are part of the body's endocrine system of hormone-producing glands. It also includes the pituitary, thymus, parathyroid, pancreas, and part of the ovaries and testes, so disruption of any part of this important system means trouble ahead![7]

The blood composition and function were both seriously disrupted. As blood is needed to carry oxygen and valuable nutrients to every cell in the body, and also to remove carbon dioxide and other waste, and any disruption in this system affects the entire body.

Cell growth was also influenced and structural changes occurred in chromosomes. The body has billions of cells and any problem here can disrupt DNA. Our body has 23 pair of chromosomes in every human cell, so cell disruption is not good news.[7]

Dowse:

1. Can regularly eating microwaved food create an imbalance in red and white blood cells?
2. Can regularly eating microwaved food upset the body's lymphatic system?
3. Can a regular diet of microwaved food create structural changes in chromosomes in human cells?
4. Can regularly consuming microwaved food disrupt the thyroid gland?
5. Can regularly eating microwave cooked food disrupt the adrenal gland?
6. Can regularly eating microwave cooked food disrupt hormones?

The radiation was shown to have a direct effect on the blood constituents and hormones in the brain; these symptoms are also linked to cell problems. This makes us realize how vital it is to avoid damage to the body's cells as the results can be far reaching.

I would like to again mention that the above results are from 16 separate research projects, each with different scientists, and all have come up with the above results, so be warned![10]

Again we ask, do microwave ovens leak radiation? The answer is Yes, but the really serious widespread threat to health comes from the effect on food. It is ironic that although many scientists spend a lot of time on researching the danger to health from microwave ovens, the research seems mainly to concentrate on leaking energy, when the main risk from this form of cookery, and the real 'bogeyman', is the effect it has on the food we eat!

It's goodbye to many vitamins and that's no exaggeration, as a drastic 30–40% of essential B12 is lost. Is it only a coincidence that there is a steady increase in illnesses associated with B12 deficiency? Many people diagnosed as suffering from multiple sclerosis have in fact the symptoms of a serious B12 deficiency, and once they receive B12 injections, their symptoms improve rapidly.

Low levels of B12 are linked to wheezing in asthma, and the number of asthma sufferers is increasing, particularly in children,[6] so it's time to ask the question, 'Are these sufferers perhaps children whose diet includes microwaved meals?'

What about Alzheimer's disease, colitis, fibromyalgia, and obesity? All of these illnesses are rapidly increasing in numbers, and B12 deficiency is often a common factor. Could the increase in those illnesses be partly due to microwave cookery? Some scientists believe they have the proof, so it's a realistic question.

Microwave ovens damage the molecular structure of food, and create a decrease in levels of nutrients. As well as B12, a decrease in vitamins C and E, and essential minerals and lypotropics (these are necessary to accelerate fat removal) is this one reason why there are so many overweight adults and children today, particularly in America where this oven is used in all but 10% of homes.

The *Journal of Science of Food and Agriculture* (Vol. 83 No. 14) reported results of a study showing that when broccoli is cooked in a microwave oven, it loses 90% of its nutrients, whereas when it had been cooked in a steamer, the minimum of nutrients were lost.[14]

Dowse:

1. Can microwave cookery destroy vitamins in food?
2. Is an amount of vitamin B12 destroyed in food cooked in a microwave oven?
3. Is a diet of microwaved food linked to increase in certain illnesses?
4. Is any of the increase in MS sufferers linked to microwave cooked food in their diet?
5. Can microwave cooking cause naturally occurring amino acids in the body to transform to a toxic form?
6. Can regularly eating microwaved food cause haemoglobin to decrease?

A comparative study of food prepared conventionally and in a microwave oven was published in 1992 by Raum and Zelt, showing microwave ovens produce an alternating current whose force causes production of unnatural molecules. Also naturally occurring amino acids change shape and transform into toxic forms, and more bad news is that haemoglobin decreases and cholesterol levels increase.[12]

The Freedom of Information act reveals the facts!

Now that the Freedom of Information Act enables the general public to request the release of details of research carried out several decades ago, it is making all sorts of useful and startling research results available to us. Some of this new information, as well as being helpful and interesting, is also telling us that scientists have known of the dangers of microwave ovens and microwaved food for several decades.

Here is a brief summary of the results of Russian and German research reported by researcher William P. Kopp, who worked for the Educational and Research Operation at Portland, Oregon. This brilliant researcher was forced to change his name, and had to go into hiding, and flee his country, after this report was made public. To ensure his work was not in vain, here are a few stark facts, as I hope you will want to be informed, and pass the facts to your friends and family.

Carcinogenic compounds in every food microwaved!

William P. Kopp's research results showed carcinogenic compounds were formed in almost every food tested under normal microwave cooking conditions. These included prepared meats, milk and cereal; some amino acids were also carcinogenic; raw, frozen and cooked vegetables and fruit too were victims.

There was a 60–90% decrease in nutritive value of vitamins, and essential minerals were also casualties,[1] so this is positive confirmation that when eating microwaved food regularly, we do need to supplement our diet with the missing vitamins and minerals!

So when you are tempted to use your microwave oven to save time, remind yourself that microwave radiation created cancer-causing agents in meat, milk and cereal, and digestibility of fruit and vegetables altered. Proteins in meat will also be destabilized and vital nutrients decreased.

You can't fool plants

If you are in the habit of microwaving a cup of water for a quick cup of tea, then think again, as big changes occur in water when it has been bombarded with radiation. I had proof recently when I experimented by planting seeds in two separate pots. One plant I watered with microwaved water, heated in a friend's microwave, and the other plant was watered with rainwater from the garden water butt. The seeds watered with rainwater thrived, while those watered with microwaved water died. This was confirmation to me that liquids, as well as solids, lose nutrients when heated in the microwave oven.

I chose plants for my experiment as I know plants are very sensitive to energy and nutrients. This is shown when you plant seeds in two pots, and for three weeks give one plant some healing energy, while ignoring the other plant. Very soon you will notice the plant receiving the healing energy is growing much faster than the other plant.

I was first asked to do this exercise sixteen years ago when sitting in a Healing Circle, and the leader gave each of us two little pots, and asked us to heal one for three weeks and ignore the other one. I found this very difficult, and kept apologizing to the other plant, and assuring it I would give it lots of healing when the exercise was over.

When I complained to the leader at the end of the three week period that it was an unfair exercise, she smiled and explained that the purpose of the exercise had been to teach us that we cannot choose to heal one person and ignore another!

Are your instincts confirming that those research results telling us that microwaved food appears to create new molecules and energies are correct? It does ring warning bells, as these molecules are not naturally occurring in the body. But surely this is a known fact, that the human body does not happily accept foreign visitors! As these are not normally present in the human diet, and are artificially produced, it is hardly surprising changes in the blood and body's energy balance occurs.

I agree that some of the research was done several decades ago, but the radiation has not changed, even although the model of oven may be more sophisticated, as results today are exactly the same, but on a larger scale, so the problems has escalated, since many more people today use a microwave oven.

Biological effects – lots of it!

Today a large amount of Russian research literature is becoming available for the Western world to view, which very convincingly shows the harmful effects of exposure to radiowaves and microwave frequency, and that accepted standards do not give safe protection to users.

This includes loss of memory, difficulty in concentration, bad sleep patterns. These symptoms occur in a statistically higher percentage if individuals are exposed to regular range-emission field effects of microwave apparatus, from either ovens or transmission stations.

Has your sixth sense told you not to befriend your microwave oven? Have the above facts confirmed your intuition was correct? It's quite amazing how often we get a strong gut feeling about something, but ignore it, and usually it is right. I regularly hear people say 'I had a feeling about that. I should have listened'. When I mention the microwave's damaging effect on food and health, so many people hastily assure me they only use it to reheat food, and never use it to cook food. That's kidding yourself, as the damage is the same whether you are cooking or reheating the food. I hope I have succeeded in convincing you that there are possibly serious long term health effects from eating microwave cooked food, or being exposed to their energy field.

I would like now to give you some information about Swiss research which will confirm the above symptoms and assure you that it is not 'all my imagination'!

A very brave scientist!

Swiss food scientist Dr Hans-Urich Hertel in 1989, in his research on microwaves and health, unearthed some alarming information, but was silenced by a Swiss court. Results of his eight-week research confirmed changes in the blood including reduced haemoglobin and cholesterol values. The results also showed the body's natural cell repair mechanism was disrupted, and instead of producing water and carbon dioxide, cells produced hydrogen peroxide and carbon monoxide.[15] Carbon monoxide is formed when carbon dioxide is heated in a limited air supply.[6]

Dr Hertel and Dr Blanc's research showed a decrease in vital contents in the blood, and as the blood acts as a delivery service to transport nutrients and oxygen to every part of the body, a breakdown in this service is a serious health risk. Another function of the blood is to collect carbon dioxide and waste from the body's cells. Our blood is used to carry carbon dioxide to the lungs, allowing the body to breath it out. As well as transporting oxygen, blood also transports important minerals, hormones and salt; these are only a few of the functions of the blood, which travels and circulates around the body in under one minute.[9]

The white cells (leucocytes) are blood cells which are an important part of the body's defense system against disease, and microwaves create an imbalance in red and white cells, which has serious implications.

Lymphocytes are a type of white blood cell and part of the lymph vascular system, and chemical alteration in food molecules has been shown to cause malfunction in the lymphatic system. As

197

all parts of the body are interlinked, trouble in one area starts a chain reaction.[7]

This is one of the facts the Swiss court silenced, although the facts are now available to governments in all countries. Please believe that it is not only blood which is affected, as our lymphatic system is also damaged.

When the body's lymphatic system is upset, look out, and as the microwaved food creates an inability to fight cancers, is it surprising there is such a dramatic increase in sufferers of this terrible illness?

The function of the lymphatic system

The lymphatic system has an important role to play as it carries fluids around the body. These vessels carry foreign particles, and excess fluid from the body's cells and tissue, so when the lymphatics malfunction, the body's defenses are down. Is this part of the reason for so many immune related illnesses?

The lymphatic system, or lymph vascular as its sometimes known, affects most areas of the body, as it's composed of lymph vessels, lymphoid organs and tissue, including the spleen, the thyroid, and the tonsils.[7] It's not just the adult body that suffers, as our children and babies are also victims, so let me tell you about baby's milk.

Don't destroy baby's milk!

The old saying 'breast milk is best' today needs to have the added words 'unless heated in the microwave oven'. Research by Richard Quin *et al.*[9] showed conclusively that you should never heat breast milk in your microwave, as the process reduces important natural immunological properties, that Nature intended should be passed from mother to offspring.[2]

Confirmation of this fact came from a group of scientists at California's Stanford University School of Medicine, where the research has shown that when breast milk is microwaved at high temperatures ranging from 72 to 98°C, the results displayed a very marked increase in the activity of all the anti-infective factors tested.

Dowse:

1. Are some immunological properties of expressed breast milk destroyed when milk is heated in a microwave oven?
2. Are any nutrients destroyed when baby's milk formula is heated in a microwave oven?
3. Does heating baby's milk formula in a microwave oven disrupt valuable amino acids?

Please phrase the dowsing questions in several different ways and you will still get confirmation of these facts. Start the question with 'Can' rather than with 'Will' as the health of some people can be affected more than others by eating microwaved food. So although research has shown it can create harmful health effects, it may not affect everyone who eats microwaved food. But be sure to cleanse your pendulum before you dowse!

Can I once again remind you of the importance of cleansing your pendulum of negative energy before asking the questions, to eliminate the possibility of getting wrong answers. Also please remember to place a light of protection around your body each time you dowse.

One frightening fact was that *E. coli* growth at this range of temperatures, was a staggering 18 times higher than the control human milk. When the milk was heated to 20–25°C, the *E. coli* growth was five times the level of the control milk. This research confirms that microwave radiation and baby's milk are not a 'good mix'.[13]

The Lancet on December 9 1989 reported research results by Dr Lita Lee of Hawaii, who showed that microwaving baby milk formula played havoc with important amino acids, and one of these, L. proline, became a neurotoxin, and the really bad news is that this is poisonous to a baby's nervous system, and to the kidneys.[9] Many mothers today use baby formula, so the baby is in fact being fed damaged milk, as when the formula is microwaved, it acquires toxins during the process. When mother's milk or milk formula are heated in a microwave oven, a change occurs, and there is often a loss of valuable vitamins. Doctors and midwives have told us for decades that mother's milk contains a built in immunity, giving the baby some protection, and this natural protection is destroyed by the process of microwave heating, and when these are destroyed, the irreplaceable beneficial properties are lost for good.

Expressed milk, when microwaved, loses some vital protective properties, so although it takes longer to prepare, and junior may be screaming loudly, heat the bottle in warm water, as your baby will thank you!

Further confirmation came from Vienna, when a study reported in *The Lancet* demonstrated that the effect of heating milk in a microwave oven showed the process disrupted proteins and amino acids. As a result of this research, Lusec *et al.* effectively warned the world that the procedure can lead to functional, structural and immunological changes. This is a very serious statement, so this team of scientists in Vienna must have been pretty sure of their facts, as their reputation was at stake![3]

These scientists have given us a warning! They cannot all be wrong, so do we ignore their facts, and hope these foreign molecules will not attack our family's health? Perhaps it's time to consider the facts, and decide just how much you really need a microwave oven?

Your body has its own electrical circuit

Yes the body does have an electrical circuit, and this can be broken by microwaved food. We all have an electricity charge, which comes from the Universal energy – it comes down through the body, into the ground, and then back to source. This ongoing energy supply can be disturbed by damaged food molecules, and so the body runs below par, thus it will be slow to respond to treatment for illness, or patients may lack energy, or feel as though they are not centreed.

Dowsers, radiesthesiasts, kinesiologists and many alternative therapists have known of this disruption for many years, and agree that the electrical circuit going through the body is the most common cause of the body's energy being out of balance. I always check this system when treating a patient, and invariably the link is broken, and they need to be reconnected to source. Once this has been repaired, their body responds to treatment. Medical science is often looking in the wrong direction to find an answer to health problems, as most research on microwave ovens and health is related to the emissions, when in fact they should be concentrating on the effect of eating microwaved food with altered molecules, and the presence of free radicals.

Look out for free radicals

These harmful menaces are highly reactive. They are by-products created by the effect of the heating process on raw vegetables, particularly root vegetables, which creates the cancer-causing free radicals.

Free radicals aren't the only health problem linked to the microwave oven, as the eyes and testes can be severely damaged by exposure to energy leakage from the oven.

Guard your eyes

Do you remember the scare in the early 1980s, when there was lots of publicity about housewives in America who developed cancer in the eyes, which was blamed on standing close to their microwave oven. Always remember to protect your eyes, when using the microwave oven, as the eyes are very vulnerable to the powerful emissions, and can suffer irreparable damage when you stand in front of the oven which has a bad seal, when it is switched on, as this non-ionizing radiation has an extremely dangerous cumulative effect.

201

Beware! there are no warning signs of itch, pain, or other irritation to remind you of the danger. Regular exposure to these emissions can cause damage, because the eyes are a low circulatory area of the body, and also have a low cooling effect, so they are more sensitive (the lens is the most sensitive part of the eye) as the rise in temperature is greater there than in other parts of the body with good circulation.

The circulatory part of the eye, when exposed to excessive heat from the microwave, because of its circulatory system being unable to provide enough cooling, would literally cook like an egg, and the same applies to the stomach, bladder, intestines, and testes. It was proved in 1987 that microwaves hitting the eyes cause lasting damage, and any housewife whose microwave seal is faulty, and who unwittingly exposes herself to emissions from a microwave at eye level, could suffer serious eye damage or blindness, as the most sensitive part of the human body is the lens of the eye.[4]

Metal frames out – plastic frames in!

Metal spectacle frames are the height of fashion today, but as far as health is concerned your eyes are better protected when you wear old fashioned plastic frames. Why? The simple answer is that the metal frames of the spectacles act as an antenna, and focus the microwaves to your eyes and your brain. Never ever stand in front of the microwave oven when it is cooking food, and always take off your metal framed 'specs' before using the oven! I know they look old fashioned but for the same reason I always wear plastic frames when using my computer.

Men – your testes are at risk

Another area it's important to protect is the male testes, as these are sensitive to temperature change. The sperm can only be formed at lower temperatures than the body heat. Accidental exposure to emissions can alter, or even kill, your sperm.

Could this be one of the reason for the drop in level of male sperm count? And should we be concerned about the long term effects? The answer is Yes.

Now from your body to your food.

Remember – restaurants zap your dinner!

Going out for a meal is a treat, but to eat out regularly could affect health, as restaurants use industrial sized microwave in commercial kitchens. The food manufacturing and catering industries are big scale users of the microwave oven. Most restaurants use these ovens as it speeds up the cooking process to quick thaw frozen foods, and speed up the cooking of poultry and fish.

So even if you don't use a microwave oven at home, for those of you who regularly eat out there is a fairly strong chance that you are eating microwaved food. If you eat lunch out each day, or an evening meal, you'll almost certainly be eating nutritionally damaged food. This is confirmed by research in Japan by Dr Fumio Watanabe, who found microwave-cooked milk, beef and pork all suffered reduced nutrient value.[3] Various research programmes have taken place in different parts of the world, and all show a clear and consistent pattern emerging, but is anybody listening? Rumblings have been going on and concerns raised for some time, so what does all this mean? It simply means that if you have any sense of self preservation, you'll kiss goodbye to your microwave oven and buy a steamer.

My microwave and I parted company several years ago, and I bought two steamers. I can honestly say my food tastes better, and I feel healthy, 'so listen to good advice from a wise old bird'!

To recap – here are a few good reasons to bid farewell to your microwave oven!

1. The long term effect on your brain due to cell damage.
2 Disruption of your body's vital hormone production.
3. The creation of carcinogens.

4. Disruption of your concentration and causing memory loss.
5. Microwaved food loses valuable minerals and vitamins, all essential for your good health.
6. Your immune system is weakened by the upset in the body's endocrine glands.

I could go on and on, but I hope these few facts are sufficient to ring loud warning bells, so dowse and ask your pendulum if cooking food in a steamer is more beneficial to health, than microwaving food. My advice is Get Rid of It! But if you cannot bear to part with it, or don't have any other form of cooking, then please remember the possible health risks to all members of your family, as damage to the body's cells and glands is often irreparable.

As I am writing these facts, I can't help having a quiet chuckle, as I can very clearly hear my mother's words, when nearly thirty years ago I bought my first microwave oven. It was my pride and joy, but did not impress my mother when she came to visit, as she was full of prophesies of gloom. Her sixth senses thoroughly convinced her that this method of cooking food was not natural, and was not healthy. Alas she has been proved right, and is probably sitting in the world of spirit, saying 'I told you so'. At least I have the courage to admit I was very wrong, and on this occasion she was correct. My mother was psychic so often knew my thoughts, and we had many clashes about modern gadgets.

She refused to have a washing machine, and when I took my children on a visit to her home, all washing was done by hand. I had to admit, although grudgingly, that my baby's terry nappies were always much whiter when they had been washed a few times by hand, proving again that there are many benefits to both the environment and health, from the 'old fashioned' methods, Today life moves at a much faster pace, so we feel that we need all of our modern day gadgets to cope with chores. Microwave ovens do make life easier, but it raises the question 'Do they also make life shorter?'.

Summary

Many housewives would probably vote the microwave as one of their most invaluable appliances, but sadly the time saved by using this form of cooking has to be weighed up against the possible damage to health caused by harmful rays given off by this user friendly gadget, and its effect on food.

When so many reliable scientists present research results showing this oven can seriously damage health, and the fact that 16 separate research projects all produced the same confirmation, that this form of cookery can damage health, it is time to listen and ask questions!

In years gone by the leakage from poor door seals was a serious health hazard, and a possible damage to eyes, but today's models have mostly eliminated that problem. Today the serious questions we must all ask are 'Does microwave cookery create unnatural molecules?' and 'Does it create new chemicals, some of which are carcinogenic?'

One factor which we must consider is the fact that a serious vitamin loss occurs when food is microwaved, particularly broccoli, which has been shown to lose 90% of nutrients. The loss of B12 has serious implications as many illnesses show a deficiency of this important vitamin, including multiple sclerosis and asthma. Other health factors to consider are that cholesterol can rise, and haemoglobin in the blood can be disrupted when microwaved food is regularly included in the diet.

It's not just the adults who are affected by this form of cooking, as babies' health can suffer if their milk has been heated in the microwave oven, and expressed mother's milk can lose its important immunological properties.

The human body has its own electrical circuit which is sensitive to invasion from powerful energy fields, so it seems wise to avoid as many sources of electromagnetic fields as possible, and to constantly be aware of the importance of protecting your body from invasion. There are many chemicals in our environment which can damage health, so it is important to keep the immune system strong and balanced. My advice to help you maintain good health is to avoid microwave cookery. You'll be amazed how much better your food tastes, and how quickly you get used to steaming food!

Endnotes

1. *Lifeforce* No. 17 reprinted from *The Truth Campaign*. Researched by William P. Kopp, extracted from *Perceptions* May/June 1996. 'Microwave Madness. The Effects of Microwave Apparatus on Food and Humans', Forensic research Document AREC, Research Document T061-7R10/10-77F05 release priority Class 1 R001a.
2. Runway, Elle, and Walther, Bridget, 'Important Information re Your Health' http://www.bridgetwalther.com
3. Wild, Marion, 'Are Microwave Ovens a Source of Danger?', *The Truth Campaign* No. 11, 2001. http://www.vegan.swinternet.co.uk
   Brodeur, P,. 1986, Mikrowellen Die Verheimlichte Gefaha Pfiemer, Wiesbaden, Berlin.
4. 'Microwaves – How Dangerous Are They?' Excerpts from the *Complete Microwave Oven Service Handbook* by J. Carlton Gallawa. Material supplied by courtesy of John C. Gallawa. http://www.gallawa.com/microtech
5. 'The Facts About Microwave Ovens', EMRAA Electromagnetic Radiation Alliance of Australia.
   Acres, USA, 1994. National Health and Medical Council, 1985. http://www.ssec.org.au/emraa/html
6. Davies, Dr Stephen, and Stewart, Dr Alan, *Nutritional Medicine*. Pan Books. ISBN 0330 288334.
7. Weston, Trevor, MD, MRCGP, *Atlas of Anatomy*, Marshall Cavendish Books. ISBN 086307 4162.
8. Becker, Dr Robert, and Seldon, Gary, *The Body Electric*, William Morrow & Co.
9. Dr Joseph Mercola, 'The Hidden Hazards of Microwave Cooking' Anthony Wayne and Lawrence Newell. http://www.mercola.com
10. Gust, Lawrence J., 'Throw Away Your Microwave'. http://healbuildings.com
11. Rainbow Network, 'Health Risks and Danger of Using Microwave Ovens for Food Preparation' Cambridge, UK.
    Gupta, Kashish, *The Ecologist*, November 2003. http://www.cam.net.uk
12. NHL Ministries, DL Publication, 'Microwave Ovens, Wave Them Goodbye. Comparative Study of Food Prepared Conventionally and in the

Microwave Oven', published by Raum and Zelt. 11992 3 (2.:43. http://blpublications.com

13. Mercola, Dr Joseph, 'The Problem with Irradiated Food. What the Researchers Say'. www.mercola.com.

14. Colby, Michael, and Epstein, Sam, *The Food and Water Journal*. Winter 1997.
Meeker-Lowry, Susan, and Ferrara, Jennifer. Food and Water Report, 'Meat Monopolies. Dirty Meat and the False Promises of Irradiation.

15. Mercola, Dr Joseph, 'The Hidden Hazards of Microwave Cooking'. Extracted from *Nexus New Times*, Vol. 2, May/June 1995. Originally extracted from the April 1994 edition of *Acres, USA*. www.mercola.com

12

Watch out, watch out, irradiation is about!

Food irradiation, like microwave ovens, is indeed a very controversial subject, as governments assure us eating irradiated food will not damage our health, while many scientists and doctors tell us a very different story. Dowsing will confirm if these warnings of the serious damage to health from regularly eating irradiated food are correct, and confirm the reliability of the research results to back their opinion. So who do we believe?

Research on rats, mice and dogs has shown chromosomal damage, cardiac thrombosis, kidney disease, cancer, internal bleeding caused by a serious vitamin K deficiency, and high death rate of fetus. Okay, we can argue that these test results all involved animals and rodents, but can we risk the possibility that humans who regularly eat irradiated food could be affected by similar health damage?

To date, there has not yet been any large scale research carried out into the long term effect on human health of eating irradiated food, but one study was carried out in India by the National Institute of Nutrition, at the Council of Medical Research in Hyderabab, on malnourished children. After being fed a diet of freshly irradiated wheat for a six week period, results of blood tests revealed the children had suffered chromosome damage, whereas the group fed on normal wheat showed no damage to chromosomes.[5]

What research results tell us

Army data on research results of animal feeding tests showed a decrease of 20.7% in surviving weaned rats, and a 32.3% decrease in surviving progeny of dogs. An FDA paper reports that dogs on the control diet weighed 11.3% more than dogs on the irradiated diet, and these poor souls developed carcinomas of the pituitary gland, which is an extremely rare type of malignant tumour.[12] So look out, Big Meat Eaters, since if meat is ever allowed to be irradiated on a large scale, you could be next to suffer this fate!

A study on rats found that within 46 days of being on a diet containing irradiated meat, a significant number of rats died. Tests found these rats had suffered a serious vitamin K deficiency.[13] Another group of male rats fed on an irradiated diet died a hemorrhagic death, suggesting non-absorption of vitamin K, which plays an important role in blood clotting.[14]

Further research involved mice fed on a diet of 50% irradiated food, and results showed the mice suffered significant increase in embryonal deaths.[15] These results present a depressing and alarming picture, and many folks take these results as a warning to avoid irradiated food in their diet.

Similar studies in the Hungarian Academy of Science in 1979 showed an increase in cancer and kidney failure in animals fed irradiated food.[21]

Dowse: and ask the following questions after you have cleansed your pendulum.

1. Can regularly eating irradiated food disrupt the vitamin K absorption in the body?
2. Can irradiation of food destroy a large amount of vitamin K in the food?
3. Can a regular diet of irradiated food create chromosomal damage in the body?
4. Can the irradiation process create new chemicals in food which are carcinogens?

Opposition to the 'zap trade' has taken an interesting turn in recent years, as several imminent scientists, all specialists in food irradiation and health, have come forward and spoken openly about the dangers to health of irradiating food. These scientists have given an unbiased opinion based on research results, and are not involved financially, so their opinion is not influenced by having shares, or being on the board of directors of any company involved in the 'for or against irradiation' war. One such expert is Professor William Au, Toxicologist at Texas University, who felt so strongly that he has sworn an affidavit, stating his research results showed irradiation is a carcinogen.[23]

Dr Geraldine Dettman PhD, Radiation Safety Officer and Biosafety Officer at Brown's University, warns irradiation is bad news, and advises us that we should be aware that irradiation is a carcinogen. It could lead to cancer and is also a mutagen and teratogen, so is an agent known to increase the incidence of congenital malformations[1] (teratogen has the ability to create monstrosities[25]). More facts from George L. Tritsch PhD, Rosewell Park Cancer Institute, NY, who says the food irradiation process increases the levels of mutagens and carcinogens in the food, and research has shown mutagenic doses of formaldehyde are formed during the irradiation of carbohydrates.

Even if you don't eat many carbohydrates, please remember that although meat is a protein, it also contains carbohydrates.

Scientist John Gofman, MD, PhD, University of California Berkeley, states research results have shown the irradiation process creates a host of unnatural and sometimes unidentifiable chemicals in food.[1]

Dr Samuel Epstein MD, who is Professor of Occupational and Environmental Medicine at the University of Illinois at Chicago, says 'Irradiation causes a host of unnatural and sometimes unidentifiable chemicals to be formed in food'. These are the words of one of the world's leading medical scientists.[22]

Studies done, in 1998 and 2001 by a team of German and French scientists, at the Federal Research Center for Nutrition in Germany and the Louis Pasteur University in France, and funded by the European Union, showed a concentration of chemicals called 2-alkylcyclobutanones (2-ACBs). These are found only in food which has been irradiated, and are known to cause DNA damage in cells, and they also promoted tumour development in rat's colon. The new chemicals are found when foods containing fat are irradiated, which of course includes beef, chicken, and eggs, and these are all on sale to the public in food stores![8]

Dr Joseph Mercola reports laboratory rats suffered serious chromosomal damage which affected the immune system, and when this important function is weakened, the body is vulnerable to all sorts of infections and immune deficiency illnesses. He also warns us the rats' reproductive system was damaged, so is there any link between the increase in couples experiencing infertility, low sperm count problems and irradiated food in the diet?[10] When you have a few moments to spare have a look at Dr Joseph Mercola's website, as there is an abundance of information on all aspects of irradiation and health.

Dowse:

1. When food is irradiated does it form new free radicals?
2. When food is irradiated does it form unique radiolytes?
3. Can unique radiolytes, formed in irradiation of food, bond to pesticides in food?
4. Can unique radiolytes, formed by irradiation of food, bond with pesticides in the body?

Did these animals and rodents die in vain? I hope not, as internal bleeding and all the other fatal symptoms suffered by these laboratory animals and rodents is a strong warning of similar symptoms in humans it future, and by then it could be too late to stop the chain reaction. I am not being theatrical when I tell you these facts, as I am only repeating what has been published in the *Journal of Nutrition* and other reliable sources.

More proof!

Following the disaster of September 11, the US Postal Service acted very rapidly to deter sabotage and introduced irradiation of all mail. A great move, but not for the mailmen, as many of them very quickly developed uncomfortable symptoms linked to handling the irradiated mail. Many mailmen complained of nosebleeds, nausea, extremely bad headaches, runny eyes, burning hands and face. We are not talking about a handful of victims: in one centre in Gaithersberg alone, 87 workers suffered uncomfortable symptoms. This was short term exposure and it demonstrates the power of irradiation.[19]

Our much needed vitamins!

Research results have shown that vitamins are depleted in the irradiation process (sometimes labeled Cold Pasteurization) and confirmation is found in the Public Citizen's publication *The Great Vitamin Robbery*, which reports results of research dating back half a century to 1956, linking nutrient loss to irradiation of food.[2]

Chicken is a great family favourite as it can be used for so many different meals, so it is a sad fact that some research results show up to 95% of vitamin A is lost,[10] and vitamins C, E, K and folic acid can all be affected.

Dowse:

1. Can a diet high in irradiated food weaken the immune system?
2. Can a diet high in irradiated food disrupt the reproductive system?
3. Can regularly consuming irradiated food upset the balance of vitamin K in the body?
4. Are high levels of vitamin K lost in the food during the irradiation process?

Vitamin K, the blood clotter

Alarm bells are ringing as cause for great concern, is the fact that research results on animals have consistently shown vitamin K level in food is greatly reduced, and this can have far reaching effects on health. Vitamin K is the name given to a group of chemical substances, and when deficient it is recognized as leading to bleeding disorders. This vitamin produces blood clotting factors including prothrombin, and can be supplemented in the diet by including turnips, lettuce, cabbage, greens, cereals, green tea and liver.[16]

Dr Robert C. Atkins in his book *Vita-Nutrients Solutions* says vitamin K shortage is the most under-appreciated cause of osteoporosis, and as many as one in three women has this deficiency. If this is the case, then all of these women who make up one third of the West's adult female population have a vitamin K deficiency which could be aggravated further by a diet of irradiated food.[17]

Another group of people who should probably steer well clear of irradiated food are those people who suffer any type of cardiovascular condition, as many people suffering from heart disease are prescribed a blood thinning anti-clotting drug. These drugs eliminate clotting by destroying vitamin K in the body, so the effect of irradiated food on the vitamin K in this group, plus the combination of the drug, could be a lethal mix.

As I mentioned earlier, an FDA paper *Food Irradiation* in October 1968 reported research rats suffered a horrible hemorrhagic death, after being fed a diet of irradiated food, so the possible vitamin K loss is serious food for thought. So are you happy about your child eating irradiated school meals?

One can't help but ask 'What effect will this bombardment of energy into our food have on our health?' The Center for Food Safety reports food irradiation depletes vitamins, corrupts amino acids and essential fatty acids, and also confirms the treatment forms unwanted chemicals which are suspected of causing birth defects and cancer.

We are hearing these facts from several different sources, so it is difficult to ignore them, and it seems very sensible to take them on board.

Dowse:

1. Is part of the increase in number of osteoporosis sufferers in the USA linked to irradiated food in diet?
2. Do a high number of osteoporosis sufferers have a vitamin K deficiency?
3. Can regularly eating irradiated food corrupt the body's amino acids?
4. Can irradiation lower the nutritional value of food?

Irradiation of school meals – no way!!

Not surprisingly, there's big concern in the USA over possible use of irradiated meat in school dinners and, rightly so, this has instigated a ban on the use of any irradiated food in any school dinners in 400 schools in 22 states, including Washington DC, San Francisco and California, which are leading the country in banning irradiated food from school cafeterias to safeguard the health of students.

In 2004 Los Angeles Unified School district also introduced a ban on irradiated meat, as they rightly believe it is very wrong to use children as a test group, since the long term effects of eating irradiated food are still unknown. In short, if research on rats shows this diet creates loss of vital vitamins, we cannot afford to expose our children to this health risk.[19,20]

Parents in the UK do not have to worry about irradiated school meals, as the sale of irradiated of food is illegal in Britain, and only herbs and spices are irradiated.

Vegetarians beware!

Food irradiation can create serious problems for many vegetarians, unless they can have a diet of mainly organic foods, as a vegetarian diet usually includes nuts, seeds, herbs and spices, all of which may have been irradiated. This means they could have a diet of mainly inferior food, as many important nutrients have been removed by radiation, and these foods do not always carry any irradiation information.

Half a century ago there was concern about the health effects of certain irradiated food in the UK, and Dr Rosalie Bertell, PhD, GNSH, past President and Founder of the International Institute of Concern for Public Health (IICPH) in her paper 'Food Irradiation' reminds us that Germany permitted irradiation of spices in 1957. This was rescinded the following year, and in 1969 Canada rescinded permission for irradiation of potatoes. In 1963 the United Sates permitted irradiation of potatoes, wheat and bacon, but rescinded bacon in 1969, after it was found that animals fed irradiated bacon suffered adverse health effects.[13]

The birth of unknown chemicals and our health!

Are you surprised that the report 'Hidden Harm' published by Public Citizen, registers concern for any type of new chemical found in irradiated food? Cyclobutanones do not occur naturally anywhere, but have recently been found to be the cause of genetic damage in rats, and genetic and cellular damage in both humans and rat cells. This chemical is found in irradiated beef, pork, chicken, eggs, mangoes and papayas. Public Citizen scientists are so concerned that they have requested the FDA to halt legalization of additional foods until these new chemicals are tested for safety.[18]

One of the biggest problem with irradiation is that this treatment can cause both nutritional content and chemical composition changes in the food, and radiolytic by-products are born. As yet very few of these new chemicals have been studied by scientists for toxicity, but one example studied in research was the chemical 2-DCB, which showed serious damage to the DNA of rats colon cells.[8]

Dowse:

1. Can regularly eating irradiated meals affect the health of children?
2. Can irradiation of food create new chemicals?
3. Can irradiation of food create the aflatoxin cyclobutanones?
4. Can cyclobutanones cause genetic damage if regularly consumed in food?
5. Can regularly eating irradiated food containing the chemical 2-DCB cause serious damage to the colon?

Your body's DNA is under attack!

Anything which disrupts the body's DNA should ring loud alarm bells, as if we become ill, from the presence of one or more of these new unknown chemicals created by irradiation in our body, we must ask the question 'Will doctors be able to treat the effects of the unknown cause?' It is hard enough for doctors to diagnose certain illnesses today, without expecting them to cure mystery illnesses.

The body's DNA is a genetic map which governs a range of bodily factors including hair, skin, sperm etc. and so when this vibration is altered, it is meddling with nature. Now must be the time for the 'turning point', as it is time to reassess the benefits of irradiation. Altering the DNA will mean all sorts of strange things can happen to our health, so at all cost any food or treatment which may alter or disrupt the body's DNA must be avoided.

Fats do not respond well to irradiation as they tend to become rancid, so does this mean that people suffering from digestive problems will find irradiated food aggravates these health problems?

Look out for aflatoxins!

Aflatoxins are bad news: this statement is confirmed by The World Health Organisation (WHO) which consider aflatoxins to be a significant risk to public health, and a major contributor to liver cancer in certain areas. These aflatoxins occur quite naturally in humid areas, where they are found in fungus spores, and also grow on certain stored foods, e.g. grains, vegetables, rice, peanuts, and cotton seed. Certain aflatoxins are known to damage important vitamins in food.

Back in 1998 the German government researchers discovered the presence of aflatoxins in irradiated food. These unique chemicals, called cyclobutanones, were shown to promote development of cancer and genetic damage in rats.[2]

For those readers who would like some technical information, alkylcyclobutanones (2-ACB) are a group of compounds generated by the irradiation of triglycerides in fat containing foods. So what are triglycerides? These are a major form of fat found in food and also produced by the body, consisting of three molecules of fatty acid combined with a molecule of alcohol glycerol. For more information have a look on the website MedicalNet.com, where there is an excellent medical dictionary giving detailed information about this subject and many others.[25]

Certain species of bacteria are immune to irradiation!

Today hospitals are finding it difficult to win the fight against the constant threat of MRSA virus, which seems to have immunity to many antibiotics, so will more trouble be ahead for them in the virus war as irradiation can spawn mutant forms of *E. coli*, salmonella, and other harmful bacteria, making them very difficult to kill?[11]

Under laboratory conditions scientists at Louisiana State University, Baton Rouge, have studied radiation-resistant strains of salmonella. The alarming news is that one of the bacteria found in spoiled meat and animal feces can survive a dose of radiation five times the approved FDA figure. It is hard to believe the bacteria survived when scientists exposed it to radiation which is powerful enough to kill a person several thousand times its size, so I cannot help but think its survival spells 'Big Trouble' in the future.[9]

We are told that irradiation 'does' kill a great many toxins and bacteria, but some dangerous toxins are not inactivated; a fine example is *C. botulinum*, as the process kills off its natural enemies. A scary fact which we are not told is that certain viruses, bacterial spores, and BSE prion can all survive the level of radiation used to irradiate meat. The US Center for Disease Control and the World Health Organization can both advise on this subject.

Where have my friendly bacteria gone?

Governments tell us that irradiation of food kills harmful bacteria, but they have forgotten to tell us that this violent treatment which zaps fresh food also kills friendly bacteria. This is a very serious fact, as these friendly bacteria are part of the body's digestive system, and when the food's natural digestive enzymes are damaged, this makes food harder to digest.

So if you regularly eat irradiated foods, and suffer digestive problems, perhaps it would be beneficial to include some friendly bacteria in your diet. Where do you find friendly bacteria? Visit your local health shop for a supply of fresh yogurt.

Mutations are here!

Are these invisible enemies gaining strength? Could we very soon see the arrival of an army of mutations in both bacteria and viruses, which could lead to potentially resistant strains – this suggestion is not so far fetched as it sounds! The possibility of mutations is no exaggeration for, as I mentioned earlier, research scientists at Louisiana State University in Baton Rouge were confronted by one very determined virus, which is found in animal feces and spoiled meat, with an immunity to normal dose radiation.

The super virus can survive radiation blasts at five times the normal level being approved by the FDS for beef. This mighty virus, named *D. radiodurans*, was exposed to between 10 and 15 kiloGrays (kGy) of radiation for several hours, to give you an idea of the extent of this virus's immunity. The radiation blast was so powerful it would have killed a person several thousand times over, so is this shape of things to come?[23] Is food irradiation going to breed monster bacteria in the not too distant future, or have I seen too many horror movies?

Dowse:

1. Can any harmful bacteria in food or animal feces survive food irradiation?
2. Can BSE prions survive the food irradiation process?
3. Can the pathogens which cause Mad Cow Disease survive the food irradiation process?
4. Can the Norwalk virus in shellfish survive the food irradiation process?

Next lets look at unique radiolytes!

Unique radiolytes – an invisible enemy!

So what are these unique radiolytic chemicals? These unidentified mysterious chemical compounds are as yet not researched for any potential harm to health. They are free radicals which can set off a chain reaction in the body, and are capable of destroying the body's valuable antioxidants. Research results show these unwelcome visitors can tear cell membranes apart, and make the body more susceptible to cancer, diabetes, heart disease, liver damage, muscular breakdown, and other illnesses which develop when the immune system is low.

Be aware of free radicals!

As I mentioned earlier free radicals are created by irradiation, and these unwanted extras can cause havoc in the body, as their interaction with irradiated food can create new chemicals which are a serious health hazard. They have the ability to bond with pesticides or other existing chemicals in the food, and form new chemicals known as unique radiolytic products (URPs)

219

Free radicals can cause tissue to degrade, and some body cells to malfunction, as they are a group of atoms with an odd number of electrons, and science has shown these can be formed by certain molecules interacting with oxygen.

These reactive radicals are capable of starting a chain effect, which creates damage to important cellular components in the body such as DNA. They can cause cells to malfunction or to die, so good old Mother Nature has given the human body an excellent defense system of antioxidants that protect the body against these scavengers.

Antioxidants, 'the good guys'!

Antioxidants play an important part in the health of the human body, as they deactivate some particles of the free radicals, delay degeneration by oxidation, and are involved in the prevention of cellular damage. When antioxidants are attacked by free radicals, the body is less able to fight cancer, other immune illnesses and premature ageing. So far as antioxidants are concerned, although they have the ability to terminate harmful chain reactions caused by these radicals, food irradiation is bad news as it creates bombardment from free radicals on a grand scale.

Many doctors believe antioxidants help to slow the body's ageing process, and prevent heart disease, but as yet there is no positive proof.

The most common antioxidant supplements are beta carotene, selenium, vitamin C, and vitamin E, so if your diet includes regular irradiated meals, it may be a good move to supplement your diet with antioxidants.

The big questions

Question 1

Bearing in mind that very little is known about the effect of irradiation on the chemicals used in pesticides, does this treatment

220

create more new chemicals, or give the existing harmful chemicals power to mutate?

Curiously I have not succeeded in find any information on the effects, and are you like me, wondering if research on this subject would open a hornet's nest?

Question 2

Do scientists know the long term health effect on humans from eating food which has been zapped twice? This double dose threat is an issue that requires research. How could this situation arise? Easy! If apricots, mangoes or other fruit are zapped when fresh, and then become ingredients in a pudding or fruit salad which is zapped, then exactly the same situation could occur as when meat already irradiated is an ingredient in a meat pie which is zapped, so this double dose threat is an issue that requires research. Would this double dose of irradiation cause more serious health problems, and would it create more new chemicals? We don't know the answers!

What is food irradiation?

Note that food irradiation is often labeled cold pasteurized. We know some of our food is irradiated, but what exactly is this controversial process? Don't panic as food does not become radioactive, but the energy transfer creates great heat, similar to the process of a microwave oven, and this is thought to create new chemicals.

The process involves food being zapped with an extremely powerful dose of radiation, equivalent to 30 million chest x-rays, when the food travels on a conveyor belt through a shielded chamber, and is then exposed to radiation of cobalt 60.

I hope these facts put the irradiation process picture in perspective, and give you an idea of the colossal strength of energy used in this process. Is it any wonder that so many people are concerned about the effects of this bombardment of energy on our food and our health.

How is irradiation measured? Irradiation used to be measured in rads, but now measurements are calculated in units of Gray (Gy) although reports written several years ago quote rads. In the new scale of measurements, 1 Gy is equivalent to 100 rads. In March 2001 Codex (The Codex Alimentarius is the international body, which sets the standards for all food in world trade) were reviewing a proposal to eliminate the Maximum Dose Limit for food irradiation. This is at present set at 10 kilo-Gray which is equivalent to 330 million chest x-rays, so we are talking about a very powerful Zap![24]

If you are concerned that you have been regularly eating irradiated food, then it is possible to dowse to confirm if it has affected your health. For those dowsers who have built up a good working relationship with their pendulum, please cleanse your pendulum and dowse to ask the following questions:

1. Can you please remove all harmful chemicals from my body?
2. Has my body excess free radicals?
3. If the answer is 'Yes' then ask it to please remove the excess free radicals.
4. Has my body excess unique radiolytes? Again if you receive a 'Yes' answer, ask the pendulum to please remove the excess unique radiolytes.

It is worth getting into the habit of regularly balancing your body's energy with the pendulum, and asking it to remove toxins and harmful bacteria. Now it's time to summarize the facts about irradiation and health.

Summary

In this chapter I have reported the comments of many experts so please seriously consider the words of these experts. Remember, there are new untested chemicals present in irradiated food, also some unfamiliar living enzymes. As yet there are no positive results of trials available, proving irradiated food is good for you. Just as radiation is bad for humans, so food and irradiation should never meet.

So far I have talked about the many well respected scientists against irradiation, but I must mention that there are certain bodies 'for' radiation. The United States General Accounting Office (GAO) in 2000 stated that 'Available research indicates that benefits outweigh risks'! I have not as yet succeeded in finding any research results which convince me that irradiation of food is good for health.

Regularly eating irradiated food is like eating inferior quality of food and, as I mentioned earlier, irradiated food can lose anything from 20% to 80% of many vitamins and minerals.

Food also loses vitamins A, B2, B3, B6, B12, C, E, K, amino acids, and essential fatty acids, depending on the strength of the dose of radiation, and the length of time the food is stored before being eaten. If you buy irradiated food, remember the sooner you eat it, the fewer vitamins it will be lost – that is a fact not a rumor!

What medicine?

We are all very aware of the increase in the number of people suffering from cancer, heart disease, and immune illnesses, and many of us suspect the enormous unaccountable increase is due to a number of different environmental problems. So microwave radiation and food irradiation are not the only health hazard linked to this increase in fatal illnesses, but it is wise to be aware, and where possible to eliminate, any suspects from our lifestyle.

If we become ill from the presence of new chemicals in our blood created by irradiation, do you think doctors will be able to treat the effects? It is hard enough for doctors to treat diagnosed illness, without expecting them to cure mystery illnesses.

As no research has yet been done on the effects of irradiated food on humans, it is almost certain that no research has been done on medication required to treat ill effects, so how do you heal any of the variety of illnesses linked to new chemicals formed in the irradiation of food?

Since the root cause is most likely to be linked to changes in the body's metabolism, it is essential to get the energies balanced by a therapist. This includes balancing ions, clearing meridians, removing toxins, and clearing the body of excess negative energy. As I doubt very much if my doctor would be able to improve my symptoms, my first port of call would be my pendulum, and then to visit a powerful healer, as their spirit doctors would be able to remove some of the free radicals, and help to heal the damage done.

Top scientists have given us proof that irradiation damages health, while governments assure us this food is healthy, and nutritional value does not change when irradiated,[26] so who do we believe? In the meantime, although we don't know for certain that food irradiation is putting the long term health of the nation at risk, we do know that irradiation kills certain bugs in food, but don't you think these bugs are less of a threat to human health than irradiation? They are natural, they have been in the food chain a very long time, and are not linked with DNA damage or carcinogens, so I vote we keep the bugs, as they appear to be less of a health threat than irradiation.

Endnotes

1. 'Scientists Speak Out'. http://www.foodandwater.org/irrad/scientists.htm
2. Rotem, Talya, BA, MA, CNP, International Institute of Concern for Public Health. '*Food Irradiation Revisited*', www.citizen.org/document/ACF23B.pdf
3. Bertell, Dr Rosalie, PhD, GNSH, International Institute of Concern for Public Health. www.citizen.org/documents/cyclobutanone.pdf
4. Epstein, Sam, MD, Professor of Occupational and Environmental Medicine at The University of Illinois at Chicago, *Food and Water*. Scientists Speak Out. http://www.foodandwater.org
5. Decuyper, Dr. J. D., 'The Decuyper Report. Radiation, Irradiation and Our Food Supply'. www.healthalternatives2000.com
6. Food Irradiation. Tuberose.com http://www.tuberose.com/food_irradiation.html
7. Sworn Affidavit of University of Texas Toxicologist Au raising concern about the risks posed by chemicals formed in irradiated food. William W, Au. http://www.citizen.org

8. *Food Quality News*. 'European Study Links Food Irradiation with Cancer'.
   Novis, *'Industry and Science News'*. www.foodqualitynews.com
9. Meeker-Lowry, Susan, and Ferrara, Jennifer, *The Food and Water Magazine*, 'Food and Water Report "Meat Monopolies, Dirty Meat and False Promises of Irradiation"'.
10. Mercola, Dr. Joseph. 'Food Irradiation, Questions and Answers'. www.mercola.com
11. Mercola, Dr. Joseph, 'The Problem With Irradiating Food. What The Researchers Say'. www.mercola.com
12. FDA Report, 'Food Irradiation', October 1968, Co-sponsored by the Surgeon General of the US Army.
13. Ibid, *Journal of Nutrition*, Vol. 69, No. 18, p. 21, 1959.
14. Ibid, *Federation Proceedings*, Vo. 19, pp. 1045–1049, 1960. Co-sponsored by the Surgeon General of the US Army.
15. Ibid, *International Journal of Radiation, Biology*, Vol. 18, pp. 201–216, 1970.
16. Davies, Dr. Stephen, and Stewart, Dr Alan. S., *Nutritional Medicine*, Pan Books, London, 1987. ISBN 0-33028833-4.
17. Atkins, Dr. Robert C., MD, *Vita Nutrient Solutions*, Fireside, Simon and Schuster, New York, 1999. ISBN 0-684-81849-5.
18. 'Hidden Harm', a report by Public Citizen. www.citizen.org
19. Lerman, Tracy, Organic Consumer Association. *'San Francisco Ban Irradiated Foods in Schools'*. Public Citizen.
20. Public Citizen, 'Update of Movement to Stop Irradiation of Food in Schools', February 8 2005. www.citizen.org/california and www.organicconsumers.org
21. Cummins, Ronnie, *Pure Food Campaign Newsletter*, 'Food and Bytes', June 1999. www.purefood.org.
22. Mercola, Dr. Joseph, 'The Problems With Irradiated Food, What the Researchers Say'. www.mercola.com
23. Colby, Michael, and Epstein, Sam, *The Food and Water Journal*, Winter 1997.
   Meeker-Lowry, Susan, and Ferrara, Jennifer, *Food and Water Report*, 'Meat Monopolies, Dirty Meat and the False Promise of Irradiation'.
24. *The Concise Oxford Dictionary*. Seventh edition. Clarendon Press, Oxford, 1998. L. H. Gray, Engl. Radiobiologist d. 1965. ISBN 0-19-861131-5
25. Medical Dictionary. www.medicinenet.com
26. Frequently Asked Questions About Food Irradiation'. http://www.cdc.gov/ncidod/dbmd/diseaseinfo/foodirradiation.htm

13

Do electromagnetic fields (emfs) from cell phones damage your health?

We are sometimes told by the media that exposure to electromagnetic fields can have a harmful effect on health, then we read in another newspaper, or see on television that it is not harmful, so who do we believe? Stop and think about it. What is your gut feeling telling you? If your gut is ringing warning bells, listen, and heed its warning.

When you stop and think seriously about this subject, you realize that the human body has many electrical systems, so it is not surprising that it can be disrupted by invading rays. Our brainwaves are electromagnetic, and the much underrated pineal gland is almost certainly electromagnetic, for as well as playing an important part in the production of the master hormone melatonin, it is linked to our sense of direction, and the homing device for birds.

So with these sensitive electrical systems in the human body, it is understandable that disruptions to health may occur when the body is exposed regularly to other frequencies.

I do not use a cell phone, as I dislike the powerful buzzing feeling going into my brain, but anyone less sensitive to this energy vibration is allowing transmission from their cellular phone to bombard their brain. Cell phones like electricity are modern day wonders which most of us take for granted as perfectly safe, and unlikely to ever damage our health, so are we blinkered?

Dowse: Ask your pendulum the question, 'Can human health be disrupted by regular exposure to electromagnetic emissions from a cellular phone?'

Cell phones are here to stay, and are now top of the 'Must Have One' list, as more and more parents are pressurized into allowing their child to have one, but what are the effects on health?

There are lots of questions to dowse on this subject, as a wide variety of symptoms are thought to be linked to exposure to the negative energy, and lots of facts are bandied about, but as yet no research has been carried out to prove that these toys do not have an adverse effect on health.

Can cell phone use cause health problems? The answer seems to be 'Yes', according to the many people who experience uncomfortable symptoms when using their phone, including a burning sensation, skin rash, sight problems, nausea, dizziness, and memory loss. These are the sort of symptoms you may expect an elderly person to develop, but these effects are being reported by healthy people in the 20–30 age group. Perhaps it is not really surprising as cell phones emit three separate types of radiation which we should never underestimate.

Dowse: Cleanse your pendulum then ask:

1. Can regular use of a cell phone affect your health?
2. Can regular use of a cell phone cause illness?
3. Does an electric field come from the phone's antenna?
4. Can heat travel from the phone through your brain?
5. Does an ELF (extremely low frequency) electric field come from the battery?

How's your DNA

Research results published in February 2002 in the *Journal of Cellular Biology* by Professor Theodore Litovitz and his team at the New York's Catholic University showed heavy use of a cell phone can disrupt the blood/brain barrier, and cause brain cancer, Alzheimer's, and other diseases by disrupting the body's

DNA repair system.[24] There are 334 website reporting the research of this scientist, so if you would like to learn more about his findings, there's lots of information available.

Is it a coincidence that the United States Center for Disease Control and Prevention confirm that Alzheimer's and other degenerative diseases, are considerably more common among patients whose job exposed them to emfs. I have friends and patients who suffer from this form of illness, and they have either worked in air traffic control or telecommunications, so please stop and think if anyone you know suffers from a neuro-degenerative illness, and mentally ask if their job involved exposure to electromagnetic rays. You could dowse and ask if their illness is linked to regular exposure to these energies.[25]

Is your blood/brain barrier down?

We hear regular mention of the blood/brain barrier, as certain chemicals are known to be able to enter this forbidden area, and research has shown emfs from cell phones are also able to open this security door, which protects the human brain from unwelcome intruders.

This fact was confirmed in 1977 by US Army researchers, and Swedish researchers have confirmed this fact. Professor Leif Salford and his team at University of Lund, exposed rats to emissions similar to a cell phone, and found within two minutes the rat's brain tissue opened up to allow proteins and toxins to enter.[1]

Results of a study in 2003, financed by the Swedish Council for Work Life Research, confirms that cell phones and wireless technology can damage young brains. This result was published by the US government's National Institute of Environmental Health Science, and could suggest an entire generation of teen-agers may become senile in middle age.

The team lead by Professor Leif Salford have spent 15 years studying a different angle from the rest of research results, which has mainly been on the possibility that cell phone use may heat the brain. Professor Salford's work has been on the ability of radiation to open the blood/brain barrier, and allow albumin to pass to the brain. The results consistently showed that neurons, which would not normally become senile until a person was over 60 years of age, could now occur in their thirties.[27]

This is a very serious statement and it is imperative that governments recognize this fact, and make everyone aware of the possible effects. It is no good in the future to diagnose thousands of young people suffering from ageing neuron problems, when it is too late to rectify the problems.

The blood/brain barrier is a cell layer situated between the blood which circulates in the brain, and the actual tissue of the brain. This barrier allows oxygen and nutrition inside the brain, while unwanted waste products and carbon dioxide are transported out of the brain, and so it is important that nothing disrupts the delicate balance of the blood/brain barrier as its work includes preventing several poisonous substances entering the brain. It is bad news and has serious implications, that scientists have found this door is not fool proof, and that these emissions from cell phones can open Nature's safety barrier, which is there to act as a security door to the brain.

Dowse and ask the following questions:

1. Can protein in the blood get through the blood/brain barrier?
2. Can albumin travel through the blood/brain barrier?
3. Can dementia caused by nerve damage be linked to protein in the blood/brain barrier?
4. Can Alzheimer's disease (directly linked to inflamed nerve cells) ever be caused by protein getting through the blood/brain barrier?
5. Can regular use of a cell phone cause premature ageing?

The blood/brain barrier has been shown to open as soon as you start a conversation on your cell phone, whether a short or long call. Scientists cannot yet tell how long an illegal substance stays in the human brain after a cell phone call, but it is known that in rats the albumen stayed present in their brain for several days after exposure.

Cancer research in Sweden

Results of research carried out by Mild and Hardell in Sweden on 1,600 cancer patients, who had all used a cell phone for up to 10 years, showed a very clear connection between cell phone users and cancerous tumours. A previous study by the same team of experts linked brain tumours to the use of analogue phones, and results of this recent research confirm the previous results, and this new research showed digital (GSM and DECT) cordless phones were also linked to an increase in the rate of tumours. Most of the tumours showed after 5 years use, but results also showed an increasing dose related response, within minutes of use per month, and the number of years of use.

Dowse:

1. Can regular use of an analogue mobile phone create cancerous tumours?
2. Can regular use of a DECT cordless phone increase the rate of cancerous tumours?

Results of this research is another reminder that we should treat this form of communication with great respect.[2]

Children's health and cell phones

Powerwatch Microwave News report interesting research by Professor Darius Leszczynski which shows a child's brain thickens as the child develops, and children under six years of age are very vulnerable to microwave radiation, from cell phones and other sources, as there is so little thickness for the energy held to travel through, to get to the child's brain.

1. A 5 year old child's skull is 0.5 mm thick.
2. A 10 year old child's skull is 1 mm thick.
3. An adult's skull is 2 mm thick.

These figures from the research done by the Radiation and Nuclear Safety Authority in Finland show clearly the difference in thickness between a young and a mature skull.[3] There are over 200 websites reporting the research results of this scientist' s work.

Both growing children and teenagers are vulnerable to electromagnetic rays as their brain has not yet completely developed, and so there is a risk that albumin, a water soluble protein which is normally refused entry into the brain, will be able to slip through the weak blood/brain barrier and cause damage.

Dr Gerard Hyland of the University of Warwick, with Dr Michael Klieeisen at the Neuro Diagnostic Research Institute in Marbella, Spain, and the neurophysiologist Professor Frank Schrober in Germany's combined research results showed beyond doubt that a 2 minute telephone call on a cell phone can alter a child's brain's natural electrical activity, for up to one hour after the 2 minute call was made.

A truly alarming result, and if this is the effect after a 2 minute call, then we must ask what devastating effect occurs after a 30 minute call?

Instead of using laboratory animals in the research, they chose to use humans, so this quietens the skeptics! The research showed the electrical activity of a child's brain is altered by using a cell phone, and that radio waves penetrate deep into the child's brain, not simply into an area around the ear, as some scientists believe.[4]

If a 2 minute call has an effect for up to an hour on the child's brain, then what happens to the children who make several calls during the school morning or lunch break? Does this mean they are more aggressive in the afternoon, or have difficulty absorbing information, or find it harder to concentrate? These results do make you wonder if cell phone calls are one of the reasons for an increase in unruly behaviour in schools, and why teachers are reporting they find it more and more difficult to control their pupils.

Dowse and ask questions about children's behaviour linked to cell phone use:

1. Is it possible for a 2 minute call on a cell phone to alter the electrical activity in a child's brain?
2. Can cell phone use influence a child's behaviour?
3. Can energy from cell phone calls disrupt a child's concentration?
4. Are a child's brain waves affected by regular exposure to radiation from a cell phone?

Dr Gerard Hyland reminds us that the child's brain waves are affected by emissions, and the alpha and delta brain waves of all children are constantly changing until the child reaches 12 years of age. He also reminds us that the child's immune system is usually not fully established, so the child is vulnerable to pulse radiation, and the research also showed emissions disrupt cells, leading to neurological problems, including sleep disruption and difficulty concentrating.[4]

That's pretty powerful stuff but there's more to come! Further research at the University of Utah by Professor Om Gandi shows that the body of a 5 year old child absorbs 50% more radiation than an adult, and a 10 year old child absorbs 10% more than an adult. These children are tomorrow's adults, so these facts are serious food for thought![5]

Yet another serious threat to school children is radiation which comes from their much loved cell phone, which is tucked into their belt around the child's waist, where it can be seen by friends, or else in their pocket, and although these phones are probably on standby, children don't realize that when a cell phones is on stand-by, it continues to give off radiation.

Dowse:

1. Can radiation from a cell phone regularly held against the body affect health?

2. Does a cell phone release radiation when on stand-by?
3. Does a 5 year old child absorb more radiation from a cell phone than an adult?

Protect the fetus

As well as worrying about the effect of cell phone radiation on our children, we must be aware of the threat to the fetus. We have been talking about our children's safety but what about the unborn child? questions being asked by aware scientists are 'Is it possible that pregnant women can unwittingly dissipate the heat going through their body from their cell phone to their unborn child? And if so, can it affect the baby's growth?' As yet I have not heard of any research on the fetus.

Nature protects the fetus from natural situations, but we are talking about a man-made threat. The fetus is protected while in the amniotic fluid in the womb, but as every part of the human body is vulnerable to cell phone radiation, it raises the question 'Could the fetus absorb any of the radiation travelling around the mother's body?'. So play it safe and don't take any risks with the life of the fetus, as medical experts tell us that 60% of everything which goes on our skin goes into the blood, and to the fetus.

The French government in March 2002 issued a warning to all pregnant mothers, and the advisory statement that pregnant women should ensure they keep their cell phone well away from their belly, and should not tuck their phone in their skirt. Another important point to remember is that no mothers should ever place the cell phone in the pram beside the child, as even when the phone is in stand-by mode, as it still gives off radiation.

Cleanse the energy of your pendulum, the dowse and ask:

1. Can the health of a fetus ever be affected by radiation from a cell phone regularly pressed against the mother's tummy?
2. Can the health of the baby be affected by a cell phone in their pram close to its body?

I have often cringed, when I have seen a young mum place her cell phone under the pram cover. It is the sort of thing you may do when you are not aware that your phone emits radiation while on stand by.

French scientists who studied the effects of radiation on 6,000 chicken embryos exposed during the 21 day incubation period, found they were 5 times more likely to die that the control group.[6] I hear you say 'Yes but this research is on chickens and not on humans', so my answer is 'Play it safe and don't take any risks with the life of the fetus'. Remember at least 60% of everything which goes on to the mother's skin, will go through to her bloodstream and to the unborn child.

Male sperm count and the cell phone

Can your cell phone disrupt your body's fertility mechanism? It is time to consider this implication, as research results from Hungary indicate that men who regularly carry or use a cell phone may unwittingly be reducing their sperm count by up to 30%, so reducing their chances of successful fertilization.

It certainly makes a lot of sense that a cell phone carried in the trouser pocket or tucked into the trouser belt can allow cell phone radiation to travel into the user's body. The Hungarian research involved 221 men over a period of 13 months, and research results showed the sperm of heavy cell phone users had a reduced count of almost 30%. This information may not be widely reported in the media, and yes, it was carried out in far away Hungary, but these results are well worth taking on board.[7]

Dowse:

1. Can regular exposure to cell phone radiation reduce sperm count?
2. Can a cell phone attached to the body pass radiation through the body?
3. Can regular exposure to cell phone radiation damage the male sperm?

Where does the radiation go in our head?

Where do you think the radiation goes, when it enters the head? Some of it is absorbed by the skin, and by the skull, but I hate to tell you that the rest goes into your brain, and the even worse news is that it then converts to heat. Are you cooking your brains? Dr Alan Preece, an expert from Bristol University, states that when the radiation gets to the brain it will be converted to heat. [8]

Wise words come from Robert Becker (twice nominated for a Noble Prize) in his book *The Body Electric* says the human species has changed its electromagnetic background, more than any other aspect of the environment, I think we can all agree with these words. He goes on to say 'the density of radio waves around us is now 100 million or 200 million times the natural level reaching us from the sun, nor is the end in sight'.[9] That's a pretty mind blowing fact, and one that's really difficult to comprehend, so is it any wonder that certain cancers are being linked to cell phone use?

Cancer and the cell phone

Can cell phone use cause cancer, that is the big question? Governments and the wireless industry say No, and some researchers say No, but many research scientists say Yes, so you have to believe what feels right to you. There are a great many different causes of cancer, so cell phone use is not the only culprit, but anyone who uses a cell phone regularly, who has a weakened immune system, is vulnerable to cancer.

We each have cancerous cells in our body, and a strong immune system keeps them under control, but research has shown that a few moments' exposure to cell phone radiation can transform a 5% active tumour into a 95% active tumour – alarming news.[10]

Traffic police victims

Cell phones are not the only tool capable of bombarding their user with radiation, as radar police found to their cost. A study was done by researchers for the National Fraternal Order of Police, after 164 cases of cancer were reported in those officers using a radar gun, and findings prompted the state of Connecticut to introduce a ban on hand-held radar guns.[11]

Research carried out in 1992 by the New York Health Research Foundation showed radiation from a low powered analogue mobile phone caused chemical changes in the brain of the user, which are similar to those found to be present in cancerous and pre-cancerous situations.[10]

It is very difficult to avoid radiation emitted by the cell phone when in use, as this energy, as well as leaking from the aerial, can also leak from several other areas of the phone.

Dowse and ask if electromagnetic radiation comes:

1. from the phone's screen,
2. from the phone's ear piece,
3. from the phone's key pad,

and remember the transmitter in your cell phone is right there in the handset.

Yet more brain tumours

Is it a coincidence that the number of brain tumour sufferers seems to be increasing, and that is official, as the National Cancer Institute in the US reports that in one year 185,000 brain tumours were diagnosed, and they also report that in the past thirty years the number has increased by 25%, and the worrying fact is that many of the sufferers are young people.[30]

Is it surprising that the Underwriters for Lloyds of London have point blank refused to insure cell phone manufacturers against damage to users' health? Due to reports of illness from heavy cell phone usage, plus the fact that numerous law suits have been filed against this mammoth industry, had forced this decision.[28]

This is the first time since humans have been misusing has been made since humans have been stupid enough to spend time holding a device against our head, while it is continuously beaming microwave emissions against the head and body. As well as an increase in brain tumours I have heard of an increase in lymphomas (cancerous tumours) in the neck of heavy users of cell phones, and among businessmen and telecommunications workers.

It is perfectly logical that the closer you hold your antenna to your head, the more radiation is absorbed, and these emissions are shown to affect brain functions including neuro-endocrine system, and an increase of 200% in neuro-epithelial tumours occurring on the same side of the brain as the cell phone was found.[12]

Should you ever suspect you have found a cancerous lump in your body, or are suffering unexplained headaches, by all means dowse to ask if you have a malignant tumour, but whatever the answer you receive, it is important to visit your doctor as soon as possible, and it's best not to tell him you dowsed the diagnosis, as he may not be impressed!

Let's now dowse a few questions about cancer and cell phone use, but first visualize a beam of pure light running through your pendulum to cleanse it of negative energy.

1. Can regular use of a cell phone create serious disruption of the blood/brain barrier?
2. Can regular cell phone use create serious deviations in chromosomes?
3. Can regular use of a cell phone cause a malignant tumour?

We don't really think through the process of cell phone use, and stop to consider what is actually happening when we use the cell phone. It is such a common sight to see someone making a call on their cell phone, and it looks so natural, that most of us don't deliberate on this user friendly gadget.

It's everything in moderation, so we must remind ourselves that the cell phone is the only piece of equipment in existence which is used frequently by over a billion people, and sends 40% of its radiation directly into the user's head.[13]

Cell phones can cause wrinkles!!

Can you believe it! Scientists are now warning us that regular cell phone use can create an ageing effect on the skin, and that's serious! Regular use of a cell phone means the low-level radiation heats up the cells in the body and this can damage the skin, which is the body's largest organ, and so create early lines and a haggard look!

This warning makes a lot of sense, as the body's natural ability to repair damaged cells is undermined by the effect of the 'heat shock' bombardment, and it is known that non-ionizing radiation has a biological effect on the body's cells.

Nature designed the human body to constantly make good damage to cells, but regular use of a cell phone means the body is receiving frequent doses of heat shock, so is unable to go into repair mode quickly enough.

The skin is not simply a layer of wrapping which holds all the bits in a tidy parcel, it is the largest organ in the body, and is really versatile, as it consists of two parts, the epidermis and the dermis, both layers containing nerve endings and several layers of cells. It protects the body from heat and helps to keep the internal body at a constant temperature, so it is easy to understand that damage to this important organ can be done when bombarded with radiation from a cell phone. Wrinkles come too early for most of us, so we don't need extra wrinkles donated by our cell phone.[14]

Dowse:

1. When regularly using a cell phone, can the radiation damage your skin?
2. Is the skin on the face sensitive to exposure to cell phone radiation?

No amount of health warnings seems to influence young people to reduce the use of their cell phones, but perhaps if they realize their good looks may be affected, that will be sufficient deterrent to reduce time spent using their cell phone.

There are roughly 000 million cell phone users worldwide so, in years to come, will millions of us become wrinkled and senile before our time, or even worse a cancer victims? What a thought![15]

Someone's listening

One of the big problems facing many people who suffer from the effects of exposure to radiation from cell phones is that there is nowhere to get assistance, but now a specialist unit has been set to establish a safety register. The Mobile Telephone Health Concern Registry (MTHCR) is there for you, and is a safety register available to all cell phone users, and if you want information a survey form is available online, which can be downloaded (http://www.health-concern.com) or use Google or another search engine) then you can fill it in at your leisure, and fax or mail it, or simply lift the telephone and give your information. It's so easy.

The MTHCR was launched by a leading expert in this field, Dr George Carlo, to help sufferers, and works to collate all confidential information received from anyone who believes their health symptoms are radiation related. This website is filling a great gap in the marketplace, as during the first week it was formed in March 2002, 62,000 sufferers visited this website, and that was without any advertising! In the first four months it received 400,000 visitors from all 50 US states, and from Europe and Asia, which is positive proof that there are a lot of people concerned about their health symptoms related to their cell phone use.[16]

Zapped on the train!

Are you being zapped on the train? It happens every day so is it happening to you? It can be absolutely infuriating when you are trying to relax and enjoy your book or magazine, and some anti-social character proceeds to conduct long telephone conversations on his cell phone.

Why do they always seem to talk in a loud voice, so it is almost impossible to shut their conversation from your mind? I had this experience last week when I went on a coach journey to the world famous, wonderfully spiritual town of Glastonbury. An inconsiderate passenger commenced using her cell phone to make calls on the journey, and on the return trip she spent the first half hour of the journey making one call after another, telling her friends what she had done on her day visit.

This sort of invasion of your thoughts is bad enough, but to make it worse, it's now been found in reliable research results that radiation levels from cell phones build up in train carriages and coaches. As well as your nerves being jangled by loud conversation, your entire body is being zapped by the electromagnetic fields from these offending cell phones.

Something has to be done about these journey destroyers, as research in Japan at Tohuku University by Tsuyoshii Hondou and by a team of scientists found using a cell phone in a confined space of a train carriage could have a serious health risk for other passengers, particularly the commuter who regularly is in this environment.

During the research electromagnetic radiation was measured in carriages and, although it is hard to believe, the levels were above International Committee of Non-Ionizing Radiation's Safety Limits, even when a small number of passengers used their phone. Why? Because the radiation was found to build up, so did not require a lot of passengers to be using their phone at the same time. Radiation from calls made by passengers at the start of the train journey remains in the compartment, and this builds up as the journey continues, and new passengers join the train and use their cells. Exposure to second-hand radiation from cell phones has, unlike cigarette and cigar smoke, so far managed to elude adverse publicity, but that's changing! When something is invisible, tasteless and odorless, it is easy to ignore it, but this research has demonstrated that short term doses of radiation are sufficient to affect the human brain wave pattern and memory.

The radiation of the microwaves from cell phones are trapped in the train carriage, as windows are often closed, and the emfs have nowhere to go, so quite simply, they bounce back off the train carriage's metal and glass surfaces, into the carriage. This silent enemy does not discriminate, and propagates through the area surrounding the antenna. These research results were published in the *Journal of the Physician Society of Japan*,[17] and a detailed report was published in *The New Scientist*.

Dowse:

1. Can a build up of radiation from cell phones used in train carriages affect the health of any passengers?
2. When radiation from cell phones is trapped in train carriages does it bounce off the metal walls and ceiling?

Cell phone radiation seems to be able to affect health in many unexpected ways, so as well as needing to be aware of the health hazard of cell phone use in train compartments, we should be aware of the danger of using a cell phone when filling the car with gasoline.

Caution – never use a cell phone in a gasoline station

Radio telephones can ignite petrol vapor and that's official! Do you ever read the signs in petrol stations, that give the Do's and Don't's. Watch out for the sign prohibiting the use of cell phones, as this should be taken seriously. Shell Oil company posters are shown in every one of their service stations advising customers to switch off their cell phone before entering the filling station, and not switching it on again until you have left the site. They state cell phones emit electricity, so if a spark occurs close to a petrol pump, a serious fire or explosion could follow.[26]

Cell phones should not be used in any inflammable atmosphere, as should a portable cell phone be dropped in an inflammable atmosphere, its batteries may cause a spark, and since petrol vapor tends to collect at floor level, the conditions are right for a fire.

Watch your blood pressure!

Why do some people seem to have an almost pathological emotional attachment to their cell phone, in that they feel vulnerable when separated from it, and get into a real panic if they forget to take their cell phone with them when they leave home., It almost appears to be an addiction like smoking or alcohol! Could there possibly be a hint of truth in this? Is it possible that the human brain can actually become addicted to this particular pulsed radiation? This addiction sounds as though it could give you serious blood pressure problems!

Does your cell phone raise your blood pressure? The answer is 'Yes', according to the results of research by Dr Braune and colleagues in Freiburg, Germany, whose research involved measuring volunteers' blood pressure regularly while using their phone, and also heart functions, and again when their cell phone was switched on. An increase in blood pressure levels of 10–15 mmHg was noted after the phone had been switched on for a very short time.[18]

Further research on blood pressure carried out in Poland by Dr Stanislaw Szmigielski which documented dose response increases in ECG abnormalities,[19] so if you suspect your blood pressure is affected by using your cell phone, it is probably not your imagination. Dowse and ask your pendulum the question:

1. Is my blood pressure altered when I use a cell phone?

Hypertension is often a symptom of blood pressure, so if you suspect your blood pressure is higher than it should be for your age group, then dowse and ask your pendulum

2. Is my blood pressure level too high?

From blood pressure we move on to talk about melatonin.

Where's my melatonin gone?

Melatonin is a naturally occurring hormone in the body, and is a powerful anti-oxidant, so can it be suppressed by man-made emissions? Swedish research showed melatonin levels in office workers decreased during the day in those who used computers and cell phones, but remained stable on days when not exposed to emfs.

This crucial neuro-hormone protects the body's DNA against attack from free radicals, and destroys cancerous cells. It also regulates the body's important endocrine organs, and stimulates the immune system, so suppression of melatonin sets up a chain reaction which creates far reaching damage to health, disrupts sleep pattern, and speeds up the ageing process.

If you would like to learn more about the wonders of melatonin, how it can improve your sleep, and delay the ageing process, I recommend the book *The Melatonin Miracle, How it Can Help You* by Dr Walter Pierpaoli and Dr William Regelson with Carol Colman.[20]

The pineal gland is believed in the East by Hindus to be what new-age therapists in the West call the Third Eye, or the Brow Chakra. It controls your body's clock, is light sensitive, and guides your body to know when it is time to be awake. It also tells it when it is time to shut down and go to sleep, so any disruption of this gland affects the body's melatonin level, and that has far reaching effects.

Any imbalance in the body's melatonin levels are linked to mood swings, and to immune system illnesses lupus, ME, aids and cancer. The medical profession now recognize that the pineal gland's balance is linked to high blood pressure and heart problems, so any suggestion that radiation from a cell phone can disrupt the melatonin level in the body, and alter the smooth running of the pineal gland, is extremely serious.

Texting – the latest addiction!

We all know about drug, nicotine, alcohol, food, and sex addiction, but a new category has been added to this list, as we now have Text Addiction! Yes folks, it sounds hard to believe, but a number of people are becoming addicted to their text messages, so the more they use text messaging, the more they cut down on their communication skills, and are now finding that texting is easier than talking face to face with people.

This fact is confirmed by the Cell Data Association who report that, in the UK alone, 2.1 billion text messages were sent in the month of March 2004, which was a 25% increase on the same month the previous year. There are over 69 million text messages sent every single day in the UK, and when you add that figure to texts sent in other countries, it's not hard to believe that some folks are becoming addicted to this form of distance chat.[21]

The simple way to cure this latest addiction is to visit a detox clinic. Can you imagine the scenario where you have to ask your boss for time off to visit a 'texting detox clinic!' Sadly this is happening. So how does this sad state of affairs occur? Do electro-magnetic fields from the cell phone somehow stimulate a release of endorphins? When you ask friends and children about texting, it is amazing how many people admit they send a number of text messages each day. This latest addiction is becoming a serious issue, but the good news is those who recognize they have a prob-lem can receive treatment at specialist clinics.[22]

A well known addiction clinic in London has recently reported an increase in the number of patients showing compulsive beha-viour towards their cell phone dependence. So are some people spending several hours each day texting, or playing games on their cell phone? Is this source of isolation a sign that deep down they feel a need to make contact with someone? Or is this a way of contacting people without having to interact, and speak to them face to face?

What is happening to the art of conversation? Texting on the cell phone enables users to get into brief conversation with lots of people, and not give away much about themselves, so is this a bad pattern that is becoming established, or is it a passing craze?[23]

Dowse:

1. Can regular texting on a cell phone create addiction to texting?
2. Do the emfs given off by the cell phone release endorphins?

3. Can regular texting over several years reduce conversation skills?

Are safety standards really safe?

You may well ask 'Don't cell phones comply with current safety standards?' The answer is Yes, but results of some research studies suggest it seems to be time to reassess the standard.

At present safety standards for cell phones are based simply on the thermal (heating)effect on human tissue, but the European Commission Public Health Directorate has confirmed that microwave radiation from cellular phones produces a heat that affects both the body's organs and tissues.

One thing we all have in common today is that we live in a dense electro-smog! When I was a teenager in my home town of Glasgow, smog and fog were commonplace. In those days it was a nasty thick pea soup colour, which clung to your skin and your clothes. It was so dense that on many occasions we could lose the person standing a yard away, and when walking home from work we would have to hold hands, while feeling walls and counting gates, to guide us home.

Those days are long gone, and I thought the smog was a thing of the past, but alas, those dirty Glasgow, London, and New York, smogs have been replaced by a much more harmful invisible smog, created by cell phones, base stations, and power lines.

Whatever the dose of radiation from a cell phone, this is doubled if you use the phone in an area of poor reception, as the phone has to work twice as hard, so uses maximum strength energy in an effort to connect you to your call. In this situation, always hold your phone away from your head when dialing the number.

Your phone has a Special Absorption Rate (SAR)

Each cell phone has a radio transmitter and a receiver, and is designed so that it does not exceed the limit of exposure to radio frequency energy recommended by the International Commission on Non-Ionizing Radiation Protection (ICNIRP). The SAR of your cell phone may be on view, but is quite likely to be found in an inconspicuous part of the phone, or in the user's manual. The SAR is the unit used to measure the level of radio frequency absorbed by your body, while making a cell phone call. The scale is either in units or watts per kilogram (W/kg) or alternatively in milliwatts per gram (mW/G) so watch out for those letters. Your local cell phone retailer will be able to answer your questions on the SAR of your cell phone.

A book written by world respected scientist Dr George Carlo will give you answers to many questions raised, which may have been raised by facts I have quoted about the health effects of electromagnetic fields from cell phones: *Cell Phones' Invisible Hazards in the Wireless Age: An insider's alarming discoveries about cancer and genetic damage*, Carroll & Graf.2001.[29]

Please remember that some scientists tell us there are no harmful effects from regular cell phone use, but so far no scientist has proved that they are safe to use, and will not damage health!

Summary

In this chapter, I have tried to give you an insight into the type of research being done on the effects of cell phone use on our health, and particularly on the health of our children. The medical profession realize that a child's brain is not fully developed until they reach puberty, so this fact is cause for concern.

As some research results show that a child's body allows electromagnetic fields from their cell phone to travel through their delicate blood/brain barrier, into their brain, this is much more serious that it appears. The blood/brain barrier is the brain's safety door, which protects the brain from all invading toxins, so to my way of thinking, if this door is opening when it should be closed, it could allow unwelcome toxins to enter. We do not yet know the long term effects of these toxins on the brain.

246

Another threat is that if the child has a weak immune system, the open door could allow a 'negative entity' to enter, which could affect either the child's health or behaviour pattern.

As certain reputable scientists have shown that this important door opens at the beginning of a conversation, and stays open until the call has ended, this could mean that during a long call, there is unrestricted entry to any type of energy or toxin. This is particularly applicable to teenagers who enjoy spending hours talking to friends, whom they may have seen half an hour before hand!

Doctors and scientists cannot tell us what happens to the 40% of the radiation from the cell phone, which some scientists state goes into the brain. What happens to it when it gets there? We know it turns to heat, so are we slowly frying our brains? Not a nice thought.

I have also talked about the danger of keeping your cell phone tucked in your belt, or in your pocket, also the possible danger to the fetus, or to a baby when the cell phone is in its pram. Also I've reminded you of the danger of using your cell phone to make a call, while you are in a garage filling your car up with gas.

Another hazards of the electromagnetic rays from cell phones is that these rays bounce off the metal walls of a train compartment, as they travel around the train compartments, and are liable to land on the nearest passenger. Perhaps even worse is the suggestion that regular use of your cell phone can increase wrinkles on your face, now that is really serious!! If you know of anyone who is concerned that their health has been affected by regular use off a cell phone, either in their job or because they enjoy chatting on their phone, then please tell them about the Cell Telephone Health Concern Registry, as they can receive help.

Text addiction is becoming a recognized illness which requires treatment, so if you find that you want to use your cell every time you have a few free minutes, then it's time to reassess and ask yourself if this is becoming a habit? A good deterrent is to remind yourself that excess use of a cell phone can block the melatonin going into your body. When over a period of time, the levels of this important age reversing, sex enhancing and disease fighting hormone are depleted, you may begin to receive warning signs!

Cell phones are an invaluable tool which can make life so much easier, but remember it's everything in moderation, and so I ask you to please discourage your children from spending hours on their beloved cell, chatting to their friends. This tool has opened up a whole new world for children, as they can make calls, and say absolutely whatever daft, or rude, words they choose, knowing their folks can't hear the conversation. Encouraging a child to reduce their use of their most prized possession is not easy, but I firmly believe it is the right thing to do.

I am not a scientist, so I have tried hard in this chapter to be unbiased when reporting results of researched facts, and any facts not referenced are my opinion.

Endnotes

1. US Army, 'Blood/Brain Barrier, Blasting Through', The 1977. Swedish Research, 1992, *Greenhealth Watch News*, 1–8. Ibid *Microwave News*, 1.11.99.
2. Hardell, L., and Mild, Kjell Hansson, *Bioelectromagnetics*, Vol. 24 No. 3, pp. 152–159, 2003; *Int. J. Oncol.* Vol. 22 No. 2, pp. 399–407, 2003. *Electromagnetic Therapy*, Vol. 14 No .1, 2003, 'New Mild Study Confirms Previous Cancer Link'.
3. *Powerwatch Microwatch News*, June 19 2000, 'Mobile Phones Blood/ Brain Barrier Damage Fears Confirmed'. www.powerwatch.org.uk
4. Kliessen, Dr Michale, *The Ecologist*, Vol. 32 No. 5, June 2002, 'A 2 Minute Call Alters Child's Brain' .
5. Gandi, Om, 'Children Absorb More', University of Utah *Environment & Health News*, 2000, 4.4.(6763), *Electromagnetic Hazard and VDU News* 1.12.99 p. 6.
6. Best, Simon (editor), *Electromagnetic Hazard and Therapy News, WDDTY*, Vol. 9 No. 5, August 1999, Chicken Embryos.
7. Philips, Alasdair, *Electromagnetic Hazard and Therapy News*, Vol. 15 No. 1, 2004.
Dr Imrie Fejes, *Powerwatch News*, 'Regular Use of a Mobile Phone Can Reduce Sperm Count by 30%'. Research carried out at Obstetrics and Gynecology Dept., University of Szeged, Hungary.

Do electromagnetic fields from cell phones damage your health?

Published at the International Scientific Conference of Fertility Experts on June 29 2003 at
The European Society of Human Reproduction and Embryology's annual conference.

8. Preece, Alan, 'Memory Loss', *Greenhealthwatch News. Electromagnetic Hazard and Therapy,* 1.11.95, Bristol University.

9. Becker, Dr Robert O., and Seldon, Gary, *The Body Electric,* Harper Paperbacks, 1998. ISBN 0688069711.

10. '5% to 95% Active Tumors' *Environmental and Health News,* 'Mobile Telephone Sizzlers', The Environment and Health Trust 1395–1396, Powerwatch UK, 1.5.96.
Ibid. *Nexus New Times* 1.10.96.
Ibid. *The Times,* London 3.5.96 (626).

11. Workers Health International Newsletter No. 34. December 1992, 'Radar Gun Hurt Police Officers', Wyncosh, New York. ISBN 71688972100.

12. Mercola, Dr Joseph '200–300% Increase in Neuroepithelial Tumors. Concern About Cellular Telephone Use and Human Health', Arch 2002. www.mercola.com

13. *The Ethical Consumer,* November 1999, 'Brain Tumors on Side of Head Phone Used' 'Frying Your Brains'.

14. *Skin. The Atlas of Anatomy.* Introduced by Weston Trevor MD, MRC, GP. Marshall Cavendish Books, 1985. ISBN 0863074162

15. Mercola, Dr Joseph, 'Mobile Telephones Brain Tumors', Uhlig Robert. www.mercola.com

16. Carlo, Dr George, 'Mobile Phone Health Registry'. RCR Wireless News. http://www.health-concern.org

17. Maisch, Don, EM Facts Consultancy, PO Box 96, North Hobart 7002, Tasmania, 'Trains Trap Mobile Phone Radiation', BBC Online Health 1.5.02.

18. *The Lancet,* pp. 1857–1858, June 20 1998, 'Cell Phones and Health' Radio Frequency Safe. www.rfsafe.com/article 2592.html.
19. Blake-Levitt, B, *Wave-Guide,* Guest Essay. 'A Clear Call. America Unplugged'.
'A Guide to the Wireless Issue', Szmigielski findings. http://www.wave-guide.org

20. Pieroaoli, Dr Walter, and Regelson, Dr William, with Colman, Carol, *The Melatonin Miracle and How it can Help you,* Pocket Books, 1995. ISBN 0671534351

21. Ananova Ltd, *Ananova News,* 'UK Will Send 23 Billion Text Messages this Year'. http://www.ananova.com/news/story/sm_858377.html/menu= news. technology.mobilephones

22. Maisch, Don, EM Facts Consultancy. *The Mercury,* Tasmania. Source: *The Courier and Mail* by English, Ben.
23. *Wired News,* October 25 2003, 'Tech. Addicts Need Textual Healing'. http://www.wired.com/news/wireless/0,138,60936,00.html
24. Litovitz, Professor Theodore, *Journal of Cellular Biology,* February 2003 Worthington, Amy, New York Catholic University. http://www.cam. net.uk
25. United States Center for Disease Control and Preservation.
26. Shell International Ltd.
27. Maisch, Don, EM Facts Consultancy.
    Reidlinger, Robert, *The Province,* October 14 2003.
28. Safe, R. F., 'Insurance Problems Facing Mobile Phone Manufacturers'. http://www.rfsafe.com/article 2628.html
29. Information on RF Exposure/Specific Absorption Rate (SAR) MT50 Page 1. my-siemens.http://www.siemens-mobile.com.mysiemens/cda/ channel/standard/popup/sar/o,1175
30. 'Brain Cancer Rates in US Increase 25%'. http://www.rfsafe.com/article2628

14

Dowsing earth energies, water and spirits

Dowsing to find fresh water

Dowsing for water could be a very useful skill in years to come, with threats of terrorists poisoning drinking water supplies, and experts telling us that the world will be short of water, and that in fact future wars will be fought over water, rather than oil. Now is the time to learn the importance of dowsing to establish that the underground water is fresh and reachable!

We know that a very large percentage of the water on this planet is ocean, and a small amount is drinking water, and we are told by the experts that much of the world's drinking water is contaminated. Also a great deal of underground water supplies are also contaminated, so perhaps in years to come we will be so glad that we learned to dowse!

Dowsing for water is something we associate with farmers drilling bore holes, and it does seem extremely unlikely that under normal circumstances we will ever need to dowse to find supplies of fresh water. As there are so many disasters prophesied for the planet, it is well worth knowing how to find water, and the important questions to ask, should an emergency ever arise.

When you search for underground water, as well as dowsing to find the water supply, you must establish the depth of the water supply, the flow and capacity, and the quality of the water, whether it is stagnant or drinkable, before you start to drill or dig.

To locate underground water it is preferable to use rods instead of a pendulum, as the pendulum is difficult to control if there is any wind blowing. Hold the rods in your hands and walk over the area, while mentally asking the rods to show you a sign, when they cross over underground water. Don't be very surprised if you find that the rods will give a violent jolt when you are walking over water, as rod movement is usually abrupt, so leaving you in no doubt of the answer.

Now the fun starts of trying to establish if the water suits your requirements, as perhaps there is another underground stream nearby, which has a greater capacity, and is nearer the surface. By dowsing the following questions, you will get a fairly clear picture of the quality of the water. Ask the following questions:

1. The most important question is: Is it practical to bore here? You could find that there is solid rock between the water and the earth's surface, and it is not practical to drill in this area.

2. To establish the depth of the water, ask if it is more than 50 ft below the earth's surface? If the answer is 'Yes', then ask if it is more than a 100 ft below the earth's surface? If you are intending to dig for water, you must keep looking, until you find a supply which is nearer the surface, as there is no point in wasting valuable energy. If you are drilling for water, you can ask the rods if the water is more than 200 ft underground.

3. Having located the water supply, you must now establish the quality of the water, as it may be contaminated, and so harmful to health. Dowse to ask if the water is contaminated, as this would be a useless source of water.

4. Once you have found a supply of water near the surface which is not contaminated, before progressing further you must dowse and check the capacity of the flow, as when you dowse for water you probably forget to stipulate the size of the stream, so the water could simply be a little stream with a trickle of water, and not what you require.

I understand that the average family in the USA needs four or five gallons per minute to cover demands of washing machines, dishwashers, showers, swimming pools etc, but if times are hard and we are struggling to find water to survive, then we would be grateful for one gallon per minute!

When dowsing for water, it is essential that you sit down and make a list of requirements, before you start dowsing, so that you find a supply which is right for your needs, as it is very easy to waste time and energy, and suffer frustration. You will probably go through life without ever needing to search for underground water, but if you do find yourself in this situation, I hope you will remember these point, and find them helpful.

Your drinking water

Are you uneasy about drinking water from the cold water tap in your home or office? Or does it have a strong smell which concerns you? You can dowse the quality of your drinking water and establish its life force, as it could be very low.

Either fill a glass with tap water and hold the pendulum over it, then dowse and ask on a 'one to ten' scale to be shown the life force energy of the water. Many dowsers prefer to dowse over the object concerned, and the alternative is to simply hold your pendulum without it being over water, and ask the following questions, after you have cleansed the energy of your pendulum.

Is the life force of the cold water in the tap above 5 on a 1–10 scale?

You should receive a 'Yes' sign, and then ask if it is above 8 on the scale. If the life force is low, you can ask the pendulum to please cleanse the water of negative energy, chemical residue and any harmful bacteria, and raise the life force energy to its original level. Make sure you ask to be shown the 'Yes' sign when the job has been completed.

Before I drink a glass of tap water, I always hold my hands over the water and mentally run white light through the water to cleanse it of all negative energy, chemical residue and harmful bacteria. I have had so much proof that this little exercise works, as most people who have drunk the water, and have not known that I do some magic on it, say how wonderful it tastes. Please experiment as I am certain you will be delighted with the results.

Raymond Grace in his book *The Future is Yours so do Something About it* teaches a very useful method of clearing pollution from water. He advises asking the pendulum to please scramble the frequency of pollutants in the water, and then adjust the frequency to that of pure water. I use a similar method and have found it effective, so start experimenting, and you will find your drinking water tastes fresher.

Raymond also tells his readers that this exercise can be done to clear the pollution energy from water in oceans and rivers. This will have a knock on effect, as water has a memory and so remembers every thing and every energy it has been through since the beginning of time.[1]

A lot of fascinating research has been carried out on water memory by French scientist Jacques Benveniste, although science has been slow to accept the research results. If you would like to learn more about this fascinating subject, I recommend Michel Schiff's book *The Memory of Water* published by Thorsons.

You can also dowse the following questions about your drinking water, or water from a stream. It is tempting to drink fresh water from a stream, but have any chemicals run off the land, and contaminated the water?

1. Does the water contain any harmful chemical residue?
2. Has the water been contaminated with fluoride?
3. Are there harmful bacteria in the water?
4. Are any dangerous organophosphates in the water?
5. Is there lead in my drinking water?
6. Does the water contain mercury?
7. Does the water contain arsenic?
8. Does the drinking water contain lead?
9. Does water have a memory?

By asking a few questions about the quality of the drinking water, you will get peace of mind, and know your water is good quality.

Arsenic in your drinking water

Arsenic comes in two forms, organic and inorganic, and the most commonly found is the inorganic which is the most dangerous to health. Each year around six million tons of arsenic are pumped into our atmosphere and some of it is found in water.

The US Environmental Protection Agency report that arsenic in drinking water is linked to many serious illness, and the International Agency for Research on Cancer, which is a division of the WHO, also states arsenic is a known cause of cancer in humans, so dowsing to check that your drinking water does not contain arsenic is a worthwhile exercise![2]

A representative from AquaMD, the water testing division of the American Water Council, advises us that a one-time oral dose of 60,000 ppm is sufficient to kill a healthy person. This sounds a high dose, but in actual fact the amount is only the size of 1/50 the weight of a one penny coin.[3]

Arsenic is a colourless, tasteless and odourless poison, so we have no way of knowing when this poison is present in our drinking water. So how does it get into the water supply? This poison is a part of nature, and occurs in certain rocks and soil, and is also found in the atmosphere from such industrial processes as coal mining and smelting. Also it is used in wood preservatives and pesticides, so finds its way into the soil, to rivers, and down to underground water.

Arsenic is known to be linked to many serious illnesses, so it is important to dowse to establish if it is present in your drinking water. In the above list of dowsing questions, I did ask you to dowse for the presence of arsenic in drinking water, and if you received a 'Yes' answer to the presence of this unwelcome poison, then it is important to establish the amount present, as the government has a legal limit on the amount allowed in drinking water. Dowse and ask the pendulum if arsenic in your drinking water is above the government's recommended legal limit?

Lead in drinking water is bad news

Many scientists report that one of the biggest environmental threats to the health of children in the United Sates and other countries is lead, as levels are high in many homes. The Pollution Information website tells us almost half a million pre-school children in the US are known to have sufficient lead in their blood to reduce intelligence.[4]

Dowsing will confirm the presence of lead, which is known to increase certain learning difficulties including attention span, and damage the child's brain and nervous system, so where is this harmful poison to be found in the home?

1. In old paint work with flaking paint.
2. Contaminated dust.
3. Lead in garden soil.

Take a close look at the paintwork in your home and office, as any paint which has been there for several years could contain lead, so dowse and ask the pendulum if the paint contains lead. Also dowse and ask if any flaking paint in your home contains lead. Now have a look at outhouses and if you find flaking paint, then dowse to check for lead content. Lead can often be found in water and as this is a neurotoxin it can damage health, so dowsing to establish its presence is important.

Research in Israel at the Shaare Zedekk Medical Center, Jerusalem, showed that lead can travel through the blood/brain barrier into the brain, and can disrupt neurological systems and upset the body's calcium.[5]

In Holland researchers at Vrije Universiteit of Amsterdam found lead in the body of children was linked to impulsive behaviour and attention deficit problems. Further research results showed the myelin sheath is vulnerable to lead, as excess lead upsets electrochemical impulses, and they are no longer coordinated.[5]

The Franklin Institute report that 16% of delinquency is caused by excess lead in the body, so with these research results warning us about the harmful effect of lead on children, it is important to dowse, to ensure it is not affecting the health of you or your children.

Dowse for mercury in your drinking water

Mercury is recognized as a health hazard and comes from several sources including amalgam dental fillings and coal burning plants, and is the second most toxic substance on earth, after plutonium. An excellent example of the harmful effects of mercury is that the amount of mercury contained in a family thermometer is sufficient to pollute a small lake. Many people in the last decade have had their amalgam fillings removed, as they leaked mercury, which is linked to certain 'ME type' symptoms. If you would like to learn some facts about autism linked to lead, have a look at Dr Jospeh Mercola's excellent website (www.mercola.com) as he has an abundance of information to offer, backed by research.

Dowse and ask:

1. Are any of your amalgam dental fillings leaking mercury? If you receive a 'Yes' answer, then find a dentist who is experienced in removing amalgam fillings, as it is a specialist job.
2. Is a harmful level of mercury present in your drinking water?
3. Is mercury present in the drinking water at my children's school?

And don't forget to ask if it is present in drinking water at your workplace.

A 'Confidential Report' from the US Center for Disease Control states that within the first three months of life, exposure to more than 62.5 micrograms of mercury can more than double the child's risk of developing autism. More information on this upsetting subject is available from www.autismfraud.com[6]

Now it's time to talk about bottled drinking water, as quality varies considerably.

Bottled drinking water

Many folks on their weekly visit to the supermarket purchase a week's supply of bottled water, as they are uneasy about giving their family tap water, but are they doing the right thing?

The quality of bottled water varies considerably depending on its source, and I understand that some bottling plants receive supplies of water from several different sources, which are all added to one tank, so perhaps dowsing the quality of the bottled water is a wise idea!

There is a school of thought which believes that the plastic bottle gives off a harmful chemical which is bad for heath, so that's another question to dowse.

1. Ask if the water in the bottle contains the right amount of minerals.
2. Has all of the water in the bottle come from the same source?
3. Does the water contain any negative energy?
4. Is the bottled water more beneficial to health than your tap water?
5. Does the plastic bottle contaminate the water?
6. Does the plastic material give off harmful chemicals?

You will probably get some very interesting answers from your pendulum, and in some cases you will find the tap water contains more minerals than the bottled water. Remember to cleanse the pendulum before dowsing the water.

I want now to tell you some facts about geopathic stress, as it has been mentioned regularly throughout the book, and if you are not already familiar with this energy, you must be wondering what sort of energy can do so much health damage?

Finding geopathic stress

Geopathic stress is the name given to negative energy which rises from rivers and streams deep underground, and is known to weaken the immune system of anyone who is sleeping or working over any of these energy bands. So what exactly is this mysterious vibration, which is associated with so many health problems? Dowsing is the quick, easy and reliable way to locate geopathic stress lines, and this technique is used by many builders in some parts of Austria and Germany to establish the presence of these lines. In parts of these countries it is a requirement of planning permission that new buildings are built on sites where the sleeping area is clear of geopathic energy.

These rays from subterranean running water are contaminated on their way to the earth's surface, by negative energy they meet on their journey, including certain mineral concentrations, weak electromagnetic fields and cavities of negative energy.

This is not a new phenomenon, as research proving the harmful effects on health of exposure to these rays was carried out 75 years ago in Austria, and since then much research has been carried out in parts of Germany, where results all confirm this energy is bad news. In 1929 Gustav Freiherr von Pohl dowsed a complete village in Austria, and proved without doubt that illness is linked to exposure to geopathic energy. He wrote a book *Earth Currents' Causative Factor of Cancer and Other Diseases*, detailing his findings, and creating awareness of this harmful energy.[8]

Children and geopathic stress (GS)

Austrian school teacher Kathe Bachler received a research grant from the School of Education in Salzburg to research the connection between academic failure in children and exposure to geopathic rays. In her book *Earth Radiation*, she shows many diagrams of these rays crossing the bed, in relation to the child's illness. Certainly a book I recommend, for anyone who wants to know more about the harmful effects of geopathic stress.[9]

Geopathic stress affects the immune system of anyone exposed to it, whether a very young baby or an elderly person, so dowsing will establish if you or your child are sleeping over one of these harmful lines.

Young babies are very aware of these negative rays and will often shuffle instinctively to one end of their cot to avoid them, and when the mother places them back in the middle of the cot, next time she looks at them, she realizes they have again shuffled to a corner, where they do not look the least bit comfortable. Sudden Infant Death Syndrome is probably the most devastating experience parents will ever have to face, and Rolf Gordon has found that when he dowsed sites where these tragedies have occurred, the cot is situated on a GS line, so the immune system is very weak.[1] I have reason to believe that sleeping over GS energy can be a cause of some babies and toddlers having a violent reaction to vaccinations, so if your child had adverse reaction to a vaccination, dowse to ask if he is sleeping over a GS line.

Toddlers will often climb out of their bed and sleep on the floor to avoid these lines. This is not usually because they are being naughty or adventurous, it is simply that they know instinctively that they should move away from this energy line. You will often hear parents say that no matter how often they place the sleeping child back in bed, and tuck the blankets around him, next time they visit the room, he is curled up asleep on the floor. If you know of anyone whose child prefers to sleep on the floor instead of his nice warm bed, get dowsing as the child could be sleeping over one of these powerful negative lines!

Animals and geopathic stress

Animals also react strongly to these lines, and dogs will often refuse to sleep in their bed, if it is placed over one of these energy lines, while cats have the complete opposite reaction, as they love this energy vibration, and will make every effort to sleep on a line. Some time ago I was asked to clear a GS line from a barn in Scotland as the cows in stalls on one side of the barn were milking well, whereas the cows on the other side of the barn were not yielding a good supply of milk. On checking the barn, I found a powerful negative energy line running down one side of the building, where the cows were experiencing milking problems, and once these lines had been neutralized, the cows began to yield a normal milk flow, and seemed content.

At the same farm I was asked to give healing to a prize bull who looked very sad, his coat was dull and his sparkle had gone, but once I had cleared his pen of GS energy, and given him a blast of healing energy, he was able to attend the agricultural show and won first prize.

Any time your animals look unhappy, or are adamant about where they want to sit or sleep, then dowse to check if their bed is on a GS line, as they will thank you!

Symptoms of GS

How often do you hear someone saying 'Ever since I moved to this house I seem to get one illness after another?' and others who say 'I've tried everything and nothing seems to work'. These are sure signs of the presence of this negative energy. We don't read much about GS in the media, and if we ask our doctor about it, we find they have never heard of, and yet the World Health Organization has recognized the effects of geopathic stress for over a decade. They estimate this energy is present in 30% of offices, hotels, institutions and industrial premises.[10] It is blamed for symptoms including headaches, tension between staff, respiratory infections, depression, and more serious illnesses including ME (myalgic encephalomyelitis) and cancer.

Do you waken in the morning feeling tired when you should be feeling energetic? Do you waken up feeling as though you have had a night on the tiles, when in fact you've had a dull evening in front of the television? Get dowsing, as these are often warning symptoms that you are exposed to GS lines, for several hours each day or night.

261

Perhaps your desk at the office is over one of these GS lines, or your favourite chair, where you sit watching television for six or seven hours each day, or your bed could be sited over a GS line. Whether you are exposed to these lines during the day or at night when asleep, they will weaken your immune system, so that you are susceptible to illness.

I recommend Rolf Gordon's book *Are You Sleeping in a Safe Place?*, which gives lots of helpful and practical advise on the history of this harmful energy and how to get rid of it.

Before dowsing for GS, please ensure you have placed a cloak of protection around your aura, and cleansed your pendulum. To find GS lines outside in the garden it is preferable to use rods, as they are not affected by the wind.

Always remember to ask to be shown a sign when you cross over GS lines Never ask to be shown a sign when you cross over energy lines, if you are searching for GS lines, as you will get the wrong answer, since there are different types of energy lines. Start by asking the pendulum:

1. Are there any geopathic stress lines under my home?
2. If the answer is 'Yes', ask: Is there more than one GS line under my home?
3. You can then ask the question: Are more than two GS lines under my home?
4. If there are two lines, it is important to ask if they are crossing under your home, as there is double strength negative energy over the crossing point.
5. You can ask if the lines are running parallel.
6. If the pendulum has confirmed that GS is present, but confused you by saying no lines are under your home, then please ask if the GS energy is rising in a spiral?
7. You can ask a series of questions to establish the depth of the stream, e.g.: Is the depth underground more than 50 ft, 100 ft, 200 ft ...
8. Ask: Are you working over a GS line? (Your desk at your workplace could be sited over one of these lines.)

9. Is anyone in your home sleeping over a GS line?
10. Are any of your animals sleeping over GS lines? This could be the family dog, or animals in pens, or even your chickens. Should your chickens have a problem laying the normal number of eggs, then check their living area as GS could be the problem.

Ley lines

We often hear a person say 'Oh my house has wonderful energy as it is built on a ley line' which is true, if it is the site of a positive ley line, but these lines can also be negative, and give off very powerful negative energy, which can affect health. Ley lines can often be as wide as 30 ft, which means that this heavy energy will fill the entire room, so it is important to get the energy balanced once its presence is detected.

Nobody really knows the history of ley lines; some experts say they are lines which link churches and villages, and have been made by constant traffic of people walking to church over centuries. Other people believe ley lines are universal energy lines placed there by the Creator, and have been present since the beginning of time. Instead of people making the energy imprint by walking the areas, it is thought our ancestors were able to sense this powerful energy, and built their church and homes on these good energy lines.

Living over a positive ley line is a wonderful experience. But living over a negative line is a nightmare, particularly when it is combined with the presence of GS lines making a building a very unpleasant place to live, so being aware of their presence is vital to good health.

Dowse and ask:

Is my home sited on a ley line?

If you receive a 'Yes' answer, then ask: Is my home sited on a positive ley line? If you receive a 'No' sign, then ask if your home is on the site of a negative ley line.

Should you receive confirmation that your home or work place is on a negative or black ley line, then the answer will most probably ring true, as this powerful negative energy creates tiredness, low immune system and constant feeling of being below par.

You can ask the pendulum to clear the negative energy and balance the energy of the ley line but, before doing so, remember to cleanse your pendulum, clear your energies and place a blanket of protection around you. If you believe in the earth spirits, you can ask their assistance.

The world has several energy grids which surround the planet like a net. The best known are the Hartman lines and the Curry lines. These go in different directions, but both alternate negative and positive, so by dowsing, and asking to be shown a sign when you cross over a negative energy line, you could be shown one of these lines, as the grids are close enough together that there are several of them crossing each room.

If you are fascinated by this subject, and would like to learn more facts about ley lines, I recommend an excellent book *The Sun and the Serpent* by Hamish Miller and Paul Broadhurst. This book is the story of their journey dowsing the St Mary's line, which runs across the south of England, it is full of invaluable and interesting information, and reading it would be time well spent.[7]

Once you have established the presence of GS energy, it is possible to clear it by using the pendulum to do the work. Sit down and check you have a protective cloak around you, and that you have cleansed the energy of your pendulum, then ask the pendulum to please clear the GS energy from your home, and replace it with good energy. Don't forget to ask your pendulum to please show you the 'Yes' sign when it has been cleared. This exercise could take a few minutes, but you will never regret the time spent clearing this energy, as your health, and the health of your family and pets, will improve, as the immune system of anyone sleeping over these lines would be weakened.

Radon gas – the silent enemy

Radon gas claims many lives each year, so it is important to know if this gas is invading your home or office. and dowsing is a quick way to find out if radon gas is rising up from under the building.

This odourless radioactive gas, which gives no warning of its presence, is a proven Class A carcinogen so deserves great respect, and its presence should never be ignored. It is known to cause genetic disease and lung cancer, and BBC News Online reported results of findings by the Imperial Cancer Research Fund, which showed that 1,800 of the 37,000 deaths each year from lung cancer in the UK are directly linked to exposure to this gas, and in the USA figures are many times higher.[11]

The health effects are recognized by health authorities in many countries including the USA, UK and Scandinavia, and testing kits are offered to householders living in areas where this colourless gas is known to be present. Radon gas rises from the ground, and is formed by natural activity below the earth's surface. It is produced by the natural decaying of uranium, and is found in areas where there is granite or limestone.

This gas is the heaviest gas known to man, is eight times heavier than air, and when breathed into the lungs, particles of decay lodge in the lungs, where they emit alpha, beta and gamma radiation.[12]

This gas is measured in picocuries (pCi)[13] named after the late Madame Marie Curie who dedicated her life to researching radioactive elements. If you are concerned that there may be radon gas in your home, don't hesitate to take action, as it is important to have it checked as soon as possible. Don't ever compromise your health, as uranium has a half life of over 4 billion years, so is not going to go away without treatment from experts. For more information visit your local citizen's advice bureau or contact the National Radiological Protection Board, who can supply literature, answer questions and give advice.

Dowsing will confirm if this gas is present in your home, so cleanse the pendulum of negative energy and then ask the question: Is there radon gas present in my home?

If you receive a 'Yes' answer, you can then ask the pendulum if the gas is affecting the health of any members of the household.

If you receive 'Yes' answer from your pendulum, please don't doubt it, act now!

Since the introduction of the Ionizing Radiation Regulations, employers have a responsibility to protect their staff from radon gas, so if you are an employer, dowse and ask if there is radon gas in the building, then dowse and ask if the health of any of your employees is being affected by the presence of radon gas. Also please don't forget to check your building for GS as this could be affecting the health of members of your staff.

As well as those who are alive being affected by GS, it can also affect the smooth passing of spirits, as they can become earthbound, and trapped by the band of powerful negative GS energy.

Dowsing for ghosts and spirits

What is an earthbound spirit and why is it being a nuisance in your home? There is really nothing frightening about an earthbound spirit as it is simply the spirit of a person who has died, and not passed on to the spirit world. If you feel afraid or uneasy, and know that you are not alone in a room, yet your common sense is telling you there is nobody else present, it is probably not your imagination. When you feel your scalp tingling, and feel an icy cold shiver pass over your body, or a cold draught close to you, it is probably either the spirit of a deceased relative come to see that you are well, or an earthbound spirit who is trapped in the building.

So why are spirits earthbound? These spirits can be earthbound for a variety of reasons, and some have been known to stay in this 'between worlds state' often for many years. Most of us have known a person who during their life had no religious beliefs, and firmly believed that death was the end, so if this poor soul had no expectations of a heaven, then when they die they stay in this grey area, assuming that this is the end.

Some spirits remain in this area because they have left unfinished business, or perhaps they have strong feelings of guilt, and wish to apologize to a loved one, while others believe that as they have sinned in this world, they are not good enough to be allowed into heaven, so linger in this state until some kind person guides them to the light.

One group of spirits who deserve our sympathy are those who are held back by the love of their partner, who do not want to let go of their spirit, and have made a shrine of their belongings. The power of love is very powerful, and this powerful energy can block a spirit's exit from this world, so they linger waiting for their partner to pass, or to be released.

Another group who need sympathy are those whose religion taught that they had to go through purgatory before going onwards, and are afraid to face this terrifying ordeal, so choose to stay in the between-world state.

When a building has powerful GS, it is not uncommon to find at least one earthbound spirit in the building, trapped by the band of negative energy, and when the energy has been cleared, the spirit is free to move on its journey. I have cleared many buildings of GS where there have been trapped spirits, and it is always an easy task to help them to the light, as they are relieved to hear a friendly voice.

Dowsing will tell you if there are earthbound spirits in your home or workplace, or confirm if the cold draught is the spirit of a visiting relative, so sit down and place protection around your body, then check your pendulum's energy has been cleansed, and now you are ready to find out about these spirits.

Start by asking:

1. Does the mind live on after death?
2. Do trapped spirits have freewill?
3. Do earthbound spirits hear my words when I mentally speak to them?
4. Do these spirits sense the love I send to them?

Ask if there are any earthbound spirits in your home. If the answer is 'Yes', then ask: Are there more than two earthbound spirits in your home? There can sometimes be several spirits from different generations present, and some may have lived on the land before your home was built.

If you would like to know the identity of the spirit, you can dowse and ask their sex, age at death, and ask if they lived in the house in the past? Did they live on the site before your home was built? You can also find how they died, from illness, enemy bomb etc. – the questions are endless.

Do you want to do some detective work and ask questions at the Family Records Office or electoral roll, or perhaps an elderly neighbour may remember the person who lived there many years ago. Dowsing to trace the identity of an earthbound spirit can be exciting, and it is satisfying when the answers all begin to make sense.

Rescuing an earthbound spirit

If you are concerned about the spirit's emotional state, you can ask

1. Are they lost?
2. Or would they like your help to meet their friends and family.

Remember there are a few folks who may have had a feud or upset, so do not want to see their family! In that case you can ask if they would like to meet old school friends? Or work colleagues.

Please don't ever be afraid of an earthbound spirit as these lost souls are usually so relieved to have a friendly contact, and you are more than likely the first contact they have made since they died, so they will do no harm.

Some spirits are very frustrated as they cannot understand how they can see us, and yet we ignore them. They don't realize we cannot see them, or hear their words, unless of course we are a medium. The human mind never dies, so the spirit's thoughts are crystal clear. By calmly speaking to them, either mentally or aloud, it is possible to encourage them to leave your home, and go to the light. It is possible to send an earthbound spirit to the light with the aid of the pendulum, so start by asking the spirit if they would like to go to the light to meet their loved ones. When you receive a 'Yes' answer, you can mentally send them love, and ask the pendulum to please assist them to the light. When you feel they have moved on, you can then ask the pendulum to please confirm they have gone to the light.

Again I say that by mentally speaking to the spirit, they will hear what you say, as their mind is still alive, although they no longer have their body, so ask them to go to the light, as their family or friends are waiting to welcome them. Usually this message is sufficient incentive for them to move onwards. When a spirit smells strongly of booze or tobacco, and is obstinate, refusing to move on, then it is time to call in a experienced rescue medium or therapist.

Do animals see spirits?

Cat and dog owners have all at one time seen their pet's fur on its back stand upright for no apparent reason, or watch them as they stare intently at the wall, when there is nothing to be seen. Another time a dog will give a low growl, and you know he is aware of an invisible presence which you cannot see, so let's ask the pendulum to answer a few questions about our psychic pets.

1. Can animals see spirits?
2. Do animals go to Heaven?
3. Do they welcome us when we arrive there?
4. Do animals know if a person has a negative attachment?

Animals, like humans, know which people they like and dislike, and recognize those with negative energy. How often have you seen a friendly animal firmly ignoring a person who is trying so hard to befriend them?

5. Can animals heal? Many people relate tales of how their animal gives them healing energy, so dowse and ask if your pet gives healing?

Reincarnation – the answers?

The next subject to dowse is reincarnation, as this is a very controversial subject, which when raised in any group of people can create strong arguments!

1. Ask: Do all human souls reincarnate as humans?
2. When a soul reincarnates, does it join a familiar group of souls?
3. Do souls reincarnate to have lives in other planets?
4. Does the mind live on after death?
5. Does Purgatory exist?

These are the sort of questions uppermost in many people's minds, so dowsing will give you the answers, although to get the correct answers it is important to ensure you have cleansed your energies, and cleansed your pendulum before you start to ask the questions.

Do near death experiences occur?

Before closing this chapter, I would like to list a few questions to dowse information about near death experiences (NDEs), as there is now proof that these events do occur. Many doctors argue that the experience is simply an effect, created by a shortage of oxygen to the brain, an increase in carbon dioxide or the effects of drugs, but those who have experienced this experience will tell you some convincing facts.

1. Ask the question: do NDEs occur?
2. During an NDE, does the spirit temporarily leave the body?
3. Do more than 5% of seriously ill patients have a NDE?
4. Are death bed visions real?
5. When we die are we shown the events of our life?

Astral travel

Astral travel, like near death experiences, occurs when the spirit leaves the body for a short time, so let's ask about this form of free travel, as today you can attend a course to enable you to take part in this 'free travel' when out of your body

1. Are humans able to astral travel?
2. Is it correct that animals astral travel?

3. Can humans be taught to astral travel?
4. Do some people astral travel while asleep?

The answers to these questions will give you food for thought, and enable you to put forward a convincing argument when discussing this controversial subject with friends!

It is so easy to get in touch with the spirit world with the use of your pendulum, and you will be able to get the answers to many unanswered questions, about the world of spirit, the angelic kingdom and your guardian angel. Have you ever wondered if you have a spirit guide? Or what is the name of your guardian angel? By dowsing the alphabet you can find their names and nationality.

Every time you think of a question about the spirit world or about deceased loved ones, you should write it down on a large notepad, and when you have a list of questions to ask, sit down and cleanse your energy, and your pendulum's energy, and ask your pendulum to give you the correct answers.

If you ever feel that the answer is wrong, then ask the pendulum if it is the correct answer, and don't be surprised if it says 'No', as sometimes we ask questions when we should not at this time know the answers.

Dowsing will give you the correct answers to so many questions provided your pendulum has been cleansed and your energies have also been cleansed of negativity. It is always worth asking a question twice, and using slightly different wording each time to confirm the answer

Have I succeeded in arousing your interest in dowsing? I hope this book has opened up new ways to use the pendulum to assist in your everyday life. Whether it is walking on the beach and being drawn to a pebble, by asking a few questions you will be able to establish its history: was it used by an ancient culture as a weapon, tool or healing stone? Or you may want to track down an electromagnetic energy beam, so please try dowsing, as it's using your body's own reflexes as a way to reach the intangible. We don't really know the source of dowsing responses. It will remain one of life's little mysteries for years to come, but we are all born with this gift, so please use it and enjoy it.

Summary

Dowsing is a basic tool which can be used to help resolve all sorts of different crises, and in years to come we may be very glad we have learned to dowse if we are faced with a water shortage due to freak weather conditions caused by global warming, or the action of terrorists. Should our water ever become contaminated, or be in very short supply, you must remember to dowse that the underground water you locate is fresh drinking water, and that there is sufficient supply to justify digging or boring for it.

As well as searching for underground water supplies, please remember you can use your pendulum to dowse the quality of the drinking water in your home, and bottled water from the superstore.

Lead is a health hazard so, if you live in an old house, be sure to dowse for the presence of lead in your drinking water, and lead in old paint on doors, as lead can travel through the blood/brain barrier in children, and affect their intelligence. Also dowse for the presence of arsenic, as this is in the atmosphere in industrial areas, and is known to damage health.

Another enemy is mercury, so dowse and check that your amalgam fillings are not leaking mercury, as this constant release of mercury can have a very damaging effect on health. Before you eat fish or seafood, always dowse to check it is free from mercury. If your pendulum tells you the fish contains mercury, you can ask the pendulum to remove the mercury, but to get the correct answer to this important question, you must make sure you pendulum has been cleansed!

In this chapter I have talked about certain earth energies, also explained how to use the pendulum to locate geopathic stress from underground water, and the effects it has on good health. If you live in an area where radon gas is found, then you can use your pendulum to dowse and ask if this harmful gas is seeping into your home. When in doubt, call in the experts as radon creates a serious health risk.

Finally I have explained how you can locate an earthbound spirit which may be causing a disturbance in your home, also how you can find answers to the subject of reincarnation. For those readers who like something a little different, I have told you how to dowse to confirm near death experiences, or confirmation that you have astral traveled!

To dowse outside, as I mentioned earlier, it is often more practical to use rods, as your pendulum can be affected by the wind. A couple of old metal coat hangers can be used as rods, so start experimenting before an emergency occurs! Happy Dowsing!

Endnotes

1. Grace, Raymond, *The Future is Yours, Do Something About it*, Hampton Roads Publishing, 2003. ISBN 1571743901
2. Massey, Rachel, *Rachel's Environment and Health News*, No. 722. April 12 2001.
   EPA Office of Water. Technical Fact Sheet, 'Proposed Rule for Arsenic in Drinking Water and Clarification to Compliance, and New Source Contaminants Monitoring' (EPA 815-F-00-011), May 2000.
   World Health Organization, *Water Sanitation and Health*, 'Guidelines for Drinking Water Quality', 2nd Edition, Vol. 1 No. 1, Geneva: WHO 1993, pp. 41–42.
3. Mesquita, Richard Aqua MD, *Arsenic, the Hidden Poison in Our Drinking Water*, The American Water Council. http://www.mercola.com
4. Environmental Defense, The Pollution Website, 257 Park Avenue South, New York.
5. The Franklin Institute Online, *The Human Brain Protection*, MacArthur, John. 'Children Are Most at Risk From Lead' from *The Human Brain, How Lead Violates the Brain. Brain Res.* (2), 168–176, July 27 1998.
   Neurochem Res., (4), April 24 1999, pp. 595–600,
   Biochem Pharmacol., 41(4), p. 497, February 15 1991.
6. Jones, Jane, *Greenhealth Watch News*, No. 8611. 'Mercury and Autism' National Pure Water Association. http://www.ehn.clara.net
7. Miller, Hamish, and Broadhurst, Paul, *The Sun and the Serpent*, Pendragon Press 1989. ISBN 09515183 13.

8. Frieherr von Pohl, Gustav, *Earth Currents, Causative Factor of Cancer and Other Diseases*, Frech-Verlag, 1987. ISBN 3-7724-9402-1.
9. Bachler, Kathe, *Earth Radiation, the Startling Discoveries of a Dowser.* Wordmaster Ltd, London, 1989. ISBN 0951415107.
10. Gordon, Rolf, *Are You Sleeping in a Safe Place?* available from Dulwich Health, 130 Gipsy Hill, London SE19 1PL.
11. BBC Online, Health. 'Natural Gas a Cancer Menace,.' Wednesday May 24 2000.
12. Radonseal. Penetrating Concrete Sealer. 'Radon Makes Homes Radioactive'. http://www.radonseal.com
13. *The Home Buyer's Guide to the Environmental Hazards,* The Consumer Law Page. Alexander, Hawes and Audet. LLP http://www.consumerlawpage.com